American Governance and Public Policy Series

A series edited by Barry Rabe

Selected Titles in the Series

Budgeting Entitlements: The Politics of Food Stamps
Ronald F. King

Conflict Amid Consensus in American Trade Policy
Martha L. Gibson

Controlling Technology: Citizen Rationality and the NIMBY Syndrome
Gregory E. McAvoy

Federalism and Environmental Policy: Trust and the Politics of Implementation
Denise Scheberle

Lobbying Together: Interest Group Coalitions in Legislative Politics
Kevin W. Hula

Policy Entrepreneurs and School Choice
Michael Mintrom

The Politics of Ideas and the Spread of Enterprise Zones
Karen Mossberger

Taking Aim: Target Populations and the Wars on AIDS and Drugs
Mark C. Donovan

How Governments Privatize

THE POLITICS OF DIVESTMENT IN THE UNITED STATES AND GERMANY

Mark Cassell

GEORGETOWN UNIVERSITY PRESS
Washington, D.C.

Georgetown University Press, Washington, D.C.
© 2002 by Georgetown University Press. All rights reserved.
Printed in the United States of America

10 9 8 7 6 5 4 3 2 1   2002

This volume is printed on acid-free offset book paper.

LIBRARY OF CONGRESS CATALOGING-IN-PUBLICATION DATA

Cassell, Mark.
    How goverments privatize : the politics of divestment in the United States
and Germany / Mark Cassell.
        p. cm.—(American governance and public policy series)
    Includes bibliographical references and index.
    ISBN 0-87840-879-7 (case : alk. paper)
        1. Privatization—United States. 2. Resolution Trust Corporation (U.S.) 3.
Privatization—Germany. 4. Germany. Treuhandanstalt. 5. Disinvestment—
United States. 6. Disinvestment—Germany. I. Title. II. American governance
and public policy.

HD3885 .C38 2002
338.943'05—dc21
                                                        2001040798

For Amy

Contents

List of Figures and Tables   viii

List of Abbreviations   x

Preface and Acknowledgments   xiii

Prologue   1

1   Introduction: How the Resolution Trust Corporation and the Treuhandanstalt Managed the Sales of the Century   3

2   Bureaucratic Outputs   25

3   Personnel, Culture, and Organizational Structure: The Impact of Administrative Characteristics on the Performance of the RTC and THA   75

4   Structured Choices and Consequences   131

5   The Impact of Task Environment on Performance   171

6   The Impact of National Institutional Environments   195

7   Strategic Bureaucracies and Their Consequences   229

Appendix—Interviews   259

References   267

Index   293

List of Figures and Tables

Figures

2.1	RTC and THA Rates of Divestment	31
4.1	THA Governing Structure in Summer 1990	135
4.2	THA's Management Board Structure in January 1991	137
4.3	RTC Governing Structure in 1989	139
7.1	Agency and the Policymaking Environment	250

Tables

1.1	The Argument: Links in the Chain	17
2.1	Summary Comparison of THA and RTC Mandates	26
2.2	Comparison of the Types of Assets and Forms of Privatization	27
2.3	Treuhand Cumulative Activity, 1990–94	32
2.4	Pace of Resolutions and the Value of Assets Passed Through to Receiverships Following Resolution, 1989–95	33
2.5	RTC Asset Sales, 1989–95	33
2.6	Summary Comparison of RTC and THA Secondary Goals and Programs	36

LIST OF FIGURES AND TABLES

2.7 No. of THA Firms Assessed by Management
Committee and Grades through 1992   43

2.8 Investment in East German Industrial Firms   46

2.9 Cumulative Employment Commitments, Guarantees
Enforced through Penalties, and Actual
Employment in Privatized THA Firms, 1991–94   48

2.10 Annual Investment Commitments, Guarantees
Enforced through Penalties, and Actual
Investment in Privatized THA Firms, 1992–94   49

3.1 Comparison of THA and RTC Administrative
Characteristics   76

3.2 THA and RTC Personnel Practices and Challenges   79

3.3 THA Salary Expenditures, 1990–95   87

3.4 Development of THA Employment, 1990–94   88

3.5 RTC Administrative Expense Budget,
Third Quarter 1990   89

3.6 Average Salaries of THA Employees   91

5.1 Estimated Value of THA's Original Portfolio
of Enterprises, 1990–92   181

6.1 Comparison of German and U.S. Governance
Structures   197

6.2 Representation of the THA's Fifteen Regional
Branch Office Advisory Boards   212

6.3 RTC Fees and Expenses Approved for Payment
between January 1992 and July 1995   220

7.1 Variation in the Implementation of Reforms   252

List of Abbreviations

AG	Aktiengesellschaft (Stockholding Company)
AHAB	Affordable Housing Advisory Board
BGH	*Bundesgerichtshof* (Federal Court or High Court)
BGHZ	*Amtliche Sammlung der Entscheidungen des BGH in Zivilsachen* (Publication of decisions of the federal court in civil cases)
CBO	Congressional Budget Office
DMBilG	*Gesetz über die Eröffnungsbilanz in Deutscher Mark und die Kapitalneufestsetzung* (Opening DM Balance Sheet Act)
FADA	Federal Asset Disposition Agency
FDIC	Federal Deposit Insurance Corporation
FHLB	Federal Home Loan Bank
FIRREA	Financial Institution Recovery, Reform, and Enforcement Act
FRG	Federal Republic of Germany
GAO	U.S. General Accounting Office
GDR	German Democratic Republic (East Germany)
GG	*Grundgesetz* (Basic Law or Constitution)
GmbH	Gesellschaftën mit beschränkter Haftung (Private company with limited liability)

LIST OF ABBREVIATIONS

KG	*Kammergericht* (Chamber Court)
MWOB	Minority- and Women-owned Businesses
MWOLF	Minority- and Women-owned Legal Firm program
NJW	*Neue Juristische Wochenschrift* (Weekly publication of judicial decisions)
OVG	*Oberverwaltungsgericht* (Upper administrative court)
REFCORP	Resolution Funding Corporation
REOIS	Real Estate Owned Inventory System
RTC	Resolution Trust Corporation
RTCRRIA	RTC Refinancing, Restructuring, and Improvement Act of 1991
THA	Treuhandanstalt (German Trustee Agency)
THG	*Treuhandgesetz* (Treuhand Law passed June 17, 1990)
VwGO	*Verwaltungsgerichtsordung* (Administrative Law Order)
VwVfG	*Verwaltungsverfahrensgesetz* (Administrative Procedures Act)
ZIP	*Zeitschrift für Wirtschaftsrecht* (Publication of business law decisions)

Preface and Acknowledgments

How does a government voluntarily decrease its span of control during fiscal and economic crisis? How do governments privatize state holdings and state responsibilities? What is the appropriate mix of inputs that generate the outputs policymakers seek when divesting of large sums of public assets? More specifically, what factors help to shape the process and outcome of privatization? These are the central questions taken up in this comparative account of two agencies—one in the United Sates, another in Germany—charged with the privatization of hundreds of billions of dollars of assets following two separate crises.

Although these crises in the late 1980s and early 1990s consisted of very different events, they produced similar bureaucratic responses. The U.S. real estate boom transpired into the worst economic bust since the Great Depression. Between 1980 and 1990 more than 1,200 savings and loan institutions had failed while another 600 were broke but remain open for business. The industry lost $20 million a day, and its collapse left the federal government saddled with the burden of what to do with the troubled financial institutions and their even more problematic assets. Policymakers were suddenly thrust into a position of having to play a significant and direct role in shaping financial and real estate markets. To put it another way, the savings and loan debacle—in addition to threatening the integrity of political leaders—forced the U.S. government to recreate and reshape private property on an immense scale. That is, assets were taken over by the government and were then transformed in order (1) to appeal to private buyers, and (2) to achieve a variety of goals specified by Congress.

Across the Atlantic there was little hint of crisis as young people climbed atop the Berlin Wall in November 1989 to celebrate the end of communism in the German Democratic Republic (GDR). Reality, however, soon kicked in as the federal government—first East Germany's and, after unification, West Germany's—assumed title to over 45,000 economic entities employing more than 4 million people in the former East Germany. Policymakers suddenly faced the daunting task of converting the command economy of the former East Germany into a modern, social market economy.

Although the crises themselves differed, the political responses were similar. In both cases, the federal governments took charge of the process, creating a new federal bureaucracy to take over the assets and institutions, manage them, sell them, and if necessary, liquidate them. The U.S. Congress created the Resolution Trust Corporation (RTC) in August 1989 as part of the Financial Institutions Recovery, Reform, and Enforcement Act (FIRREA). In March 1990 the former GDR created the Treuhandanstalt (THA; translated "trustee agency") as part of the first of a series of laws passed by the East German Volkskammer that would shape the agency and eventually make it part of the Federal Republic of Germany (FRG).

Governments throughout the world confront enormous challenges when divesting. Whether it be poorly performing bank loans in Japan and Korea, military bases in the United States, or real estate in eastern Europe, the challenge of public divestment is more than just a question of how to map an abstract optimal path to economic efficiency. Divestment programs, particularly ones that affect large regions, economic sectors, or populations, are the stuff of politics and administration. They are the product of (1) competing interests, whose values and views on economic efficiency differ dramatically; (2) administrative factors, which determine the capacity of any divestment program and structure a program's very purpose; and (3) a national architecture of institutions within which an entire divestment process is embedded.

Conventional wisdom expressed in the public management and privatization literature is that the management of such enormous tasks as divestment is typically done poorly, and that government strategy is likely to be inefficient. This study of two agencies presents a more complicated understanding, one that because it highlights the importance of institutional context and managerial structures (often neglected in privatization studies) for the choice of government strategy is ultimately more useful to policy practitioners and scholars alike.

The book's audience includes four distinct groups. In the first are readers simply interested in the historic events that occurred in the aftermath of the savings and loan crisis and German unification. What happened after the United States closed all those savings and loans? What happened after West Germany incorporated East Germany? How were all those economic entities resolved? At what cost? Who benefited? Who lost? These are empirical questions addressed in this book.

A second audience consists of those interested in exploring and applying alternatives to the traditional public sector structures. Specifically, this book considers how such administrative alternatives can shape the public and private goods created by government. How were these two agencies able to attract armies of contractors? What impact did outsourcing have on their performance? Did decentralization hurt or help the process? The chapters that follow answer these questions by examining the independent role that administrative structures and processes played in defining how the THA and the RTC created property.

This book also examines the origins of the two agencies in terms of the choices, motives, and constraints of German and U.S. legislators and executives. Thus, a third audience for this book includes readers interested in electoral connections. How do legislators and executives structure bureaucratic solutions to challenges they cannot avoid, that offer little political capital, and which pose potentially high political costs?

And finally, this is a comparative study. It's not just about a single case. Rather, the target audience is readers interested in developing insights into divestment that can be applied across situations and nations. The book draws upon the rich literature in comparative political economy to assess how the capacity of each state to shape its economic structures was affected by the interaction between, on one hand, the agencies' administrative structures and processes; on the other, state-societal governing relationships in Germany and the United States. The study thus combines two great literatures in political science—public management and administration and comparative political economy. Up to now these have rarely been bridged. The payoff is not just a clearer picture of privatization, but a more general understanding of how new bureaucratic structures interact with national policymaking environments to shape state capacities.

Any errors and mistakes in this book rest squarely with the author. However, I could not have completed this project without incurring a number of significant debts. Donald Kettl's extraordinary support and constructive comments epitomized the best of what an adviser should be. Graham Wilson and Leon Lindberg read and commented on far more drafts than I'm sure they would care to recall. My numerous conversations with Joe Soss over single-malt scotch and double espressos were indispensable in helping me to understand my own arguments. Also, this book would not have been comprehensible without the help of William Cassell, Amy Hanauer, and Susan Hoffmann, who each applied to the manuscript the essential and needed skills of clarity, patience, and a keen eye for spotting gratuitous academic prose. Other individuals important in this project include Wolfgang Streeck, David Soskice, John Witte, Anne Khademian, Peter Katzenstein, Steve Casper, Bob Turner, Wolfgang Seibel, Bob Hanke, Ilona Köhler, Sig Vitols, J. Rogers Hollingsworth, Pepper Culpepper, Orfeo Fioretos, and the anonymous reviewers at Georgetown University Press.

In addition, this research would not have been possible without the willingness of dozens of respondents to share their perspectives on the Treuhandanstalt and the Resolution Trust Corporation. It is their stories and experiences that provide the basis for the central insights from this text, and for that I am eternally grateful.

I also wish to acknowledge the financial support I received from the Wissenschaftszentrum Berlin für Sozialforschung (WZB), the Social Science Research Council, the Institute for Contemporary German Studies in Washington, D.C., the University of Wisconsin-Madison, and Kent State University's Research Council. I would not have been able devote myself fully to this research without it.

Prologue

The U.S. Resolution Trust Corporation and the Federal Republic of Germany's Treuhandanstalt were public agencies responsible for the largest transfer of public assets to the private sector in history. Yet to walk into the headquarters of the Resolution Trust Corporation or the Treuhandanstalt in the early 1990s was to experience anything but formidable, powerful, or imposing organizations. The Resolution Trust Corporation, headquartered in a plain brown building identified only by the three small letters "R - T - C" located just above the door, welcomed guests with a tiny lobby, several tired-looking security guards, and a log book to record the names of those who entered. The building's location in Washington suggested not power but subservience: It was on 17th Street, otherwise known as "Gucci gulch" because of the high density of lobbyists, within clear sight of its primary bureaucratic guardian, the Federal Deposit Insurance Corporation (FDIC). It was just down the street from the White House, its political guardian waiting to shield the agency from its enemies and from itself.

To visit the upper floors of the Resolution Trust Corporation in 1990 or 1991 was to witness chaos in action: floors divided into ever-changing temporary carrels, small offices, and employees costumed in bankers' clothes moving through the maze. By 1994 employees appeared less anxious and were eager to talk about the "Wild West Days" when "RTC" stood for "Round-the-Clock" organization. There

1

was little indication of stress on the faces of employees whose agency had sold close to a half trillion dollars' worth of assets in five years. Instead, they had the sort of relaxed look that comes at the end of a successful election campaign. As one employee put it, "I just want to make sure I'm not the last one to turn off the lights."

The central offices of the Treuhandanstalt in these years also lacked the presence one would expect from what former German Chancellor Helmut Schmidt described as "the second most powerful government in the six east German states" (Schmidt 1993, 110). The agency was housed initially in the dreary socialist-style office building on East Berlin's Alexander Platz. Following unification the Treuhandanstalt's headquarters was moved to Leipziger Strasse, one of the most infamous addresses in all of Germany. The building was Adolf Hitler's first architectural contribution to Berlin. Built in the 1930s to house Herman Goehring's Luftwaffe, the monstrous monument to fascism was placed adjacent to the Gestapo headquarters and just down the street from Hitler's own office. Following the Second World War the building housed the puppet cabinet of the German Democratic Republic, the council of ministers. And finally, in 1991 a small black-green plaque was hung upon the building identifying its post-unification tenant: "Treuhandanstalt."

1

Introduction:
How the Resolution Trust
Corporation and the
Treuhandanstalt Managed
the Sales of the Century

This is a story of how two remarkable public agencies managed two of the greatest public sales of assets in the twentieth century. One agency is the Resolution Trust Corporation (RTC), created by the U.S. Congress in August 1989 to sell the billions of dollars' worth of assets assumed in the wake of the largest financial disaster in the United States since the Great Depression. The second agency is the Federal Republic of Germany's Treuhandanstalt (translated "Trustee Agency," hereafter referred to as "THA"), created after the fall of the Berlin Wall in 1989 to carry out the privatization of East Germany's economic assets.

Both agencies were charged with a similar mission: to transfer to the private sector what amounted to the largest sum of public holdings and assets in history. Such a task entailed creating public organizations capable of taking inventory of large quantities of complex assets, evaluating what were often unwanted assets of poor quality, and transferring them to the private sector, all while under enormous external pressure. The sheer size of their portfolios assured both agencies an influential role in shaping their nations' economic and political systems. Senator Tim Wirth (D-CO) remarked on the eve of the RTC's creation that the agency's impact and cost would be "bigger than the combined cost of the assistance provided to Lockheed, Chrysler, Penn Central, New York City, and for good measure, you can throw in the Marshall Plan" (*Cong. Rec.* 1989). The THA, as the immediate employer of 4 million workers and owner of 8,000 of the largest firms, according to an influential labor economist, "completely reshaped the industrial landscape in eastern Germany" (Kühl 1997, 121).

A number of well-written accounts detail the individual experiences of both agencies.[1] Many of these accounts offer excellent historical descriptions and documentation of what each agency did. Relatively little work, however, has focused on developing a theoretical framework with which to explain the factors that led to the outcomes of the two organizations. Instead, the best accounts treat the creation and subsequent activity of each organization as a set of neutral events. Politics, however, is about who gets what, when, where, and—most important—why. Moreover, until one can identify the relevant variables and can predict their impact on the RTC and THA's behavior, we cannot know how findings about their behavior must be modified to serve as prescriptions or lessons for behavior in other situations. When the two agencies are examined together, interesting new puzzles emerge that show the need to understand the factors that contributed to the agencies' behavior.

EMPIRICAL PUZZLES

One set of puzzles centers on outcomes. This book seeks to explain three basic bureaucratic outcomes: (1) speed of privatization; (2) treatment of secondary goals; and (3) patterns of accountability.

Speed of Privatization

By any measure, the RTC and THA privatized at a remarkable clip. Starting completely from scratch with no staff or organization, the American agency closed its doors a year ahead of schedule, having seized and resolved 750 insolvent savings and loan (S&L) institutions (nearly 40 percent of the industry) with assets in excess of $465 billion, nearly twice the amount held by the largest private sector holding companies.

The THA immediately took possession of more than 8,000 former state-owned companies, which included more than 45,000 plants with a total workforce of 4.1 million, roughly half of the total workforce in the German Democratic Republic at the time of the fall of the Berlin Wall (Kühl 1997). On December 31, 1994, the agency closed its doors, having privatized or closed 98 percent of its portfolio.

Although the agency began with 8,000 enterprises, its portfolio increased over time due to the splitting up of firms. Of the 12,162 enterprises transformed over the four-year period, 6,546 (54 percent) were sold to the private sector. An additional 7,600 enterprises were partially privatized, meaning that only a part of the firm was sold while the rest was shut down and sold off for parts. Wendy Carlin (1994, 132) reported in 1994, "There is general agreement that the Treuhand has been successful in one respect: it set the objective of rapid privatization and this has been achieved."

At the same time that both agencies shared a similar drive to privatize, the THA privatized at a much greater pace than the RTC. In an early critique of the RTC, appropriately titled "A tale of two bailouts," the *Wall Street Journal* (31 October 1991) reported: "If Germany's Treuhandanstalt manages its still-vast holdings . . . at its current rate, it will liquidate itself altogether in a few more years. RTC, meanwhile, just grows and grows. Is anyone still in charge of economic policy in Washington?"

How did so much get privatized so fast in both countries? And why were assets divested even more quickly in Germany, a country with a social market economy and a history of a strong state, than in the United States with its liberal economy and weak state?

Treatment of Secondary Goals

A second bureaucratic outcome explained in the book is the treatment of secondary goals. In addition to privatization, both agencies were required by law to achieve ancillary goals for which there were significant vocal constituencies. Yet both agencies largely minimized other legislative goals, opting and ultimately succeeding in carrying out a very narrow form of privatization despite constant pressure from legislators and societal groups to expand their interpretation of privatization. The RTC's enabling legislation, the Financial Institutions Reform, Recovery, and Enforcement Act (FIRREA), included three specific mandates designed to channel the resources of the RTC toward particular societal groups. The goals included maximizing opportunities for minority- and women-owned contractors, maximizing availability of affordable single- and multifamily

5

housing, and protecting local real estate and financial markets from asset dumping. Of the three goals, only the protection of local markets and concerns over dumping was given a great deal of attention. The agency was slow to implement Minority and Women-owned Business (MWOB) and Affordable Housing programs (MacDonald 1995; GAO 1992b, 1991c; CBO 1993). Over time both these trends changed. Under pressure from Congress, and after a good portion of the institutions and assets had been sold, the agency made progress in developing its MWOB and Affordable Housing programs. Alternatively, after fears of dumping disappeared, the agency focused attention on ensuring that its sales practices were competitive.

Similarly, the THA's enabling legislation required the agency to do more than just privatize quickly. The Treuhandanstalt Law, which passed June 17, 1990, and later became Article 25 of the Unification Treaty, instructed the agency to identify firms that could be saved from liquidation and then to carry out a restructuring program that would make them competitive in a market system. The THA was compared to the Kreditanstalt für Wiederaufbau, the public enterprise established in West Germany after the Second World War, which provided low-interest loans and support to firms to help them rebuild (Czada 1996a). The agency's own management committee determined that more than 85 percent of its firms had a future with the right restructuring plan and capital investment.[2] Yet with the exception of a handful of very large and politically important enterprises,[3] restructuring was conducted in a passive manner: drastically downsizing workforces; dismantling firms into pieces; and selling off what was of value (Seibel 1994; Priewe 1993; Klemmer 1990; Kühl 1997; Kemmler 1994; Czada 1996b; Ganske 1991; Carlin 1994, 140).[4] The very restrictive form of restructuring was followed despite the fact that active restructuring and investment enjoyed significant support from vocal constituencies, such as labor unions (Kemmler 1994; Fichter 1993; Wagner 1993).

Why did these agencies wind up ignoring important ancillary goals even though these goals had vocal constituencies?

Patterns of Accountability
A final bureaucratic outcome explained in this book is the pattern of accountability shared by the agencies. Given the importance of the RTC and the THA's missions and the enormous attention both

6

received, the extent to which the agencies successfully evaded societal and political accountability is remarkable. While neither agency was shy about promoting its sales successes, the information systems necessary to conduct effective and accurate accounting of their behavior were typically either poorly developed or put in place only after most of the privatization had occurred. The lack of controls became the subject of serious criticism, particularly by the legislative auditors: the U.S. General Accounting Office (GAO) and the German Bundesrechnungshof (Bundesrechnungshof 1992, 1993; GAO 1994a, 1991b, 1992a, 1992c, 1991a).

Much of the current bribery scandal involving former Chancellor Helmut Kohl is directly connected to the THA's privatization activity (Cohen and Tagliabue 2000).[5] During its short existence, the THA was plagued with numerous cases of fraud and scandal. This is remarkable, given Germany's bureaucratic legacy, characterized by a high degree of honor and military sense of control and organization. The THA, however, seemed particularly vulnerable to fraud. Its scandals are the subject of a number of well-documented books (Kampe 1994; Suhr 1991; Christ and Neubauer 1991), federal audits (Bundesrechnungshof 1992, 1993), and Parliamentary Hearing Reports (Treuhandanstalt 1994c).

One of the most recent cases featured a shipbuilding company, Bremer Vulkan. Vulkan purchased shipbuilding facilities in the troubled region of Mecklenburg-Vorpommern in 1992 from the THA. Vulkan received DM1,5 billion (about $90 million) in subsidies from the THA to transform the East German firm into a modern competitive enterprise. The purchaser, however, used DM716 million (approximately $49.6 million) of the subsidy illegally to, among other things, funnel money into a troubled West German subsidiary (*Der Spiegel* 1996).

The agency's internal and external auditors lacked the necessary number of employees to monitor the activities of the agency and its firms. Auditors also lacked the expertise and knowledge concerning the various industries they were expected to monitor. The federal prosecutor who headed Germany's equivalent of the Inspector General's office within the THA remarked, "The politics of the THA was to empower the buyer and to treat controls as a necessary evil. The signal from the top to lower level employees was unfortunately not: Work carefully and with thought. The signal was rather: If something comes up, we'll help you" (Kampe 1994, 166).

The RTC also struggled with maintaining effective oversight. The GAO and the Office of the Inspector General were both critical of the agency's oversight systems, particularly the inadequacy of information management systems to monitor contractors and track the progress of assets. When it began, the RTC was one of the top risks for fraud in the federal government, according to the GAO. And as late as 1994 the GAO reported, "RTC and FDIC are vulnerable to fraud, abuse, and mismanagement because they do not systematically screen applicants or current employees to determine if they have been found culpable in the losses that caused federally insured institutions to fail. The Corporations have no systems designed to screen prospective employees to determine if the Corporations make culpability determinations; they have no systems to verify whether they or a conservatorship institution currently employ the individuals deemed culpable" (GAO 1994a, 3).

Yet despite the significant problems of oversight, very few major cases of fraud and scandal occurred. In most instances, a contractor overcharged or underperformed. Given the vast sums at stake and the enormous potential for abuse and conflict of interest that existed, it is somewhat surprising how few scandalous episodes occurred in the RTC in comparison to the THA. Despite operating under a much more open system, the RTC experienced nothing like the number of cases of fraud and abuse that were raised during the Treuhand Investigatory Committee hearings and that are still being discovered, as the case of Bremer Vulkan shipbuilding company reveal.

How could such important agencies manage to avoid societal and political accountability so successfully? Furthermore, what explains the difference in the magnitude of the oversight and accountability problem experienced by the RTC and THA? Why were oversight and accountability particularly problematic in the country where the public sector is held in greater esteem?

In addition to bureaucratic outcomes, the comparison of the RTC and the THA raises a number of theoretical questions not easily explained with reference to the scholarly literature.

INTRODUCTION

THEORETICAL PUZZLES

Neither agency conformed to expectations developed in the public administration, management, or political economy literature. Classical organizational theory says that public bureaucracies consist of finite, bounded jurisdictions of authority and responsibility with efficiency made a function of specialization and coordination between divisions.[6] Yet in the RTC and THA, boundaries and jurisdictions were ephemeral, constantly in flux, and often unclear to those in the organizations. There was little specialization and even less coordination.

Bureaucratic theory states that public bureaucracies are hierarchical with clear lines of authority; that they have stable patterns of obedience; and that they employ personnel who share a strong belief in the legitimacy of the system of authority.[7] The RTC and the THA adopted highly decentralized structures in which clear lines of authority and hierarchy were not well established. The managerial practices, structures, and culture of both agencies resembled a private firm rather than a public organization. Employee incentives were based much more upon market mechanisms than on hierarchies, organizational loyalty, or allegiance to a particular public mission. The agencies relied on short-term contracts designed to ensure that values of the individual were aligned with those of the organization. Allegiance was made a function of self-interest rather than acquired through socialization into the organizations' values. Employees within both organizations claimed that it was a strong adherence to the market or private sector model of administration that made their organizations less political and thus more effective. Notwithstanding such claims, what is important about both agencies is that, in contrast to the Weberian idea of "government of laws and not men," the RTC and THA represented a government of individuals and firms. That is not to say that there were no rules or norms. Much of how the agencies defined and implemented privatization, however, was left to the discretion of the individuals and firms hired by the RTC and THA.

Scholarly and more popular literature suggests that public bureaucracies are at best slow and inefficient; at worst they are unaccountable, self-perpetuating, and budget maximizing (Niskanen 1971; Tulluck

9

1965). Policy implementation in "cooperationist" countries like Germany[8] and "adversarial" systems such as those in the United States are said to be plagued with inefficiencies (albeit for different reasons) that make their executive agencies particularly ill equipped to respond to society's problems.[9] Yet as noted above, both agencies privatized at an astonishing pace before closing their doors.

In sum, the comparison of the RTC and THA is revealing on several fronts. Both agencies were created at roughly the same moment in history in two different but highly advanced industrial capitalist countries.[10] Both were given the unenviable task of transferring large sums of public holdings to the private sector at a time when their countries' economies were particularly vulnerable. Neither agency was given much of a plan, and both enjoyed a great deal of autonomy and freedom to carry out their task. Although German unification and the collapse of America's financial system in 1989 garnered widespread attention among scholars, policymakers, and the public, it is the story of the public bureaucracies that resolved them that may provide the most important lessons in the decades ahead. This book explains what factors contributed to the bureaucratic outcomes in the two agencies. In answering these questions, I also hope to shed some light on the theoretical puzzles as well.

THE ARGUMENT IN BRIEF

The behavior and actions of the RTC and THA are the result of independent factors in the political economic environment, the choices German and American legislatures made for them in regard to legal status and mandate, and a set of administrative factors that, to a large extent, were under the agencies' control. All of these combined to shape the RTC and THA's sense of mission, which in turn drove behavior. The mix of factors also combined in a unique way that allowed the agencies to build rapidly the capacity to function (and even become innovators) in the highly sophisticated and private world of asset sales and management. At the same time, the factors undermined the capacity of both agencies to achieve ancillary goals and establish an effective oversight mechanism.

INTRODUCTION

Bureaucratic Outcomes

Chapter 2 sets the stage for this investigation by describing the bureaucratic outcomes produced by the two agencies. As outlined above, the central focus of this book is to explain three basic outcomes: (1) Speed of performance: How did so much get privatized so fast? (2) Treatment of secondary goals: Why did the agencies largely ignore these important goals even though the goals enjoyed vocal constituencies? and (3) Patterns of accountability: Given the importance of their missions and all the attention they received, how did these agencies evade societal and political accountability?

Administrative Characteristics

The most proximate source of explanations for these bureaucratic outcomes can be found in the agencies themselves. Carl Friedrich (1978, 401) noted that administrative officials, by virtue of their managerial positions, are able to participate continuously and significantly in the policy process long after a legislative decision is made. Specifically, these outcomes were shaped by three administrative characteristics: (1) Styles of personnel management, that is, the recruitment and compensation strategies of the RTC and THA; (2) Organizational structures and distributions of responsibility and authority in the two agencies; and (3) Organizational culture—the set of values and beliefs held by employees and promoted by the leadership of both agencies. The influence of each of these administrative characteristics is compared in chapter 3.

These administrative variables enabled the RTC and THA to change their capacity to take action, and they shaped the way the agencies interpreted the public goals assigned to them. The structure, personnel, and organizational culture explain the increased capacity of the agencies to take inventory of assets, structure them into a marketable form, and then market them when many observers believed the task too difficult. The extensive recruitment of personnel with private sector experience in areas such as asset sales and management, the management of financial institutions (in the U.S. case), and the management of private firms (in the German case) coupled with a decentralized organizational structure, meant that

11

both agencies could quickly buy the expertise they needed. At the same time, the decentralized structure, along with high turnover, merit pay, the dependence on private sector personnel, and contractors, weakened organizational allegiance and internal coordination of information systems. This in turn made accountability and oversight difficult.

The second way in which administrative factors affected the behavior of the RTC and THA is in shaping the way in which the agencies interpreted their assigned missions. An organization's mission lies at the heart of its culture. I use the term "mission" in the classical sociological sense: the shared sense of purpose that leaders build into an organization over time, enabling it to survive and prosper if leaders seize the opportunities presented by the environment (Selznick 1949).

In interviews with managers in both agencies, it was clear that the concept of "mission" was a loaded word, for it was typically understood in terms of a second meaning in contemporary management practice: a mandate handed down from above, intended to direct behavior. It was in this second sense that RTC and THA managers bristled at talk of their "mission," for mission in this sense—a directive from outside (Congress or the German Bundestag)—can constitute a threat to "mission" in the first sense—the unifying purpose that permits the organization to thrive.

Considering mission in the first, sociological sense, the central purpose or emphasis that was understood by employees was transferring assets to the private sector as quickly as possible. That is, while employees in both agencies were cognizant of the list of tasks legislators had assigned, their focus was clearly centered on rapid divestment.

Structural Choices

Administrative characteristics influence outcomes, but they are not "uncaused causes" in the policy process. They are directly shaped by the actions of political principals who establish mandates and make structural choices designed to promote desired political ends. Legislative and executive principals seeking reelection had strong reasons to be concerned about the RTC and the THA. Not only were both created in the midst of enormous political and economic turmoil, it was clearly understood by all policymakers involved that the actions or inaction of the RTC and THA would have significant lasting consequence on the economic health of their respective countries.

Political principals in both countries shared economic and political concerns. Given their sizable portfolios, the overriding economic concern centered on the impact agencies would have on domestic markets. Many viewed the RTC as a threat to already vulnerable real estate markets and called for restrictions or price floors on the sale of its portfolio (Vandell and Riddiough 1992). Some viewed the ownership of such a large amount of securities by the public sector as the cause for instability in the financial markets and called for the immediate liquidation and sale of institutions and assets (Litan 1990). Still others hoped the agency might use the troubled thrift institutions and their assets to provide some type of public goods such as affordable housing, reinvestment in urban communities, and opportunities for disadvantaged groups and small businesses (Waldman 1990b). Since the greatest beneficiaries of the savings and loan bailout were the wealthiest in society many felt that it was only fair that the RTC should be used to provide some direct benefits to the disadvantaged.[11]

The THA was also seen as a powerful force in shaping the economic future of the new unified Germany. Birgit Breuel, the agency's longest serving president, described the organization as "the largest holding company in the world." Helmut Schmidt, the former West German chancellor, called the THA the second most important government agency in eastern Germany (Schmidt 1993). Like the RTC, the THA was viewed with a mixture of hope and concern. The agency's actions clearly affected all sectors of the five new eastern German states.

A strong belief echoed by all sectors of society and discussed extensively within the country was that the agency should direct its privatization efforts toward rebuilding and restructuring eastern markets (Nägele 1994; Hickel and Priewe 1994). At the same time, active engagement in restoring the competitiveness of eastern firms was viewed with concern by western competitors whose production before the fall of the Wall was well under capacity. Many of these groups held a strong belief that the THA should be little more than a short-term sales agency, facilitating the quick transfer of public assets into private hands.

In addition to economic concerns, politicians in both countries worried about the political ramifications attached to the agencies' activities. Specifically, legislatures were concerned about the agencies' budgetary impact, the uncertain future costs associated with funding the RTC and THA, and the electoral impact overseeing (and thus being connected to) two agencies charged with such difficult and largely thankless tasks.

Scholars of the bureaucracy such as Terry Moe argue that bureaucratic structures are the result of political conflict and compromise among competing principals who control the agency in an environment of great uncertainty (1989). In the case of the RTC and THA, administrative characteristics (and hence, outcomes) were strongly influenced by three sets of structural choices: (1) the passage of conflicting and vague mandates; (2) establishment of hybrid legal identities; (3) the establishment of off-budget financing mechanisms; and (4) the governing structures of the two agencies.

While this book draws upon Moe's central insight, it differs in several ways. First, Moe restricts his view of politics of structural choice to *public* agencies, explicitly contrasting this to the process of designing private firms. This book extends Moe's view of structural choice to a *public/private* hybrid. Second, Moe's central argument is that public agencies are designed to be ineffective. The approach taken here centers on trying to understand how concepts such as "efficiency" and "effectiveness" are in part products of institutional arrangements. Finally, this work examines the range of "choices" by considering how the transference of public responsibilities to the private sector or the use of market-oriented structures in the public agencies emerged from political processes in the United States and Germany.

Bureaucratic Task Environments

In addition to being shaped by the mandates and structural choices made by principals, the RTC and THA were also influenced by the sheer tasks they confronted. Specifically, it was in the course of attempting to fulfill their missions that agencies confronted a number of challenges—over which the agency had little control—that strained the ability of principals to oversee the actions and outputs of the agencies (Wilson 1989, 158). Although neither U.S. nor German legislative bodies planned it, the size and complexity of the RTC and THA's tasks quickly transformed the agencies. The task challenges led managers to be more likely to emphasize the most measurable forms of outputs. It also led to considerable conflict within the organizations as operators faced the difficult situational imperatives and managers confronted the constraints imposed by politically influential constituencies.

In considering how task environments mattered for the two agencies, this book focuses particular attention on the RTC and THA's high level of dependence on third parties, which in turn was a function of the overwhelming nature of their task. The reliance on third parties affected the organizations in crosscutting ways. First, it increased the organizations' capacities by allowing them to tap a market immediately for much-needed experts who could, in turn, be quickly deployed to accomplish the tasks at hand. Second, dependence on third parties constrained the organization because it, in a sense, made both agencies beholden to exigencies of the market. And finally, as Dietmar Braun's (1993) work shows, dependence on third parties gave third parties a great role in defining the purpose of the organizations. All three effects can be seen in both the THA and RTC.

Their administrative characteristics, their actions, and their strategic choices were all influenced by (1) the volume of assets they had to privatize; (2) the nature of these assets; and (3) in the RTC's case, the existence of a shadow agency (the Federal Deposit Insurance Corporation) with mandates and priorities that differed from the RTC. Chapter 5 analyzes how these factors contributed to the behavior of the agencies.

Systems of Governance

In addition to structural choices made by principals and political and/or task environments, there was a third factor that the THA and RTC had little control over: the national systems of governance in which they were located. Governance is the process of coordination or regulation of transactions and includes the institutions and norms that facilitate the coordination of transactions and productive activities within and among sectors (Sako 1994, 19). National systems of governance integrate a nation's regulatory culture with its regulatory institutions[12] (Dyson 1992).

The three areas in which institutions and culture combined to influence the behavior of the RTC and THA were the beliefs and attitudes concerning (1) state and policymaking institutions; (2) markets and economic regulatory structures; and (3) bureaucracy and bureaucratic structures. Germany and the United States differ along each of these ideological and institutional fronts, and thus the impact on the agencies' behavior varies as well.

The influence of German and U.S. systems of governance help to account for THA and RTC outcomes in two critical ways. First, they define the context in which principals acted as they established and designed the agencies. Second, they define the context in which the agencies carried out their work. Chapter 6, therefore, analyzes how the combinations of the nationally specific institutional structures and regulatory culture mediated the creation and actions of the two agencies.

Conclusion

Chapter 7 concludes the argument by linking the stories together to draw a set of lessons concerning the ways in which institutional context, administrative structures, and process matter in shaping the outcomes of public agencies. Table 1.1 summarizes the outline of the argument developed in the book.

ANALYTICAL APPROACH

Although there are a number of ways to study how and why public bureaucracies function, the approach taken here places both agencies explicitly at the center of the analysis. This means first opening up the black box of the organization to study its administrative structures and practices. Second, it entails looking outward to take stock of how a public bureaucracy's administrative structures and practices conform to the larger or "macro" system of governance specific to a country. Such an approach is typically messy since it is largely inductive and requires immersing oneself in the agency and its personnel rather than testing a set of clean models and assumptions with a data set. Nonetheless, "getting one's hands dirty," as some scholars argue is necessary, allows the researcher to understand the project better—in this case by identifying how the organization's personnel perceive and understand the public problem they are charged to address

Table 1.1

The Argument: Links in the Chain

Outcomes (chapter 2)	Administrative Characteristics (chapter 3)	Structural Choices (chapter 4)	Bureaucratic Task Environments (chapter 5)	Systems of Governance (chapter 6)	Conclusions (chapter 7)
Rapid privatization	Organizational culture	Establishment of conflicting and vague mandates	Unpredictable circumstances including large quantity of poor assets coupled with weak markets lead both agencies to become "coping" organizations	Beliefs and attitudes about the state and policymaking institutions	Administrative structures and processes matter
The minimization of secondary goals	Personnel management strategies and techniques	Establishment of hybrid legal identities		Beliefs and attitudes about markets and economic regulatory structures	Institutional context matters
Lack of accountability	Organizational structure and delegation of authority	Establishment of off-budget financing mechanisms	Managers focus on measurable outcomes	Beliefs and attitudes about the bureaucracy and bureaucratic structures	
			High level of conflict within organization		
			Influence of third parties in shaping purpose		

17

(Hirsch, Michaels, and Friedman 1987). The approach is particularly relevant in the case of the RTC and THA because of the extent to which both agencies eschewed a "classical" and "bureaucratic" model of public administration.

The approach offers several advantages. First, it creates the opportunity to explore what effects administrative structures have on bureaucratic outputs. Although an abundance of rhetoric favors or opposes adoption of private strategies for public agencies, it remains extremely difficult to answer the simple question: How do breaks with the traditional model affect an organization's performance and behavior? One problem is that it is difficult to find comparable cases from which to draw clear conclusions. Donahue (1989), for example, shows that even in cases of public tasks as narrow and specific as garbage collection it is difficult to find comparable cases.[13] The comparability problems increase with the complexity of the public task.[14] In addition, even when one studies a single case over time, such as education, it is hard to draw out exactly how a change in the administrative structure affects policy outcomes.[15]

And finally, efficiency itself poses a problem.[16] Traditional policy analysis borrows much of its theoretical power from microeconomics and typically begins by assuming an optimal outcome.[17] In the private sector, variables such as profit, growth, and share price serve as useful measures of outcome. In the public sector, however, clear outcomes are not always possible or desirable since the public sector is often asked to pursue conflicting sets of goals.[18] Agents often play an important role in determining how these broader sets of goals are defined, and efficiency can change over time in response to the political environment.[19] The problem is manifold when one compares across countries with different ideas of what constitutes a good society. Relying on the perspectives of those in the agencies relieves some of these difficulties. Those engaged in the management and sale of assets can articulate what they perceive to be the organizations' strengths and weaknesses, missions, and definitions of efficiency. It is their stories that provide the data for identifying the key factors that influenced privatization.

A second advantage of the approach taken here is that it identifies the politics of administrative structure. In his classic work *The Administrative State,* Dwight Waldo (1948) argued that despite their proponents' claims to be apolitical, the concepts of efficiency and economy which guided prewar public administration were highly political. Referring to their use against the progressive movement in the 1920s, Waldo noted that efficiency and economy have been used as weapons of attack and defense in a political struggle. They are difficult to define precisely because they are regarded as ultimates, in terms of which other concepts are defined. At the same time, theories of organizational structure that ignore the definition of success or effectiveness "fail to examine whose interests, whose goals, and whose preferences are to prevail in organizations" (Pfeffer and Salancik 1978).

A comparison of the RTC and THA's administrative structures and strategies illustrates how these allegedly apolitical structures shaped regional economic development, distribution of public and private resources, and distribution of political power. Given the impact on their countries' economic and political systems, nowhere are the political stakes associated with bureaucratic structure more plain than in the origins of these two public agencies.

In short, the experiences of the THA and the RTC bring into focus the political elements of privatization. The activities of the agencies constituted what Harold Lasswell (1950) defined in 1950 as politics: "Who gets what, when, and how." At the same time, the cases illustrate how the domains of conflict and terms of debate were also shaped by the administrative strategies and structures adopted by the organizations.

A final advantage of the organization-centered approach, as applied to the THA and RTC, is that it allows one to address how deviations from traditional models of public administration are possible. What political conditions give birth to breaks from the bureaucratic norm? The stability of bureaucratic institutions often makes it difficult to explain such breaks.

Case Selection
The most important reason for choosing these two cases is the similarity in management. Both organizations relied heavily on market mechanisms, entrepreneurialism, and decentralization. Second, the agencies share similar control and oversight relationships to institutional actors. The political nature of the two crises facilitated the

creation of organizations whose autonomy from institutional actors was substantial when compared to other, more traditional public agencies. Third, the activities of these highly controversial agencies were richly documented by governments, scholars, and the news media. Fourth, both agencies only recently closed their doors. Many individuals involved with the agencies are still accessible and can clearly recollect their experiences and, in some cases, provide documentation. And finally, the broader institutional environments, such as the legal system, the organization of government, and the economic system, are different enough to cause variation in the links between bureaucratic structures and outcomes. The comparison presents the opportunity to focus attention on the role the broader institutional architecture plays in shaping agency behavior and outcomes.

A final feature that makes the RTC and THA comparable is that although they shared certain internal structures, they existed in different countries.[20] The approach adopted here considers explicitly how the agencies' structures interacted with their countries' systems of governance. It focuses on how their similar breaks from traditional models of public administration played out within the two different systems of governance.

Methodology and Data

The methodology utilized in this work is a qualitative case study comparison of two most-similar cases. Building on the insights of James Q. Wilson, I studied both organizations from the perspective of (1) operators—the rank and file public and private agents who worked on the front lines; (2) managers—individuals involved in organizing work and delegating responsibility; (3) executives—leadership in the agency; and (4) institutional actors—organized social interests such as unions or business associations.

During a two-and-a-half-year period between 1995 and 1997, I conducted 80 semistructured, open-ended interviews with management and front-line employees in both agencies (see appendix A). In the case of the RTC, I conducted 45 interviews at two of the largest regional offices—Dallas, Texas, and Newport Beach, California—and with employees at the RTC headquarters Washington, D.C. In the case of the THA, I carried out 35 interviews throughout 1995 and 1996 at the agency's headquarters in Berlin as well as in the surrounding region. I also used approximately 50 additional interviews conducted by two German research teams between 1993 and 1995.[21]

The interviews illustrate the connection between institutional environment, managerial structure, and agency outcome. The interviews are supplemented with documentation produced by the agencies, government auditors, legislative hearing staff reports, or from scholarly and periodic literature. The emphasis in interviewing was less on attaining a large enough sampling than on looking for repetition. Enough interviews were conducted to identify with confidence patterns emerging from answers given by respondents. The number of interviews for each set of actors therefore varies.

Secondary sources of data are used to supplement the findings. These include assessments performed by government auditors in both countries such as studies performed in the United States by the GAO and Congressional Budget Office (CBO); and internal memos written in Germany by the Bundesrechnungshof (Federal Auditor's Office). In both cases, interviews took place with the auditors themselves. Statistical data and records compiled by both agencies offer another valuable secondary source of data. And finally, a good deal of information derives from accounts by journalists and scholars.

NOTES

1. Studies of the RTC include Tucker, Meire, and Rubinstein (1990); MacDonald (1995); Kettl (1991a); Bowers (1992); as well as numerous audits by the General Accounting Office and the Congressional Budget Office. There are far more studies of the THA. Some of the best include include Dininio (1999); Seibel (1997); Kemmler (1994); Seibel (1992); Sinn and Sinn (1992); Carlin and Mayer (1994); Fischer, Hax, and Schneider (1996); and Dodds and Wächter (1993).

2. The THA's management committee ranked each firm's chances. By the end of 1992 only 14.2 percent of firms fell into categories five and six, the two worst categories, indicating little hope for survivability (Schwalbach and Gless 1996, 188).

3. See Phyllis Dininio's (1999) account of the THA's bias toward restructuring some of the largest firms.

4. Kern and Sabel (1996) describe several exceptions that, because of their exceptional status, largely support the general rule that the THA minimized goals other than rapid privatization.

5. The scandal surrounding Helmut Kohl and his Christian Democratic Union party (CDU) is complex. Kohl admitted to receiving more than $1 million in illegal political funds from 1993 to 1998 (Boyes and Bremner 2000). The CDU received an additional $2 million illegally in 1991 and 1992. A Parliamentary Investigations Committee looked into allegations that the CDU and Treuhandanstalt officials were the recipients of bribes. The most notable case involved the French oil company Elf-Aquitaine, which purchased the Leuna oil refinery from the THA. The newspaper *Die Welt am Sonntag* reported that Elf bribed Treuhand officials. Elf is also suspected of artificially inflating construction costs at the refinery and making suspicious donations to the CDU. Complicating matters has been Kohl's steadfast refusal to reveal who donated the money to him or the CDU. In addition, two-thirds of all of Helmut Kohl's documents were destroyed during the lame duck period following Kohl's defeat in the 1998 election and the takeover of the new Chancellor Gerhard Schröder. The documents included information related to the sale of the Leuna oil refinery, many other privatizations, and the controversial sale of thirty-six tanks to Saudi Arabia in 1991 (*Der Spiegel* Staff 2000). In the end, the CDU paid $6.5 million in fines. Kohl reached an agreement with the German prosecutor's office to pay a $143,000 fine and acknowledge a "breach of trust" for accepting illegal cash donations (Finn 2001). The London *Daily Telegraph* reported, "Helmut Kohl, the fallen giant of German politics, has agreed to accept a face-saving legal deal that will allow him to emerge from the country's worst post-war scandal shamed, but without a criminal record (Helm 2001).

6. The classical model was most clearly articulated by Luther Gulick (1937) in the 1930s while he chaired the Brownlow Committee, which advised President Franklin Roosevelt on the reorganization of the executive branch.

7. Weber's views were first made accessible to an American audience through two translations of portions of his work that appeared in 1946 and 1947. Numerous later editions also occurred. See, for example, *From Max Weber: Essays in Sociology*, translated and edited by H. H. Gerth and C. Wright Mills (New York: Oxford University Press, 1958).

8. Roman Herzog, Germany's president, described the German policy system in the following way: "What is wrong with our country? In brutal terms, the loss of economic dynamism, the paralysis of society. Instead of producing decisions, debates turn into rituals. At the end, the problem is usually put off. The status quo prevails. Everybody waits for the next subject" (Whitney 1997).

9. For an account of the differences between cooperationist and adversarial policy systems see Steven Kelman's work (1992). For historical comparisons see Andrew Shonfield's classic (1969) *Modern Capitalism*. For more contemporary comparisons see Michel Albert's study (1993) of the insurance industry *Capital-*

ism vs. Capitalism and Lester Thurow's (1992) *Head to Head.* For books that look at the difference in regulatory policy see Kelman (1981); Hollingsworth, Boyer, and Streeck (1997); Hollingsworth, Streeck, and Schmitter (1994); Brickman, Jasanoff, and Ilgen (1985); and Badaracco (1985).

10. The Treuhand was actually created by the last government of the German Democratic Republic roughly six months prior to unification. Upon unification, however, the agency was firmly housed within the West German Ministry of Finance. And decisions about its governance were made by the unified German government.

11. In one of the few studies that have looked into the question, the Southern Finance Project surveyed 54 of the largest failed S&Ls and found that deposits of more than $80,000 made up 32.1 percent of total deposits. In several instances, these large balances represented up to 70 percent of an institution's deposits.

12. "Regulatory culture" refers to what Gerhard Lehmbruch (1992) calls the "institutionalization of meaning" or what Ikenberry (1988) calls "the nation's normative social order." It refers to how individuals in a society perceive the institutional arrangements that govern them such as the state, the market, unions, or some combination of the three. "Institutions" refers to what Douglass North (1991, 3) calls "the humanly devised constraints that shape human interaction" or what Peter Hall (1986, 13) calls "the formal rules, compliance procedures, and standard operating practices that structure the relationship between individuals in various units of the polity and economy."

13. Donahue (1989) notes that communities' different geographic features, service providers, and variations in the capacity to recycle or dispose of trash make it difficult to find cases to compare in order to say with confidence what impact privatization or some administrative reform had on the organization.

14. Privatization, for example, involves myriad social, historic, political, and economic factors that are often specific to a single country. As a result, most comparisons of privatization—whether of public assets or public responsibilities—typically present individual cases rather than attempting comparisons. For U.S. examples see Donahue (1989) and Gormley (1991). For several examples of international effort at comparing privatization experiences see Dobek (1993); Wright (1994); Vickers and Wright (1989); and Estrin (1994).

15. The battle over vouchers in public schools is an example of what should be an ideal research design: measure students who participate in a public school voucher program against students in the rest of the district who do not participate in the program. Yet as John Witte's study of the Milwaukee voucher program shows, even this case is far from simple. Among the difficulties were

the fact that participants in the programs were not a representative sample of the entire district. They were poorer and more likely to be African American. Moreover, even across the same socioeconomic and racial classes, students in the program come from parents who are on average more educated and more involved in their schools. If the outcome is student test scores, for example, it is unclear whether vouchers or parental involvement or some combination are the cause of variations. That is not to say that it is impossible to isolate the impact of certain administrative reforms. But it is an inherently frustrating task that grows with the complexity of the policy (see Witte and Thorn 1994; Witte 1992).

16. For a discussion of this point see Schneider (1995) and Stone (1996).

17. Cost-benefit analysis, for example, borrows concepts and assumptions from microeconomics to determine the efficiency of a policy.

18. For a good account of the important differences between public and private sector see Rainey (1992).

19. For an excellent account of the role agents play see Katzmann's (1980) study of the Federal Trade Commission.

20. A burgeoning body of scholarship recognizes and seeks to understand the application of market-based practices to reform the public sector as an international phenomenon (see for example Donald Kettl [1997]; Jon Pierre [1995]; Guy Peters [1996]; and Jan Kooiman [1993]).

21. One team, headed by Wolfram Fischer, was the *Treuhand Forschungsprojekt* (Treuhand Research Project). A second team of researchers, headed by Professor Nils Diederich, conducted interviews of THA employees as part of a project titled *Kontrolle öffentlicher Unternehmen* (Controls of Public Corporations). The interviews were used to supplement and verify my own work.

2

Bureaucratic Outputs

If the United States and Germany had decided to maximize the proceeds from the sale or disposition of assets as quickly as possible, both countries could have simply put firms and assets up for auction. The potential economic and political impacts such an enormous transfer might have had on their respective national economies led the legislative creators of the Resolution Trust Corporation (RTC) and Treuhandanstalt (THA) to supplement rapid privatization with a set of additional goals (for a comparison across agencies see Table 2.1).

The Financial Institutions Reform, Recovery, and Enforcement Act (FIRREA) required the RTC to privatize thrifts and their assets quickly. It also required the RTC to minimize the impact of these transactions on local real estate and financial markets; maximize the availability and affordability of housing for low- to moderate-income individuals; and maximize the opportunity for minority- and women-owned businesses (MWOBs) to participate as contractors, buyers of institutions, and purchasers of assets. Similarly, the Treuhandanstalt Law, passed on June 17, 1990, by the East German Volkskammer and later incorporated into Article 25 of the Unification Treaty, required the agency to "privatize state-owned enterprises as quickly and fully as possible" and to "establish the competitiveness of as many enterprises as possible and thereby secure and create jobs." Furthermore, the RTC and THA shared an implicit mandate of public organizations in all democratic countries, namely to ensure that effective accountability

Table 2.1

Summary Comparison of THA and RTC Mandates

RTC	THA
Rapidly resolve failed thrifts and their assets	Sell state-owned enterprises as quickly as possible
Minimize impact on local real estate and financial markets	Renovate as many enterprises as possible to secure and protect jobs
Maximize the availability of housing for low- to moderate-income individuals	Liquidate and close enterprises that have little hope of surviving
Maximize the opportunity for minority- and women-owned businesses to participate as contractors and buyers	Develop effective oversight and accountability
Provide effective oversight and accountability	

and oversight mechanisms were in place to maintain the integrity and legitimacy of the organizations and their governments.

Neither agency was given instructions on how it should pursue its legislative mandate. Nor did political principals prioritize what outcomes the agencies should pursue. The impact of structural designs assigned the two agencies by political principals is discussed in chapter 4. What is important to understand is that the RTC and THA were largely left on their own to fill in the blanks for how privatization should be implemented. This chapter discusses how the agencies filled in those blanks, how, in particular, their legislative mandates were put into practice.

Three categories are compared across agencies: (1) the pace and content of privatization; (2) the achievement of secondary goals; and (3) the patterns of accountability observed within each organization by various auditors.

PACE OF PRIVATIZATION: SIMILARITIES AND DIFFERENCES

The RTC managed to dispose of its portfolio in less than six years while the THA took four and a half years to dispose of the industrial assets of what, until 1989, had been one of the largest economies in

Table 2.2

Comparison of the Types of Assets and Forms of Privatization

	RTC	THA
What types of assets were in their portfolio?	Thrift institutions and their branches Mortgages Real estate Deposits Cash and securities	Industrial enterprises

What form did privatizations take?	Sale of thrifts and their branches (Resolution) through:
	    Purchase and assumption
	    Insured deposit transfer
	    Insured deposit payout
	
	Sale of assets sold as part of resolution
	
	Sale of assets while in conservatorship
	
	Sale of assets while in receivership
		Whole privatization (sale to private entities)
		
		Partial privatizations
		
		Reprivatization or restitution
		
		Management buyout
		
		Liquidation and closure

the world. Painting the agencies' stories in such broad strokes, however, obscures the enormity of their tasks, the substance of their accomplishments, and important differences in performance.

Table 2.2 compares the types of assets privatized and the forms that privatization took across the two agencies.

Types of Assets

The collapse of the U.S. savings and loan industry, which began in the late 1970s and peaked a decade later with the demise of more than a third of the industry, gave rise to one of the most complex domestic challenges the country faced since the early 1930s. The government had to assume the ownership of close to 750 ailing thrift institutions along with their assets. Assets included everything from large tracts of real estate in the Southwest to housing projects in the Northeast to billions of dollars' worth of mortgages backed by collateral scattered throughout the entire country. The level of sudden government ownership was not lost on international analysts who viewed it as peculiar that a conservative American government was taking such bold steps to nationalize a good portion of its economy. *The Economist* staff (1990, 24) noted in an article titled "Who'll Bid for Dallas?":

> It is tempting to see the RTC—now the world's largest property operation—as just another stage in the gradual progress of America towards socialism. The federal government has long owned much of the land in western states. . . . Now the government has nationalized a goodly chunk of the property business. Should President Bush get round to explaining the RTC to President Gorbachev, he may find his Russian guest congratulating him on his grasp of the elements of the command economy.

As the quotation suggests, the savings and loan crisis put the United States in the peculiar situation of suddenly owning a sizeable portion of the nation's financial industry.

When it began operations August 10, 1989, the RTC had 262 thrifts under its control and approximately $104 billion worth of assets.[1] By April 1990, the figure had ballooned to 400 thrifts, and the agency had instantly become the largest financial institution in the world. Ultimately, the RTC assumed control over 747 institutions and their assets. It was instructed to dispose of more than $460 billion worth of assets that included $210 billion in loans and mortgages, $161 billion in cash and securities, and $30 billion in real estate. To appreciate the magnitude, consider that in 1995 the two largest American private holding companies, Citibank and BankAmerica, owned assets valued at approximately half of the RTC's portfolio.[2] The uniqueness of the event made it even more surprising that it was matched in scale by an equally obscure German agency at roughly the same point in time.

To the THA fell the task of transferring to the private sector more than 8,000 former state-owned enterprises (SOEs), which later grew to over 13,000 firms. The SOEs included over 45,000 plants employing more than 4.1 million workers. The THA's portfolio centered around large-scale conglomerates known as *Kombinate.* Firms covered the entire spectrum of an advanced economy including mechanical engineering, energy, chemicals, textiles, and clothing. The *Los Angeles Times* (November 17, 1991, D3) described the THA's activity as the "biggest, most hectic, and most controversial going-out-of-business sale the industrial world has seen."

Forms of Privatization

The THA and RTC privatized in several different ways that reflected the complex nature of their portfolios. The RTC resolved failed thrifts that had been taken over by the government by legally separating assets from the thrift institution. Once a failed thrift was taken over by the federal government, it was placed under RTC management in what was known as "conservatorship." Thrift resolutions occurred in one of three ways.[3] Under the first option, known as a "Purchase and Assumption Agreement," the RTC was required to pay the full value of a thrift's depositor base immediately, net an amount that covered the value of the depositor and/or customer base, a thrift's name and branch offices, and the thrift's assets. The buyer purchased the assets and assumed the liabilities.

Under a second option, known as an "Insured Deposit Transfer," the government paid buyers the full value of the thrift's depositor base, net an amount that covered the value of the customer base. The third option was an "Insured Deposit Payout," where the government simply closed the institution down and paid off the debts and depositors.

In all three types of resolution, most of a thrift's assets remained with the RTC, where they were sold separately as part of what was called a "receivership." The privatization of RTC assets occurred in three different forms and in several different ways. A large number of assets were sold while under government management as part of the conservatorship operation. In conservatorship, managing agents (employed by the agency) reduced their portfolio by (1) selling assets, (2) marking down and discounting the book value of assets, and (3) allowing assets such as securities to mature. It is impossible to know how much of a reduction in assets occurred as a result of markdowns. Although the RTC published a book value, the figure is unreliable.

Appraisals were conducted both at the beginning and during the conservatorship operation. Conservatorships account for over $212 billion in sales and collection on assets. The overwhelming number of assets reduced were cash and securities which totaled $113.8 billion or 53 percent of the total volume of conservatorship assets. In fact, 71 percent of the RTC's entire portfolio of cash and securities was liquidated in the conservatorship operations.

As noted previously, assets were also included in the package of thrift sales. Thrift resolutions account for approximately $53.5 billion in assets sales. A third way in which assets were sold was in receivership. Receiverships accounted for nearly $130 billion in asset sales.

In carrying out its mandate, the German agency faced six separate divestment options. The most popular option from the THA's perspective was to sell the entire enterprise to a private buyer. If a buyer for the entire enterprise could not be found, the agency partially privatized a firm by first breaking up the conglomerate and selling the core businesses. A third option, used often in the cases of schools and utilities, was for the THA to transfer the enterprise or its parts to a local government. A fourth option was to return the firm or parts of the firm to groups whose property had been taken away by the Nazi or Communist regimes.[4] A fifth alternative was to allow the employees or managers to purchase the firm through a "management buyout." Finally, the sixth option the THA had was to declare bankruptcy and sell off the thrift's assets through a liquidation proceeding.

The differences in the types of assets the two agencies privatized makes it difficult to provide a quick comparison of the two agencies' actions. However, keeping in mind the different forms of privatization allows one to draw some conclusions about the comparative pace of divestment. Figure 2.1 illustrates the differences and similarities across the two agencies.

Both agencies divested themselves of their portfolios at a dramatic pace. Following the unification of East and West Germany in October 1990 and the placement of the THA within the Ministry of Finance, the THA quickly privatized more than 4,800 firms, as well as nearly 25,000 smaller retail enterprises (BvS 1995, 5).[5] By the end of 1991, nearly 40 percent of the agencies' holdings had been divested. Most were sold to private buyers, though a significant number, 865,

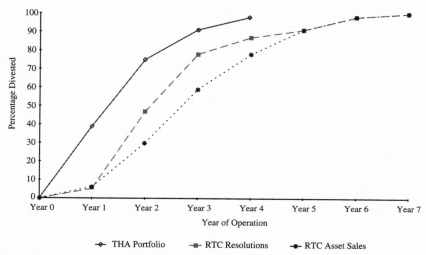

Figure 2.1   **RTC and THA Rates of Divestment**

were closed and liquidated. Table 2.3 reports the THA's divestment activity over time.

Schmidt and Siegmund (1996) note that during the initial period the agency conducted "free sales" (though several privatizers with whom I spoke sarcastically referred to them as "fire sales") of the most desirable firms. In many cases, state-owned enterprises had signed cooperation agreements with western companies even before the establishment of the THA. Negotiations between the THA and interested parties occurred without any formal procedures, and arrangements worked out between the SOE and western firm were largely accepted as a fait accompli.

Later, when faced with the more difficult-to-sell assets, the THA privatized at a slower rate and chose to close and liquidate firms more frequently. In 1991 the agency privatized 5.6 firms for every one it closed. A year later 2.4 firms were sold for every one that was liqui-dated. During the later years of its operation, the agency also con-ducted far more management buyouts, transfers to local governments, and restitutions. What stands out is the overall pace of divestiture, which remained fairly constant throughout the agency's existence. The agency did not alter its central tendency to divest itself of as many

Table 2.3

Treuhand Cumulative Activity, 1990–94

Activity	1991	1992	1993	1994
THA portfolio of all enterprises	10,663	11,780	12,246	12,354
Enterprises in THA ownership	7,502	3,143	1,059	192
Rate of divestment[a] (%)	39	75	91	98
Privatized enterprises[b]	4,852	5,456	6,180	6,546
Reprivatized enterprises[c]	527	1,188	1,573	1,588
Community ownership	145	319	261	265
Other privatizations	0	0	85	45
Liquidations	865	2,249	3,196	3,718
Management buyouts	854	1,946	2,425	2,697

Source: THA cited in Kühl (1997, 120).

[a]Total number of enterprises transformed as a percent of portfolio by end of 1994.

[b]Including 7,600 parts of firms and 25,030 "small" privatizations (e.g., retail trades, restaurants).

[c]Including 2,670 parts of firms that were given back to their previous owners.

assets as quickly as possible. The THA expected the cost of renovation or reinvestment to be borne by the private investor, not government.

The RTC also privatized at a rapid pace, though there were several important differences that distinguished the American agency from its German counterpart. The RTC not only sold or closed thrifts through its resolution procedure, it also sold thrift assets. Tables 2.4 and 2.5 describe the pace of thrift resolutions and asset sales, respectively.

Both tables suggest a similar pattern that is different from the THA. The RTC was initially quite cautious. Three attempts in 1990 to mount ascending-bid, property-by-property auctions were each canceled because of the excessive due-diligence costs imposed on buyers by the RTC (Vandell and Riddiough 1992, 117). As complaints from private investors mounted, the agency's philosophy and procedures changed dramatically.[6] Rather than seek the highest return on each asset, the RTC's strategy shifted to an aggressive drive to package and sell off combinations of desirable and undesirable assets well below book value. Noting the change, a *Wall Street Journal* article stated,

Table 2.4

Pace of Resolutions and the Value of Assets Passed Through to Receiverships Following Resolution, 1989–95

Year	No. of Resolutions	Total Assets at Resolution ($ billions)	Total Assets Transferred to Buyer ($ billions)	Assets Transferred to Receivership (%)
1989	37	10.8	2.20	79.6
1990	315	96.0	23.90	75.1
1991	232	78.1	16.17	79.3
1992	69	35.5	5.43	84.7
1993	27	7.5	2.73	73.6
1994	64	15.3	2.98	80.5
1995	3	1.7	.08	95.2
Totals	747	244.9	53.49	78.2

Source: RTC (1996).

Table 2.5

RTC Asset Sales, 1989–95

Year	Total Assets Transferred to Buyer during Resolutions ($ millions)	Asset Sales in Conservatorships ($ millions)	Asset Sales in Receiverships ($ millions)	Total Assets Sold ($ millions)
1989	2,200	22,648	243	25,091
1990	23,900	59,333	11,774	95,007
1991	16,170	55,275	40,066	111,511
1992	5,430	33,836	39,029	78,295
1993	2,730	29,774	17,389	49,893
1994	2,980	10,044	14,041	27,065
1995	80	1,112	7,262	8,454
Totals	53,490	212,022	129,804	395,316

Source: RTC (1996).

"They've [the RTC] said, 'Let's forget about what this was worth five years ago'. . . . Their philosophy has changed to sell, sell, sell" (cited in Vandell and Riddiough 1992, 119).

Table 2.4 shows that during the first six months only thirty-seven resolutions were carried out. The following year resolutions increased tenfold. Between August 1989 and January 1991, the agency resolved 352 institutions, and by 1992, 584 institutions had been resolved. In its report the RTC Task Force stated, "The RTC's record is unprecedented and unequaled—352 institutions were 'resolved' in the 17 months between August 1989 and January 1991 . . . double the amount that was planned for the first three years" (U.S. House 1991, 8). Altogether, in resolving the institutions, the agency performed 495 purchase and assumption agreements, 158 insured deposit transfers, and 92 insured deposit payouts.

A similar story applies to the sale of assets. In the early stages of its operation, the RTC behaved cautiously, but it accelerated in the third year with an increase in bulk sales and securitizations. Table 2.5 shows the annual sale of assets by their book value and how they sold: in conservatorship, as part of the resolution, or in receivership.

During its first six months, the RTC divested approximately $25 billion worth of assets. This was an extremely small amount, about 6 percent, of total holdings. A year later, the agency sold $95 billion worth of assets or about a quarter of its holdings. At that point much of the RTC's remaining asset portfolio was also the least desirable. During its third year, the RTC sold more than $111 billion in assets, which constituted nearly half of the agency's entire asset portfolio. This was a major increase in the pace of privatization and corresponds to observations made by real estate finance experts Kerry Vandell and Timothy Riddiough (1991, 119), who compared the change in the agency's behavior to the shift from Jekyll to Hyde.

In summary, the RTC and the THA divested themselves of their portfolios at an extremely rapid pace. It is difficult to imagine *any* organization selling off $400 billion in assets along with 750 weak financial institutions, as the RTC did, or 13,000 industrial firms, as the THA did. The fact that these were public organizations that accomplished the feat in seven and five years, respectively, gives one pause. The data indicate that it was the United States, a much more liberal economy than Germany, that acted in a far more cautious and careful manner.

Treatment of Secondary Goals

In addition to rapid privatization, the RTC and THA were instructed to pursue another set of goals. Employees and observers of the agencies often referred to these as the "social" or "political" goals and responsibilities, as opposed to the "economic" or "core mission" of the agencies. Table 2.6 presents a comparison of the secondary goals written into the RTC and THA's enabling legislation.

The THA was required under law to "establish the competitiveness of as many enterprises as possible and thereby secure and create jobs." Firms that could not be saved were to be closed and their assets liquidated. The RTC was required by law to minimize the impact on local real estate and financial markets, maximize opportunities for MWOBs as purchasers and contractors, and maximize affordable housing for low- and moderate-income households. The fact that these additional goals made it into the enabling legislation of both agencies with no specific priority given to rapid divestiture suggests that there was strong societal support for these secondary outcomes.

Yet with two important exceptions, there is general agreement among academic observers, public auditors, and agency employees that both agencies minimized these secondary legislative goals despite constant pressure from legislators and societal groups to expand their interpretation of privatization. The exceptions include in the THA's case the active restructuring of a handful of large firms; in the RTC's case the protection of local real estate and financial markets from the adverse effects of the agency's divestments. The following offers a more detailed account of these outcomes.

Minority- and Women-Owned Businesses

Under Section 1216c of FIRREA, the legislature required the RTC to "prescribe regulations to establish and oversee a minority outreach program . . . to ensure inclusion, to the maximum extent possible, of minorities and women and entities owned by women . . . in all contracts entered into by the agency." The Oversight Board, a governing body created to oversee the agency, directed the RTC to develop by January 31, 1990, an MWOB outreach program to provide for (1) the active promotion of the outreach program to eligible firms and individuals; (2) the development of an ongoing monitoring mechanism

Table 2.6

Summary Comparison of RTC and THA Secondary Goals and Programs

	RTC			THA	
Mandated Goals	Maximize contracting and purchasing opportunities for minority- and women-owned businesses	Expand the supply of affordable housing for low- and moderate-income households	Minimize impact on local financial and real estate markets	Restructure firms	Guarantee employment and investment
Agency Program or Initiative	MWOB program MWOLF program[a] Interim capital assistance program[b]	Single family disposition program Multifamily disposition program	Prevented from selling thrifts below 95 percent of their book value in certain states	Passive restructuring Management KGs Creative privatization Atlas program	No specific program A general policy of taking price, employment, and investment guarantees into account

[a]Minority- and Women-Owned Legal Firm program designed to increase the hiring of MWOB firms for legal services.

[b]Program aimed at assisting minority-owned financial institutions in purchasing thrifts.

to allow evaluation; (3) a definition of what constitutes an eligible individual or firm; and (4) a process for identifying and certifying eligible MWOB contractors.

The RTC was slow to implement its MWOB program (GAO 1991e). While the agency did adopt interim guidelines for the program by the January 1990 deadline, it took another year and a half before final rules were established and the program was completely under way.

The interim guidelines were vague and lacked clarity. They included, for example, no mechanisms for identifying, certifying, or promoting MWOBs.[7] Bruce Vento (D-MN), chairman of the Task Force on the RTC, issued a report in March 1991 that stated, "Clearly the RTC, while it is awarding some contracts to minority- and women-owned firms, has not reached an equitable level of activity. . . . The RTC revised its bidder selection procedures to, among other things, assure that a sufficient number of minority and women-owned firms were represented in the pool. But obviously, this program hasn't helped" (U.S. House 1991, 35–36).

During its first year and a half of operation, the RTC let 4,594 contracts and awarded 6 percent to minority-owned firms and 11 percent to women-owned firms. Most of these contracts were in the area of real estate brokerage. No contracts were awarded to minority-owned firms for services involving architecture, engineering, appraisal review, financial investigation, litigation, marketing/leasing, security services, or surveying. No contracts were awarded to women-owned firms for marketing/leasing, litigation services, property tax consulting services, security services, or surveying.

In April 1991, the RTC formally transmitted the draft MWOB program policy to the Oversight Board for review. The board expressed concern that the policy did not fulfill FIRREA's requirements. Final regulations were approved and published in the *Federal Register* on August 15, 1991. The rules adopted required firms to register with the RTC, certifying their MWOB status and specifying the service they could provide.

Over time, the RTC made progress in hiring more MWOB contractors. In accordance with the RTC Refinancing, Restructuring, and Improvement Act of 1991 (RTCRRIA), the RTC awarded bonus points on both technical and cost portions of the contract evaluations to MWOB firms and to firms that committed to substantial MWOB participation. The agency also moved the head of the MWOB up to the level of vice president, on par with resolution and asset management. Noting the changes, a government auditor stated:

> The most significant step the RTC made toward developing an effective MWOB program was when they elevated the job to the position of VP, made it a division, and increased staffing. But this didn't occur until 1992, three years after the agency started. At that point the RTC increased the staff both at the headquarters and in the field and established concrete goals instead of merely vague mandate.

RTC officials at the national office concurred with the auditor's statements. With each refunding of the agency came managerial reforms that standardized procedures, increased oversight, and placed the MWOB program higher on the agency's agenda.

By 1992, after the agency had divested much of its portfolio, the RTC significantly increased its use of MWOB contractors. Of the 45,928 non-legal contracts that were let during that year, 12.4 percent went to minority firms, and 22.3 percent went to nonminority, women-owned firms. A year later, 14.6 percent of non-legal contracts went to minority firms, and 28.7 percent went to nonminority, women-owned firms.

The agency increased its use of MWOB for legal work through the development of the Minority- and Women-Owned Legal Firm (MWOLF) program. By 1993 the agency awarded 56 percent of its legal contracts to MWOB firms (U.S. House 1994, 48–49).

Finally, the RTC also increased its efforts to aid in the acquisition of minority-owned thrifts by minority bidders. Under the interim capital assistance program, the RTC lent acquirers up to two-thirds of the capital required to set up a new thrift institution and receive FDIC insurance. In 1994, John Ryan, the RTC chief executive officer, reported that of the twenty-nine minority-owned institutions that had failed, twelve were acquired by like-minority bidders, nine were bought by majority bidders, five were paid out, and three remained unresolved (U.S. House 1994).

Affordable Housing

As with its MWOB program, the RTC moved extremely slowly in developing and implementing an Affordable Housing Disposition Plan (AHDP). Referring to the affordable housing program, a national sales staffperson who worked for four years in the agency said, "The RTC did not really have a program set up until 1991–92." Heather MacDonald's (1995) work, supported by GAO audits and congressional testimony, notes that the "first years of [the RTC's] existence produced disappointing results for the housing advocates who had argued so strongly for the disposition plan" (558). A congressional briefing paper on the Operation and Performance of the RTC to the House Banking Committee noted, "The RTC's efforts at implementing the low-income housing goals of FIRREA have been minimal" (U.S. House 1990a). Although the agency acquired the bulk of eligible housing properties between 1989 and 1992, it was not until 1992 that the affordable housing program began to work as intended.

The RTC reported in 1990 that it had sold 64 single-family properties directly to state agencies and 2,728 single-family properties (36 percent of total holdings) through clearinghouses at an average price of $36,694 per housing unit. By June 1992 the RTC reported that it had made available 28,819 single-family properties. Of these, it had completed sales on 9,529 (33 percent), accepted offers on another 9,943 (35 percent), and 5,235 (18 percent) were still for sale. The remaining 4,112 (14 percent) were passed through the program's exclusive listing period without being sold to an eligible buyer.

Although the RTC increased the pace of sales, exact figures on sales of single-family homes to qualified buyers are difficult to establish because of the agency's poor record-keeping. The agency was negligent in enforcement of directives about data. For example, until the RTC issued a directive on certification of buyer eligibility in June 1992, at least two regional offices (Southwest and West) did not require documentation of buyers' income (GAO 1992f, 6). In addition, third parties, such as real estate brokers and other contractors, were required to verify buyers' income, yet the GAO could only establish that 35 percent of purchasers under the AHDP in the Southwest and West had provided documentation to third-party contractors

(GAO 1992f, 7). Finally, there was inadequate verification of the owner-occupancy requirement. To ensure that affordable housing would be used by those who needed it rather than by speculators, FIRREA required that buyers use the property as their principal residence. This was later clarified to mean twelve months. Purchase offers accepted by RTC after May 6, 1992, included a deed restriction to enforce the requirement. By May 1992, however, only four of RTC's fifteen field offices had begun testing for occupancy.

A similar picture emerges with multifamily properties. During its first three years, the agency experienced only limited success selling and preserving multifamily affordable housing. The RTC reported in February 1992 that since its inception the agency had offered 744 eligible properties for sale with a book value of $1.2 billion. Of those, it had closed sales transactions on 127 properties (17 percent) and accepted offers on another eighty-four properties (11 percent). About 20 percent of the total assets were still in the ninety-day marketing period and 37 percent had passed through but remained unsold. About 15 percent of the properties were not sold while in the program and subsequently were sold without affordable housing restrictions (GAO 1992a, 7–8).

The sale of multifamily units to eligible buyers was hampered by the agency's preference for bulk sales over individual sales. Bulk sales excluded smaller purchasers such as local nonprofits. The lack of assistance by the RTC to nonprofits also slowed the process. FIRREA authorized the RTC to provide up to 100 percent financing for multifamily sales to nonprofits and public agencies. The agency did not offer this assistance until January 1992 and by June had not completed any multifamily sales under the program (GAO 1992a, 10).

Initially, properties belonging to thrifts in conservatorship were not included in the affordable housing program. This meant that during the first cut at selling residential assets, the affordable housing mandates did not apply. The RTC estimated that 10 percent of eligible single-family properties in conservatorship were sold to unqualified buyers during this period. In addition, twenty-one multifamily properties in conservatorship were sold in 1990 without AHDP restrictions (U.S. House 1990b, 63). Further, MacDonald notes that discounts were not offered until a property had remained unsold for five months (and thus was no longer available exclusively to qualified buyers) despite the fact that appraisals were outdated and well above the market value (MacDonald 1995, 561).

MacDonald as well as auditors in the GAO note a systematic pattern in the RTC's reluctance to embark on a program such as affordable housing. When the agency did make progress it came only after significant pressure was exercised by Congress and a large portion of the agency's other assets had already been sold. The RTC Funding Act, passed by Congress in March 1991 (PL 102–18, 105 Stat. 58), extended the affordable housing program to conservatorships and removed the requirement that RTC get a minimum sales price for the property (Crawford 1991).

Protection of Local Financial and Real Estate Markets

A final mandate in FIRREA was to protect local real estate and financial markets. FIRREA charged the RTC with establishing "an appraisal or other valuation method for determining the market value of real property in distressed areas."[8] Market value was defined as the price at which a property would sell in a competitive and open market. Appraisals, mandated twice a year on each asset, were conducted by independent appraisers hired at the regional and consolidated offices. To protect markets, FIRREA required that real estate be sold for at least 95 percent of market value in distressed areas, which included Texas, Arizona, Colorado, New Mexico, Oklahoma, and Texas. In other areas the RTC could sell for no less than 90 percent of market value. Later, in August 1991, the RTC revised this policy to allow asset sales at progressively lower prices, ranging from 80 percent of appraised value in the first six months down to 50 percent after eighteen months.

Vandell and Riddiough (1991) note that in the beginning the RTC exhibited a great deal of caution regarding the impact of its sales on real estate markets. The "dumping" of assets was a major concern during the first year and a half of the RTC's operation. Regional and national advisory boards became forums for local interests to express their concern about how much real estate the RTC would put on the market. A countervailing point of view was that holding assets off the market created a great deal of uncertainty about the future and thus, by keeping assets from being sold, negatively impacted markets. In the end, the RTC's sales activity had little impact on local markets since the RTC did not create new properties or assets.[9] The primary concern among agency salespeople was to ensure that enough bidders participated to allow the competitive market to function. If there were enough bidders and the price on the asset was below book value, it meant that the appraisal was incorrect rather than that dumping had occurred, according to an RTC official in charge of auctions.

Restructuring of Firms

The Treuhand Law required the THA to (1) identify firms that could be transformed into competitive enterprises and (2) carry out a restructuring plan. The agency fulfilled the first part by creating an independent advisory body known as the management committee (Leitungsausschuß), consisting of approximately eighty consultants from the most elite management consulting companies in the world. The management committee was responsible for evaluating the restructuring and privatization plans of firms that had liabilities in excess of DM10 million. More than 5,000 firms were evaluated by the committee, and each received a grade according to a scale from one ("company operating profitably") to six ("company not capable of being restructured"). Various elements were taken into account including the accuracy, completeness, and assumptions underlying the corporate strategy and balance sheets submitted by firms. A breakdown of grades through the end of 1992 is shown in Table 2.7.

Only 23 percent of firms fell into categories five or six. At the same time only 2 percent of firms were determined to be profitable and in need of no immediate infusions of liquidity. The overwhelming majority—more than 70 percent—were given a reasonable chance of being salvageable but required some combination of immediate liquidity and restructuring.

Despite the large number of firms that were deemed salvageable, the agency did relatively little to actively transform struggling SOEs into competitive enterprises through new investments of capital, preferring instead to let the private buyers carry out restructuring plans. The exception to this general pattern was a handful of the largest and most politically important East German firms that were "saved" by the federal government in response to external pressures.

Table 2.7

No. of THA Firms Assessed by Management Committee and Grades through 1992

Grade	No. of Firms	Percentage
1	101	2
2	320	6
3	1105	21
3.1	998	19
4	1548	29
5	343	7
6	852	16

Source: Schwalbach and Gless (1996, 188).
The interpretation of each grade is as follows: 1: Company is operating profitably; no further need for restructuring. 2: Company expected to become profitable; virtually no further need for restructuring. 3: Corporate strategy appears successful. 3.1: Definite take-over purchaser must be identified, otherwise demote to group 5 or 6; liquidity requirement is necessary. 4: Company appears capable of being effectively restructured; strategy not yet sufficient; alternative strategies need to be established. 5: Capability of restructuring company appear dubious. 6: Company not capable of restructuring; liquidation or bankruptcy necessary.

In her study of East Germany's privatization, Phyllis Dininio (1999) documents how, despite the THA's open commitment to "promoting the formation of small and mid-sized firms," the agency did very little active restructuring during the first two years of operation. Instead, the agency practiced what Marc Kemmler (1994) refers to as "passive" restructuring—providing initial support (through loan guarantees) to meet payroll costs while simultaneously dismantling and downsizing firms. Studies and accounts from individuals hired by the THA to manage its firms indicate that the THA refused to devote resources for new equipment, capital, or research and development. A firm manager recruited by the THA to run two of its firms put the matter in the following way:

> My role as manager was to turn the company into something that could be privatized. I worked on three different plans. They were designed around

using the proceeds from the sale of land to restructure the company. The Treuhand would have none of it. They told me that the land was separate from the enterprise and not under my control. Each time I tried to pursue a different proposal that would turn the company around it was rejected. I would characterize the agency as negative consulting: I never saw a single case where they would say 'you can do this.' They always said you can't do this or can't do that. Why was there no positive consulting? Probably because that was not their job.

In short, restructuring that was specifically designed to reorient the enterprises toward new markets or developing new products was discouraged.

In a speech in November 1991, THA President Birgit Breuel stated the need to preserve the industrial cores of eastern Germany "under any circumstances."[10] The newfound religion led to several restructuring initiatives including the development of Management Kommanditgesellschaften (Management KGs) in December 1991, the Creative Privatization Program in May 1992, and the Atlas Program in April 1992.

Management KGs, or limited partnerships, placed business executives in charge of restructuring selected THA firms on a for-profit basis (Dininio 1999; Kern and Sabel 1996; Geppert and Schmidt 1993). Business executives contracted by the THA directed the restructuring and profited from the eventual privatization. The THA withdrew from the daily management of the firm but remained owner and provided capital. The agency sought out mid-sized firms (with 400–500 employees) that were classified as viable but had significant restructuring needs and no prospective buyers. Ultimately, with a great deal of fanfare, the Management KG initiative involved no more than sixty-nine firms with a total of 31,600 employees and "remained an ancillary operation since the agency did not establish them 'across the board' or 'on principle,' but instead founded them 'according to need' or to the availability of a business partner (Dininio 1999, 57).

In May 1992 the THA launched the Creative Privatization Program, an effort to allocate greater personnel resources to restructuring and selling of large firms or "industrially and trans-regionally significant firms with more than 250 employees." The agency invited the managers of 800 large firms to propose medium-term capital investments and then negotiated financing for the projects. Dininio notes that in the end, however, the Creative Privatization Program "deployed substantial managerial and financial resources to only a dozen or so very large firms. . . . The [program] amounted, in effect, to little more than an authorization of ad hoc interventions in large firms" (Dininio 1999, 57). The ad-hoc interventions created "restructuring islands" in the East (Cadel 1994).[11]

Finally, a third program known as ATLAS (Ausgewählte Treuhandunternehmen vom Land Sachsen angemeldet zur Sanierung) was established in April 1992 (Nolte 1994; Kern and Sabel 1996). The program linked the THA, the state of Saxony, and societal groups to save "regionally significant" companies. The state of Saxony identified 215 THA firms it considered regionally important based on the number of employees, their importance for supply networks, or their research and development potential. As with previous initiatives, few firms actually received capital, and those that did were very large. By the end of 1993, the ATLAS program provided DM55 million to thirty-eight Saxon firms, mostly in the metal and textile industries (Nolte 1994, 36).

Dininio's examination of the THA's restructuring supports a more general trend within the agency to not invest in new restructuring proposals. The policy of leaving "active restructuring" to purchasers is reflected in the differences in the level of investment per employee between THA and former THA firms that were privatized (see Table 2.8).

The data from the German Institute for Economic Research point to dramatic differences in investment between THA-owned firms and those that were formerly THA-owned. The differences occurred in firms of all sizes but were particularly pronounced in smaller firms where the ratio of investment between THA and privatized firms is approximately one to five. For example, in those firms surveyed with more than 500 employees the investor spent approximately DM 32,000 ($21,000) per employee, whereas the THA-owned firm invested approximately half that, DM 18,200 ($12,100). The difference was even more dramatic in smaller firms. For example, in those firms with between twenty and 500 employees, the survey reported

Table 2.8

Investment in East German Industrial Firms
(in DM thousands)

Firm Size (employees)	Total	< 20	20–499	> 500
THA Firms	16.5 (142)[a]	5.0 (7)	12.9 (113)	18.2 (22)
Privatized Firms	29.8 (958)	23.7 (189)	28.0 (725)	32.6 (44)

Source: Carlin and Mayer (1995). Data from a survey conducted in the winter of 1993–94 supplied by the German Institute for Economic Research (*Deutsches Institut für Wirtschaftsforschung*), Berlin.

[a]No. of firms in parentheses.

that DM 28,000 ($18,600) was invested per employee compared with the DM 12,900 ($8,600) that was invested in the THA firms.

In short, the THA did little active restructuring, preferring instead to let buyers (who would ultimately bear the financial risks) take on the responsibility. Restructuring initiatives were begun in 1991 and 1992, although they were primarily focused on large firms and done in an ad-hoc fashion. Relying on data collected from eight representative surveys conducted of privatized firms on behalf of Germany's Bureau of Labor, Jürgen Kühl concludes, "Almost half of all privatizations transferred only parts of firms—the more successful parts—to the new owners. But there was no concept of reindustrialization. . . . The THA ceased privatization operations in 1994, and left the public budget with a debt of DM270 billion. . . . Instead of reconstructing firms before privatization, the THA strategy contributed to a rapid deindustrialization in all industrial sectors and in almost all regions" (Kühl 1997, 139–40). In line with the agency commitment to allowing buyers to carry out any new investments, the THA negotiated contracts with clauses guaranteeing investment and employment levels.

Employment and Investment Guarantees

To fulfill what it perceived as its "social" mandates, the THA took into account three types of currencies: price, a commitment by the buyer to retain a minimum number of employees, and a commitment by the buyer to make investments in the enterprise after it was sold.[12] Employment guarantees were for annual levels of full-time employment.[13] Job creation programs or part-time work were not included. Investment guarantees were for investments in capital equipment or plant construction. The purchase of additional land, for example, did not count. Contracts signed by the agency and investors were typically for no more than three years.[14] Job and investment commitments were thus guaranteed only for a limited period of time. Clauses were included that allowed firms to renegotiate the terms of their contracts if, for example, their ability to remain viable was jeopardized by changes in the market. Initially the agency "encouraged" or "suggested" that firms meet their commitments. Later, penalty clauses were included in contracts that required the purchaser to pay fines for failing to meet investment or employment commitments.

Subsidies were included in the sale either directly or in the form of a negative price. The agency, in essence, paid buyers to take the assets off the state's hands. In this way, Czada and others note that it makes sense to think of the THA less as a sales agency than as a purchaser of business proposals (Czada 1996b). The agency negotiated among the mix of currencies to satisfy its mandate of rapid privatization, restructuring, and closure. Discounts on sales prices or increases in subsidies were typically offered in exchange for job commitments and investment guarantees.[15]

Tables 2.9 and 2.10 summarize the THA's performance in negotiating employment and investment guarantees over time.

The THA reported that from its start through 1994 it had successfully protected 1.5 million jobs and persuaded buyers to invest DM211 billion in privatized firms. While the agency's reported findings suggest the agency was successful in achieving its secondary goals, questions and concerns were raised by the federal government's accounting office and various research groups that studied both types of commitments.

First, the type of data collected systematically and reported to the public make it impossible to evaluate effectively the costs and benefits of employment and investment commitments. A study of employment and investment guarantees (Bundesrechnungshof 1992) by the federal auditor found that in 75 percent of the contracts reviewed,

Table 2.9

Cumulative Employment Commitments, Guarantees Enforced through Penalties, and Actual Employment in Privatized THA Firms, 1991–94

Year	Employment Commitments	Employment Guarantees Backed by Penalties	Actual Employment in Firms	Commitment Backed by Penalties (%)	Actual Employment as a Percentage of Employment Commitments
1991	930,262	223,455	247,518	24	27
1992	1,400,677	447,987	497,567	32	36
1993	1,486,750	559,759	617,000	38	44
1994	1,505,000	426,503	510,700	28	34

Source: Treuhandanstalt, Ministry of Finance cited in Sitte and Tofaute (1996, 10).

Table 2.10

Annual Investment Commitments, Guarantees Enforced through Penalties, and Actual Investment in Privatized THA Firms 1992–1994 (in DM billions)

Year	Investment Commitments	Investment Guarantees Backed by Penalties	Actual Investment in Firms	Commitments Backed by Penalties (%)	Actual Investment as a Percentage of Investment Commitments
1992	9.73	1.33	3.07	14	32
1993	19.33	9.47	13.20	49	68
1994	21.90	9.13	12.13	41	55

Source: Bundesanstalt für vereinigungsbedingte Sonderaufgaben (BvS) (1995, 3).

THA agents entered negotiations with no prior concrete expectations about job or investment guarantees. The agreed-upon commitments were typically below those that had been initially proposed by the buyer.

Several agency employees explained that investors viewed employment and investment commitments as a means to achieve a lower price (increased subsidy) and in some cases to renegotiate the contract later. As long as employment and investment commitments were either unenforceable or within the range of what the buyer would have adopted in the absence of the legal commitments, no real cost was imposed on the investor. The THA pushed for lower commitments to demonstrate that it was being effective at protecting jobs. As one agent put it, "If a company that had 8,000 employees puts down in writing that it will keep 800 and in the end keeps 1,000, the labor force is reduced by 7,000 but the THA can say not only that it guaranteed 800 jobs but that investors exceeded their contractual obligations." Thus, looking strictly at the aggregate investment and employment commitments says little about how successful or efficient the agency was in spending the public's resources to maintain jobs or improve the competitiveness of eastern industry.

Even more problematic are the raw data on investment and employment commitments. The agency's figures blur the distinction between the various types of contracts and commitments. The THA negotiated three types of guarantees. The first specified precise employment and investment levels that were enforced through penalty clauses. The penalty clauses took one of two forms: either a certain increase in the price of the enterprise per unfulfilled commitment or, alternatively, a certain amount independent of the contract price of the asset.[16] A second variation involved contracts in which timetables, investment, and employment guarantees were clearly defined but there was no penalty clause included. Finally, a third variation was "soft" contracts in which investors committed themselves in principle to target levels of investment and employment and no penalties were involved. Although all three contracts were "guarantees" in theory, the reality was that only those enforceable through penalties were actually binding.

The THA information system was inconsistent in its reporting. One study found that on a single day (May 31, 1994) three different agency estimates were reported for the number of jobs secured in 1992. An investigatory committee in the Bundestag commented that the agency was plagued with methodological problems in its data reporting, including unsubstantiated data, inconsistencies, irregularities in calculating data, and simply wrong information. Even the *Final Report of the Treuhandanstalt*, published in English and made available to researchers, makes no reference to the percentage of the investment and employment guarantees that are enforceable.

The distinction between enforceable and general commitments is significant. Tables 2.9 and 2.10 report on enforceable employment commitments, unenforceable commitments, and actual employment levels in privatized firms. The data draw upon THA data and research conducted by a number of research groups that assessed the impact of the THA's policies.

There is a significant difference between employment commitments generally and employment commitments that contractually obligate the buyer through penalties. In 1991, for example, the agency reported that 930,262 jobs had been preserved through commitments by buyers. Of that figure, however, only 24 percent were contractually ensured. Furthermore, studies based on the THA and the Ministry of Finance's data note that 247,518 jobs were actually secured. Similarly, in 1993 the general figure for employment commitments reported by the THA rose to nearly 1.5 million. In fact, however, only 38 percent of the jobs were guaranteed contractually, and only 44 percent actually existed.

Second, job commitments guaranteed through penalties declined following 1993. This is explained by the expiration on the contractual obligations and points to a further weakness in the data reporting system: although the THA reports the overall level of investment and employment commitments, no information is given regarding how long commitments are in effect. The average is reported to be between two and five years.

A similar phenomenon applies to investment guarantees. Table 2.10 reports on the investment guarantees between 1992 and 1994.[17] It shows that the THA secured investment guarantees from buyers that substantially exceeded the guarantees required under the sales contracts. In this respect, the THA was highly successful. By 1994, according to the THA's figures, contracts negotiated by the THA had contributed to nearly DM30 billion in investments to privatized firms. On the other hand, in comparison to all investment guarantees, the actual investment falls far short of promised investment reported by the agency.

Two final issues are important regarding investment and employment guarantees: (1) the agency's collection of data on commitments; and (2) the position the THA faced when commitments were not met. The THA and later the BvS collected information from investors through questionnaires sent to the firm management. Employees in the Contract Management Department rarely conducted on-site visits. In many cases firms failed to return questionnaires. More problematic, however, was that the incentives built into the agency's data collection system created a bias toward over-reporting job and investment commitments on the one hand, and under-enforcement by the agency on the other.

Firms faced a strong incentive to report figures to the THA that exceeded their contractual obligations. This was particularly true in cases of investment guarantees, which were far more difficult to track and validate than employment guarantees. Since few firms would voluntarily impose penalties upon themselves, those that failed to meet their obligations were either unlikely to report their progress to the government agency or likely to ask for their contract to be renegotiated. For example, *The European* reported (July 8–11, 1993, p. 34) that the buyer of a textile company, Faser AG, had invested only a fraction of the DM100 million ($60 million) originally committed. The case is troublesome in part because the buyer had received a sizable subsidy from the THA, much of which was to cover the investment commitment, and in part because the agency found out about the investor's activity only after workers in the company complained. The incident points to a further problem in the monitoring of contracts.

In particular, there was little incentive on the part of the THA (or now the BvS) to develop any extensive investigatory capacity or to be aggressive in monitoring contracts even though large subsidies were transferred to buyers. This was true for two reasons: first, it was quite costly to set up monitoring systems across different industries and branches; and second, every investor caught cheating reflected poorly on the agency overseeing control of the process. In other words, the agency's own reputation was enhanced when it could claim that industries had exceeded their investment and job guarantees, and conversely, the agency's reputation declined when reports raised questions about the integrity of contracts. A young manager in the contract management division who had spent several years in the agency after obtaining his law degree put the matter clearly: "Any investigation that undermined these findings was seen to undermine the agency."

There is evidence to show that the THA did little to hold firms accountable when they did not fulfill their guarantees. For example, Kühl (1997) writes that firms reduced their workforce by 20 to 30 percent after the THA had transferred ownership:

> Some firms had made no promises on jobs; some had no agreements on penalties; some kept on parts of the workforce for some time before dismissals; some found their initial expectations of a rapid upswing disappointed, having made this a condition for retaining jobs. Only a very few privatized firms have been asked to pay the fine of DM5,000–DM20,000 per job promised—a sum which would bring firms close to bankruptcy if they had to pay it (124).

The manager in the division described the difficult position faced by the agency:

> What do you do if the company says we cannot meet these employment commitments and stay viable? Do you slap on fines that may send the firm into bankruptcy? The reality is that the THA, and later the BvS, can do very little. We imposed maybe 766 million marks in fines, and maybe DM 20 million were actually paid. In most cases fines were levied against bankrupt firms. Why levy fines against a company that's hurting?

More common was the case in which a firm would seek to renegotiate its contract in order to reduce its sales price (or increase the subsidy) or change one of the commitments. One report suggests that more than a thousand firms renegotiated their contracts in 1995 (Schwenn 1995).

PATTERNS OF ACCOUNTABILITY

While oversight and accountability are not typically thought of as bureaucratic outputs, few things are as important in a democratic system. As Fesler and Kettl note, "A constitutional system of government entails the subordination of bureaucrats to mandates and constraints of the Constitution and laws, as interpreted by the courts, and to hierarchical superiors in the executive branch" (Fesler and Kettl 1996, 367). An important element of bureaucratic subordination is control, the ability of citizens (through their representatives) to ensure that legislative mandates are met by their bureaucratic agents. Four essential elements of control can be seen and compared across the THA and RTC.

The first element of control is *voluntary compliance*. Employees within the agency must be counted on to follow the rules and procedures of the organization. Without such compliance, the scope and intensity of control systems would be impossible to achieve. Second, control requires the establishment of *clear standards*. The standards communicate to individuals what is expected of them and when they are subject to sanctions. Standards also convey the central oversight concerns to control agencies and, by extension, hold the controllers accountable. Third, *monitoring systems* are necessary for any control to be credible. Monitoring may be comprehensive or selective. It may also be reactive; monitors investigate complaints about mismanagement or fraud. Monitoring may done through sampling. Additionally, monitoring may concentrate on those agencies, programs, or sets of officials most prone to illegal or deviant behavior. Finally, *sanctions or penalties* are necessary to ensure the credibility of a control system.

The RTC and THA were plagued by serious and systematic oversight problems in all four areas. At the same time, the accountability problems were significantly worse in the German agency. The German agency's pattern of accountability was at least partly the culprit during the bribery scandal that broke in late 1999 involving former Chancellor Helmut Kohl and his Christian Democratic Party (Cohen and Tagliabue 2000). Other scandals involving the THA are the subject of a number of books (Kampe 1994; Suhr 1991; Luft 1992; Christ and Neubauer 1991), federal audits (Bundesrechnungshof 1993, 1992), and Parliamentary Hearing Reports (Treuhandanstalt 1994b). More scholarly work has also highlighted the significant weaknesses in the agency's oversight structure (Cadel 1994; Cloes 1992; 1991). The RTC, despite the intense scrutiny and the problems of oversight, faced relatively few major cases of fraud and scandal.

The agencies took certain steps to improve oversight in response to external pressure and once they had developed greater organizational capacities. However, the procedures and resources that were adopted to improve accountability occurred after much of the agencies' portfolios had been divested.

Voluntary Compliance

Studies by government auditors and legislative investigations indicate that the lack of voluntary compliance was a serious problem in the German agency among agency employees as well as contractors. In the U.S. case, voluntary compliance among agency employees was not a problem early on when most of the agency's employees were FDIC employees. With the increased use of contractors, subcontractors, and temporary employees, however, government auditors noted that lack of voluntary compliance with government procedures grew to be an issue.

Information on specific THA cases remains highly confidential. In one of the few cases where a subset of a parliamentary committee was allowed to study the files of thirty major privatizations, the committee found that 60 percent lacked documentation; in half the cases the creditworthiness of the buyer went unchecked; in a third of the cases no document existed in which the investor agreed to continue to operate the firm; in only 29 percent of the cases was there any competitive bidding with multiple investors; and, finally, 75 percent of the cases lacked the mandated approval from supervisors (Baumann 1994).

Testimony and interviews given by THA employees and auditors of the agency point in a similar direction. In his testimony before a parliamentary committee, Ludwig Tränkner, head of THA's Liquidation Department bragged openly to legislators that he had little interest in government guidelines (Treuhandanstalt 1994b, 935). In response to a question about his compliance with agency guidelines, he said:

> You have caught me on the wrong foot. I believe I am one of those who in his entire life has not read the rules. That's why I have employees. . . . In this case I must unfortunately admit that they (agency guidelines) are too long and too broad. I don't know if you've seen them, these books. . . . The fact that I paid little attention to the rules is what made me exceptional.

One employee who worked in the Dresden regional office said matter-of-factly: "We didn't spend a lot of time reading manuals. Most of the learning came from different experiences." A manager who had no experience in the electrical industry prior to being recruited by the THA and who was hired to run a large electrical firm in Berlin said, "I am a businessman and financeman. For me the basic principles in the businesses are all the same. I certainly don't require any training. I have been a manager so I know how a firm works. I know how to restructure a company. I had to develop a business concept on my own. I didn't rely on anyone. I asked, 'What do we have and what does the competition have?'" The irony is that the manager's experience, prior to the THA, had been as the managing director of a textile firm in northern Germany that had gone bankrupt. The firm he managed for the THA eventually also closed.

The federal prosecutor who headed Germany's equivalent to the Inspector General's Office within the THA remarked, "The politics of the THA was to empower the buyer and to treat controls as a necessary evil. The signal from the top to lower level employees was unfortunately not: work carefully and with thought. The signal was rather: If something comes up, we'll help you." A THA lawyer promoted to division head within the area of contract management admitted the enormity of the problem associated with the poor reporting in his agency:

> There were controlling problems. They occurred because you gave those charged with privatization enormous freedom to act. If you were to look back at the contracts worked out in the first two years, you'll often find nothing written. You'll be lucky to find a hand written note. As a result it becomes very difficult to retrace decisions and control the problems.

In parliamentary testimony, a bankruptcy lawyer hired by the THA to provide assistance in the handling of thirty firms that were either privatized or liquidated stated that she was appalled by the ways in which firm sales were handled by agents. She said that at the very minimum a seller of firms must be familiar with his product, must know something about the industrial sector, and must be aware of what the investor intends to do with the enterprise: "I found that in 100 percent of the cases I worked on, that every, I mean every, rule governing a legal privatization was broken. . . . In not a single case was even the minimum guidelines followed" (Treuhandanstalt 1994b, 796).

In contrast to the THA, RTC employees were overly cautious in their handling of thrift and asset sales and were concerned about charges that they were dumping assets on local markets and driving down prices. Anthony Downs, a noted scholar of public organizations, said that RTC agents were responding to congressional pressure by being overly cautious. He testified before Congress in 1991 that "RTC officials have developed elaborate committee procedures for arriving at sales prices and arriving at individual deals. These procedures are designed to insure that no one RTC official can be solely blamed for any decisions that subsequently look bad. In bureaucratic parlance, this is known as CYA—Cover Your Ass" (U.S. House 1991, 67). Buyers of RTC assets testified before congressional committees about the excessively bureaucratic nature of the agency.[18] Martin Rueter, senior vice president of Century 21, noted before the U.S. Senate Banking Committee:

> The ability of local RTC staff to make decisions is burdened by a well-intentioned system that stifles rather than encourages the sale process. For example, preapproval is mandatory for even minor repairs or maintenance. Procedures and document requirements vary from lender to lender. Paperwork is extremely burdensome. Trying to get answers, as we've seen, can take months or weeks (U.S. Senate 1990, 60).

At a Senate committee meeting a broker testified that a sale of a $47,000 house had to be approved by a regional RTC committee, plus four attorneys, who could not agree on the proper purchase offer form. The result was a thirty-three-page contract for a $47,000 house that required seven signatures from the buyer (U.S. Senate 1990, 61). The RTC's rigid application of its contracting procedures was criticized by the GAO (1991b).[19] An RTC regional sales officer from Dallas stated, "In the very beginning we really didn't know how the agency was going to operate. At the same time there was a lot of turnover, rules were constantly being reformulated, and don't forget the agency was under a fishbowl. . . . It's not surprising that we were a bit cautious."

As the agency stepped up its resolution and sales activities, government auditors identified voluntary compliance with governmental rules as a problem, particularly among part-time employees hired from failed savings and loans and private contractors. Three different auditors—the GAO, the Inspector General, and RTC's Office of Contract Oversight and Surveillance—issued numerous reports critical of the RTC's failure to follow procedures at all stages of the privatization process leading the GAO. In 1992 the GAO listed the RTC as one of eighteen high-risk areas that were particularly vulnerable to fraud, waste, and mismanagement (GAO 1992c, 1993b). Three years later, following a series of management changes designed to improve compliance, the agency was taken off the high risk list (GAO 1995).

Areas where compliance was identified by auditors as particularly problematic included asset evaluation and appraisal[20] (GAO 1993a; RTC Office of Inspector General 1992; GAO 1992b, 1993f); asset management (GAO 1992h, 1994b, 1993d); contractor and subcontractor oversight (GAO 1991a, 1992g, 1992d, 1992e, 1991d); MWOB and Affordable Housing programs (GAO 1992f, 1992a, 1991e); and the employment of thrift managers who were culpable in the thrift crisis (GAO 1994a).

A government auditor involved in a number of RTC audits stated:

> If you put the problems of the RTC into a single word, it's "Oversight." The view among the top RTC managers was that to correct a problem you just write a directive and it automatically gets implemented. . . . Nobody wants oversight, procedures. Anything that's procedural, people seem to resist. That's fine in situations, but not in a large organization. They didn't really spend time in a management cycle: you plan it, you do it, and you review it. RTC did very little planning, a lot of doing, and no reviewing. They changed the model to do, do, do.

A former Atlanta office employee who worked in the FDIC for three years prior to being transferred in 1989 to the RTC to work as a legal information technician testified to Congress:

> The flagrant disregard for rules and regulations is pervasive throughout the RTC. Managers often chide 'we are RTC: not FDIC' or 'this does not apply to the RTC,' therefore implying the RTC does not have to abide by the same rules and regulations as the FDIC. Management's perception that the RTC is 'a quasi government organization' has bred an atmosphere of arrogance. Since they believe they are not a full fledged government agency, they have a mandate to pick and choose which Federal government rules and regulations they want to follow, and those they wish to disregard (U.S. Senate 1993b, 123).

The Inspector General's Office and the GAO reported on several episodes that garnered a great deal of media and congressional attention. In one case Jack Adair, inspector general for the RTC, reported that the agency had paid the accounting firm Price Waterhouse roughly $7 million, or 67 cents per page for labor in the copying of documents for Homefed Federal Savings Bank. The accounting firm's markup was over 340 percent, and oversight of the contract was shown to be extremely poor. The Inspector General found that (1) the RTC's Office of Contracts and legal division were not involved in the contract; (2) an inappropriate contracting vehicle was used;[21] and (3) proper delegations of authority were not followed. Adair remarked before Congress, "Millions have been wasted. . . . RTC management disregarded policies and procedures that were put in place to protect RTC's and the taxpayer's interest" (U.S. Senate 1993a, 62).

A year prior to that an incident known as "Western Storm" also made headlines.[22] The Western Storm Project was created to reconcile the asset records of ninety-two failed thrifts with RTC's general ledger in the RTC's regional office in Denver. A $24 million contract was awarded in April 1991 to complete the work. Shortly after work began, questions developed concerning the contract award process and the quality of work performed by the contractor. The regional office in Denver was found to have acted inappropriately in contracting for the project by not following established contracting policies and procedures, not establishing realistic goals and strategies, not exploring less costly alternatives, not following delegations of authority, and inadequately overseeing the project, wasting about $3 million.

Standards

The development of clear standards was a highly controversial issue in both agencies. While societal actors and legislators often sought ways to hold the agency and its activities accountable to a definable set of standards, greater specificity was often (quite rightly) perceived as a reduction in bureaucratic discretion. Both the RTC and THA began with very few clearly defined standards. Over time, the RTC attempted to find a balance—adopting more specific rules that were sometimes excessively detailed. The THA, however, largely retained its discretionary power, deliberately not defining clear standards for judging various stages of the process.

The difference was most clear in the rules and procedures governing the use of contractors. Both agencies used many contractors, yet they took very different approaches to the issue of standards. While managers in both agencies enjoyed great discretion in engaging contractors, the RTC's procurement process for approving contracts was extremely complicated and laborious in comparison to the Treuhand's.[23] Prospective RTC contractors were required to provide extensive background documentation.[24] The information was then reviewed by the RTC to ensure that FIRREA's strict conflict of interest rules were not violated. Once approved, the contractor was registered in the agency's database. Each interested registrant was sent a "Notice of Intent to Solicit" memorandum, which defined the nature of the task and specified certain minimum capabilities. From the responses to this notice, the RTC randomly selected twenty to thirty firms to receive solicitations for service. The number selected was designed to be competitive, and the randomness ensured fairness.

Upon receipt of the proposals the agency conducted a further three-step review process. A technical panel evaluated a firm's capabilities and expertise. A cost panel ranked proposals solely on cost, and a regulatory compliance panel reviewed and verified material on potential conflicts of interest. The agency did not automatically select the lowest bid, but looked at a number of elements assigning points to factors such as cost, technical ability, and whether the contractor represented a minority- or woman-owned enterprise. Furthermore, in the case of asset managers, once selected, the contractor was then required to provide extensive quarterly disclosures documenting the status of assets and the progress of their disposition.

In contrast, few rules initially governed the THA's hiring of contractors early on. It was not until the end of 1992, nearly three years after the Treuhand's inauguration, that a control unit was set up in the agency. Several THA managers described the agency's personnel policy as "ad hoc." The individual hired to create a contract oversight division in the THA said:

Between 1990 and 1992 the number of contractors increased dramatically. There were very few rules or guidelines governing their usage, and every regional office did it differently. It quickly became very clear during this period that contractors were making out extremely well: high fees paid per person per hour. In the beginning this was viewed as acceptable because it was believed, falsely, that the person would only remain for a short period. As in the private sector, the expectation was that the contractor would depart in a couple of weeks, having completed his particular task.

This, he noted, turned out to be an enormous problem. Firms were not easily sold, and contractors remained on the THA's payroll without a great deal of control or oversight.

Hiring of contractors was done informally. A director of a large consulting company in Düsseldorf who worked extensively for the THA since 1990 said, "The auditing and consulting firms used by the THA in eastern Germany were hired because of their clients in the west who in turn had contacts in the east and the THA and somehow contact was made." The head of contract oversight who had worked in Dresden noted the freedom, particularly among regional offices: "Regional offices were big consumers of contractors. They were given a great deal of freedom to hire whom they needed. The difficulty we experienced in setting up a control unit was that every office hired differently. Sometime contracts were not even formalized."

Several problems developed as a result of the great need for contractors and the absence of much screening and coordination between offices and firms. In a number of cases, contractors from the same company were paid different fees by different offices for the same services. In other cases, auditors report that the contractors bid themselves up by playing offices against one another. These accounts are consistent with Seibel and Kapferer's (1996) account of the THA's use of contractors in the branch offices whose numbers in some cases accounted for a third or more of the staff of the branches. They write:

> The symbiotic relationship between the consultants and the permanent organization . . . showed the risk of 'rent-seeking.' The firm relationships between the consultants and the permanent organization, which at times reached the point where it was no longer possible to differentiate in day-to-day work between the consultants, engaged for long periods but at a daily

fee rate, and the permanent staff, led not only to excessively high personnel costs for the THA as a whole but apparently also to the consultancy firms becoming accustomed to these lucrative conditions and being unwilling to give them up (127).

The situation was particularly problematic in the firms themselves.

East Germany's state-owned enterprises were major consumers of contracted services. No data is available on how much firms used contractors.[25] Interviews with auditors, firm managers, and THA employees and contractors charged with overseeing the expenditure of liquidity firms received suggest that firms were much larger consumers of contractors than the agency itself. Contractors assisted in putting together business and investment plans and balance sheets. A former member of the THA's managerial committee that evaluated firm proposals said:

> These companies were extremely vulnerable. Management usually had no idea what a balance sheet or business plan looked like. At the same time they knew they had to make a strong case to the Treuhand that they were viable and worthy of liquidity. In many cases contractors, especially the biggest and most reputable companies, were viewed as a good investment in trying to secure support. From the perspective of management the cost was worth it because it was usually figured into their request to the agency.

The qualifications of consultants were rarely checked. What mattered was the extent to which the firm could secure its needed liquidity. Contractors, firm employees and managers, and THA employees all described the scene as "absolute chaos." Others compared it to the "Wild West." In a particularly graphic metaphor of the circumstances associated with the THA's use of contractors, the head of contract oversight said, "You can imagine how in this area, the lack of any ground rules, philosophy, or system can mean that you are pulled pretty hard by your nose."

RTC Striving for Balance

Throughout its operation the RTC struggled to reach a balance between giving its employees and contractors flexibility and establishing clear standards and mechanisms for holding them accountable. In some instances standards were clearly identified. FIRREA, for example, stated clearly that assets could not be sold below 95 percent of book value in certain markets. This was a clear legislative mandate. There was also a "cost-test" for deciding which resolution option should be followed. The test compares the costs the RTC must bear in a liquidation and compares that figure to the loss it would realize under different types of resolutions and under different bids. There were also detailed procedures for selecting and hiring a contractor. At the same time, the agency was criticized severely by the GAO and the Inspector General for failing to develop effective standards and procedures. An auditor noted, "RTC's contracting procedures really went through a long evolution. To start with, the regulations were very sketchy, very poorly thought through."

As noted above, MWOB and Affordable Housing programs did not fully develop until the agency had been in operation for two or three years. However, given the agency's enormous dependence on contractors, contract oversight was the area in which the agency was most vulnerable. Donald Kettl described it as "*The* central one of the bailout" (Kettl 1991b, 446).

The GAO found in 1990 that the RTC had not only failed to set up a viable contract administration structure but the auditor could "find no detailed instructions, procedures or other guidance to help regional personnel monitor the activities of contractors" (GAO 1990). Donald Kettl wrote that the lack of clearly defined rules and procedures was the agency's central challenge. He stated that the agency's manual included a single paragraph on contract monitoring, "Such language, of course, provides little guidance. . . . The lack of such oversight, as GAO has already found, can be costly (Kettl 1991b, 446).

The problem was particularly acute in the case of subcontractors who were not required to register with the contracting system. An auditor said:

> So what happened was here you've got a private system of general contractors really who were allowed to privatize a lot of the work so that the RTC would not become a huge bureaucracy. Then they were supposed to hire another level of private escort people using RTC's rules and then do a lot of the work.

Essentially what they were doing was creating something of a private sector
government agency if you think about it. That these people were supposed to
act as RTC surrogates in hiring subcontractors because the RTC didn't want
to spend the time to hire the subs or make that kind of effort.

He added, "If you go through the asset reports and look at that in
painful detail, one of the biggest problems is that the system was not
set up for tight financial control. Management at RTC just did not see
tight financial control as being one of the most important constraints
of the system."

At the same time the RTC was criticized for the lack of clear standards, it was also criticized for excessive standards. The GAO noted
that asset management contractors were required to provide up to
twenty-seven standard reports to about 125 oversight managers in fifteen consolidated field offices. Twenty of the reports were monthly
and the remaining seven were quarterly, annual, or final reports.
Contractors were required to submit all of these reports for each contract they had with the RTC. Because a contractor sometimes had several contracts with one or more field offices, the volume of data was
compounded. One contractor reported that his company's monthly
reports averaged around 600 pages. While the RTC struggled to find
a clear balance between definite standards and great bureaucratic
discretion, the THA was far less willing to take steps that might
restrict the discretion of its employees.

Following the lead of its political principals, the THA and its leadership deliberately sought to give employees and contractors the
greatest degree of freedom by providing only vague guidelines for
making decisions. In his analysis of the THA's privatization strategies,
Klaus-Dieter Schmidt notes that the THA legislation gave the agency
plenty of room for maneuvering and has "therefore not sought to
define priorities even in its internal working instructions." In its
guidelines for the Privatization Directorates, only very vague rules are
given under the heading "Decision Principles" (Schmidt and Siegmund 1996, 214). He later notes that the THA developed only minimum criteria for the privatization process, thereby giving privatization
teams "plenty of free scope in their negotiations and decisions. Normally they decide for themselves whether a given bidder is to be
selected as a buyer or not. This is seen by many as a shortcoming
since this takes a major proportion of the decision-making process

out of the range of public supervision. The THA is of a different opinion, and attributes at least part of its success in privatization to this regulation." (Schmidt and Siegmund 1996, 226).

In sum, the THA chose to adopt very few specific guidelines or standards, giving agents maximum levels of flexibility. The RTC went back and forth. At times it adopted very vague standards, particularly in judging the work of contractors. In other areas, the RTC adopted highly specific rules governing sales decisions, the use of contractors, and level of reporting.

Monitoring

Monitoring is a function of resources and integration. It requires enough auditing personnel with the capacity and the access to information to carry out effective oversight strategies. These strategies may be comprehensive, be reactive, or rely on sampling. Furthermore, in organizations as large and diverse as the RTC and THA, monitoring also demands information systems capable of tracking assets and personnel.

As in the case of standard setting, the THA largely failed to allocate effective resources for overseeing the activities of its employees, contractors, or managers within the firms. Similarly, while the RTC was subject to a significant number of audits and investigations, auditors noted that it was often impossible to know whether the agency was following its procedures because of poor management information systems and the extensive use of private contractors.

The THA was overseen by two internal control agents, the Stabsstelle für Besondere Aufgaben (similar to the Investigator General's office) and the Innererrevision, and one external control agent, the Bundesrechnungshof (Federal Audit Office). All three were highly understaffed. The Innererrevision employed twenty-three people at the end of 1991 to oversee the sale of 12,500 firms spread out over fifteen regional offices. The Stabsstelle employed six people and was firmly within the THA hierarchy. And the Federal Audit Office began with a staff of nine employees (Hickel and Priewe 1994, 76). As a result, several studies suggest that the low number of criminal cases reflects the weakness of internal controls rather than an absence of fraudulent activity.

In Dieter Kampe's (1994) investigation of the sale of an electrical company in Berlin, he writes, "The Treuhand was overseen a little bit by a lot of people, but by no one effectively" (158). As a result, write Hickel and Priewe (1994, 77), "The various control agents either were unwilling, unable or simply prevented from the exercise of their responsibility. Control was thus dispersed. The decision-making competence remained with the THA and the Ministry of Finance. Power without any check leads to abuse and, as a rule, to poor decisions."

A young auditor in his mid-thirties was hired to work in the Innererrevision in 1991 to oversee the subsidies funneled to firms and buyers of firms. In comparing his work to his previous job at Schering AG, he said:

> What I found amazing was the absolute sums that we were investigating. When I worked at Schering AG, they had fifteen auditors who performed internal audits. The company was extremely organized. It was very easy to check accounts. It got to the point where we would check the cars of employees to see if they were up to the company's standard. In the THA we wouldn't touch anything under a million marks. We had at the peak sixty auditors to cover the 15,000 firms that were privatized and the agency itself. I mean that is amazing. There was no way to achieve any sense of control.

The auditor stressed the important impact that the time deadline had on the auditing division's ability to oversee what was going on:

> The strategy in the Innerrevision was not to get too deeply into any one case. We had four weeks to perform every audit. The leader of our department had a list of audits we had to get through so there was every interest in making sure that things did not slow down. We therefore performed spot checks on various sectors and within firms. These were done according to an auditing plan worked out by the Executive Committee (Vorstand) and directors on the Supervisory Board.

Citing the case of the chemical sector, he adds:

> The basic strategy for our department was, "Don't hurt anybody and they won't hurt you." There was no interest in really delving into any one case. I have often had to fight with the head of my department to write a report. For example, I am looking into chemicals now. It's mind boggling. There is no way to tell where they spend their money. We're talking 11 billion in subsidies. When I wrote the report we were told to put it on hold for awhile. It was too political. But we're going to write the report anyway

because once you write the report it goes to the Bundesrechnungshof and they begin to investigate.

In answer to the question of why there were not more auditors assigned to monitor the agency's activities, he said:

> In part it was clearly because we could not get the manpower. Not enough available. The real problem was, however, that Breuel blocked the use of auditors. It was felt that they slowed the privatization process down. She didn't like auditors so we were highly understaffed. This feeling toward the auditing department extended throughout the THA and into the firms themselves. Basically no one wanted to see us because they believed we would make waves or slow the process down. . . . So now we have ten auditors and five secretaries. I have the entire chemical sector by myself as well as the TLG. The bottom line is that no one wants to see what is going on.

One of the THA's young turks, hired into the agency in 1992 after completing a graduate degree at Harvard University to work in contract management, also noted the link between accountability and structure:

> The THA is neither a bureaucracy nor a company, yet it is also both. . . . According to the law, the THA is a bureaucracy, but in practice it was a company. Yet in contrast to any company, never has so much money flown so easily to so many. . . . The freedom that employees here had would never occur in any firm. Decisions were made in the central and branch offices by inexperienced and pressured managers that would never have occurred in the private sector. The THA could borrow money without approval from the Bundestag whenever it needed. This was a system without checks.

A central monitoring problem confronted by the RTC was less the lack of auditing personnel than weakness in the information systems. Each regional office used different systems for managing and selling assets. Different computer programs were used that proved incompatible with those used in other parts of the country. A number of attempts were made to develop a systemwide information tracking system, but few were effective. A senior auditor who had also overseen many of the audits and reports done of the agency said, "The primary problem were controls to ensure that they were getting what they paid for. They didn't have any infrastructure and they didn't really try to put it in place until the third year. In his testimony before Congress in 1993, an RTC contract manager discussed the problems in the RTC's real estate tracking system, REOIS (Real Estate Owned Inventory System):

> The REOIS was a temporary system. . . . This system was flawed from the beginning. Too many people from too many areas of the RTC tried to be involved in the design and knew absolutely nothing about computer design and what a computer could do or could not do" (U.S. Senate 1993b, 20).

A senior GAO evaluator who conducted a number of investigations into the RTC's activities said:

> From the beginning the RTC was a data-collection nightmare. It was mandated by Congress to contract out everything. Yet there was nothing set up to oversee the contractors. Very few procedures or checks. . . . The systems to monitor things were extremely weak.

Another RTC contract manager said:

> One of the mistakes made was the lack of integration in the system. Rather than going to the private sector and saying, "Hey folks we need a system that will be fully integrated that we'll be able to load these assets onto, manage these assets, track these assets, report to Congress, the Oversight Board, IG, and GAO," they didn't. Instead they took the approach in building a system in which "this little shell never talks to that little shell." There was no systems master. As a result a lot of money was wasted developing systems that were never used, like the AMF, which cost $20 million. There is no systems integration.

The GAO reported that the lack of data, data inaccuracies, and the lack of consistent corporate-wide data hampered the RTC's efforts to assess the efficiency and effectiveness of its operation (GAO 1993c). Furthermore, the government auditor noted that limitations in accounting hampered cost control efforts.[26] The GAO wrote that the RTC "has not set up a viable contract administration structure to effectively monitor the execution of its contracts."

Wrapping Up

The RTC and THA accomplishments are remarkable on a number of levels and raise questions that are important to those interested in governance and state behavior. First, despite popular assumptions about bureaucratic inertia, these two agencies fulfilled their legislative mandate to divest what amounted to history's largest transfer of wealth from the public to the private sector. They carried out these historic tasks in a short amount of time. Yet the comparison of their experiences raises a number of important questions: How were they able to privatize so quickly, particularly given the lack of planning or preparation? Bureaucracies are generally considered to operate slowly and in a self-preserving manner. How is it possible that these two agencies managed to divest so rapidly before closing their doors? Interest group and corporatist politics are said to create incremental policies. How was it then possible that these agencies could transfer in a brief period such a large quantity of public holdings? Furthermore, one would expect a social democratic country to behave much more cautiously toward such a neo-liberal solution as rapid privatization. Even during the long periods of conservative rule in the 1950s and 1980s, West Germany had always been extremely slow to privatize state-owned enterprises.[27] Yet when one compares the two experiences, it is the American agency that moved much more slowly and cautiously early in the process. How can this be? What accounts for these bureaucratic outcomes?

Second, with the exception of restructuring some large firms in Germany and the protection of local markets in the United States, both agencies largely opted to devote resources and strategies toward privatization and rapid divestiture rather than actively pursue their ancillary mandates. The agencies focused attention on their secondary goals only after much of their portfolio had already been divested and the legislative pressure became difficult to ignore. Bureaucracies are supposed to be shaped (inefficiently, according to Terry Moe) by the demands of interest groups, particular those agencies that redistribute resources. How was it possible for these two agencies to have resisted such pressures from groups who supported the secondary goals? One would expect a social democratic country like Germany to be predisposed to embracing more active forms of restructuring. Previous West German privatization experiences during the 1970s and 1980s would suggest this to be the case. Yet the THA remained resolute in its resistance to restructuring. What factors made this possible and predictable?

Finally, patterns of accountability present a special set of puzzles. These were two agencies with enormous authority and discretion over the allocation of billions of public dollars. They were the focus of a great deal of public and media attention. How could such powerful and public organizations fail to develop effective oversight and control mechanisms? The German civil service, with its strong Prussian heritage and high standards, is said to be one of the most accountable and professional public sectors in the world. Yet interviews, reports, and studies confirm the conclusion reached by *Spiegel* reporter Dieter Kampe who wrote, "The THA operated outside the control of the Rechtsstaat. It was not bound by the traditional control systems characterized by a parliamentary democracy. The agency followed its own rules which gave strong-willed and determined managers enormous opportunity and freedom to—how it could it have been different?—pursue their own interests" (Kampe 1994, 159). How was it possible for such scandals and lapses in oversight to occur? What factors allowed an American agency to be more accountable than a German public agency?

The answers to these questions are addressed in the remaining chapters.

NOTES

1. The RTC's inventory were those institutions that the Federal Savings and Loan Insurance Corporation (FSLIC) had insured and that were placed into government conservatorship or receivership between February 6, 1989, and August 9, 1990 (later extended to September 30, 1993).

2. Citibank and BankAmerica Corporation held assets valued at $256 and $232 billion, respectively, in 1996 (*American Banker,* 1996).

3. For an excellent summary account of the RTC resolution process see Tucker, Meire, and Rubinstein (1990) and the CBO report (1993) on resolving the thrift crisis.

4. For a good account of the impact of restitution on privatization see Hall and Ludwig (1993); Feddersen (1991); Sinn and Sinn (1992, esp. ch. 4). For a com-

plete collection of all laws and treaties governing the restoration of property from June 15, 1990, to 1991 see Fieberg and Reichenbach (1992). For a discussion of the history behind such claims see especially Feddersen (1991).

5. Between March 1990 and Oct 3, 1990, 9,300 small privatizations occurred. From October 1990 through June 30, 1991, an additional 13,000 entities were sold (BvS 1995, 5).

6. A *Wall Street Journal* (Martin 1991) article titled "No sale: RTC's Many Miscues in Selling Off Property Rattle Local Markets" reported that out of 2,000 real estate investors surveyed in January 1991, "not a single one expressed satisfaction after dealing with the RTC and 65 percent said they never would again" (1).

7. The interim guides state only, "The RTC must satisfy itself that the ownership and control provision of the program's requirements are fulfilled." No criteria were provided, however, for deciding what should be included or how to develop certification procedures (GAO 1991e, 4).

8. Section 501(b)(12)(D)(ii).

9. For a full discussion of the RTC's impact on markets see Vandell and Riddiough's work (1991).

10. Breuel wrote that "'Industrial Core' is a metaphor for the attempt to find the future potential in firms, to give them a fair chance to develop, and to make possible renewed growth and regeneration from this core" (Breuel 1993a, 60).

11. The firms receiving assistance included: the steel mill EKO Stahl AG; the metal firm Mansfeld AG; the machine tool firms Heckert-Chemnitzer Werkzeugmaschinenbau GmbH and Werkzeugmaschinenfabrik Zerbst GmbH; the machine textile firm Kändler Maschinenbau GmbH; the freight-car producer Deutsche Waggonbau AG; the heavy machinery firm SKET Maschinen- und Anlagenbau AG; five brown coal pits in the Lausitz mine and two in the Mitteldeutsch mine; and the chemical triangle of Halle-Bittersfeld-Merseburg (BMF 1993).

12. The assumption that guarantees were designed to satisfy social mandates was not accepted uniformly within the agency. Dr. John von Freyend, ministerial director in the Finance Ministry, testified that the guarantees demonstrated the earnestness and seriousness of an investor and his or her business plan (Treuhandanstalt 1994a, 735). He argued that guarantees were not about "employment politics" but were designed to ensure that investors were serious about their commitment to establishing businesses in eastern Germany.

13. Rules governing investment and employment guarantees were passed by the THA's management board in November 1990. For a complete description

see *Leitlinien der Geschaeftspolitik der THA vom 16 November 1990* (cited in Bundesrechnungshof 1992).

14. For an excellent description of THA contracts in English, see Dodds and Wächter (1993) and Kuepper and Mayr (1996).

15. Subsidies took a variety of forms, including paying off the company's debt, loan guarantees, absorbing any environmental cleanup costs, and direct grants from state and federal governments. One of the most well-known cases, the sale of EKO Stahl GmbH, was written up on the front page of the *Wall Street Journal* on December 9, 1994. When the Treuhand could not find a buyer for the large steel company, located in Eisenhuettenstadt, the THA offered buyers a subsidy of $610 million on the condition that they upgrade the plant and keep 2,000 of the original 12,000 jobs. The total works out to $500,000 for each job saved. In negotiating contracts, particularly on the sale of the largest enterprises, the THA would sometimes factor in the cost of unemployment particularly in politically sensitive industries. For example, in the chemical sector the government factored that DM 300,000 per job was the opportunity cost of permanent unemployment for large chemical enterprises.

16. In the case of the sale of Bagger-, Bugsier- und Bergungsreederei GmbH, a shipping company in Rostock, the terms of the contract stated that if the number of employees falls below 900 the company agrees to an increase in the sales price by DM10,000 for each worker not hired (Treuhandanstalt 1994b, 733). In the case of the sale of Bellino Gmbh & Co., a metal working company in Göppingen, the contract committed the investor to 350 employees and 30 apprenticeships for three years. For every worker not hired the company agreed to pay a penalty of five months' wages (Treuhandanstalt 1994b, 733).

17. A number of different estimates were reported by the agency and research groups. The problem is partly due to the changing environment of firms whose investment plans shift depending on the state of the economy and their industry.

18. The RTC Task Force held a number of hearings at which public complaints were voiced. See especially RTC Task Force Hearings held on May 4, 1990, and July 30, 1990.

19. The GAO also surveyed buyers of RTC real estate and found similar results (GAO 1992i).

20. The RTC Inspector General's office noted the lack of sufficient documentation to support asset valuation conclusions. As a result, the IG was unable to tell whether the RTC had properly valued its assets according to policies and procedures (RTC Office of Inspector General 1992).

21. The task order agreement used was for obtaining asset valuation reviews, which are generally awarded on a fixed price basis and average about $30,000 per review. Adair stated, "Instead of using the task order, RTC should have assessed the nature of the work to be done, determined the appropriate expertise to accomplish the tasks, and solicited firms accordingly" (U.S. Senate 1993a).

22. For a good account of the Western Storm Project, see hearings held by the U.S. Senate Banking Committee (1992a) and the investigations conducted by the GAO (GAO 1992j, 1992g, 1992d).

23. A GAO report found in fact that RTC staff did not have to justify decisions to hire private sector contractors on the basis of lower cost or higher returns from asset sales. RTC staff revealed to auditors that justifications were not used because RTC directives require that contractors be used for asset management and disposition (GAO 1991c, 3). For additional information on the RTC's contracting process see the appendix in Senate Hearing on Contracting oversight (U.S. Senate 1990).

24. During a congressional hearing it was revealed that contractors had to answer more than 600 questions regarding their business practices and background.

25. According to contract managers, the lack of data is partly a function of the legal division between firms and the Treuhand and partly a factor of the chaos that characterized the situation. As a manager put it, "Of all the things we had to keep track of, the precise amount spent on consultants was not a high priority at the time."

26. The GAO noted, for example, that in 1992 RTC reported payments of $2 billion for professional or contract services. The agency posted nearly half of that amount to two very general accounts—"other contractual services" and "other professional services"—making it impossible to develop meaningful cost comparisons, evaluate performance, and promote efficiency (GAO 1993e, 6).

27. For a good account of Germany's experience with privatization following the Second World War, see Joseph Esser's (1989) work.

3

Personnel, Culture, and Organizational Structure: The Impact of Administrative Characteristics on the Performance of the RTC and THA

The most proximate source of explanations for bureaucratic outcomes can be found in the organizations themselves. Organizations are composed of collections of choices looking for problems, issues and feelings looking for decisions, and decision makers looking for work (Kingdon 1984; Cohen, March, and Olsen 1972). Outcomes, in other words, are most directly a function of internal administrative features.

Bureaucratic outcomes in the Treuhandanstalt (THA) and the Resolution Trust Corporation (RTC) were shaped by three administrative characteristics: (1) personnel policies—the composition of their workforce and compensation practices; (2) organizational structure—how they organized responsibility and authority within the organization; and (3) organizational culture—the shared set of values and beliefs among subgroups of employees in the organization.

Table 3.1 presents a summary comparing the content of the administrative characteristics across the two agencies.

What stands out in Table 3.1 is the degree to which both agencies differed from "classical" and "bureaucratic" models of public administration.[1] Classical theory stresses the establishment of definitely bounded jurisdictions of authority and responsibility.[2] Efficiency is a function of specialization and coordination between divisions. Bureaucratic theory parallels classical theory in its emphasis on hierarchy and the establishment of clear lines of authority. There is an

Table 3.1

Comparison of THA and RTC Administrative Characteristics

	Personnel Policy	Organizational Structure	Organization Culture(s)
Treuhand	Personnel • Short-term private sector hires including recent college graduates, retired/unemployed Western managers, borrowed executives Private contractors Compensation • Decoupled from government grade system • Generous salaries and benefits • Differential pay between eastern and western employees • Exit bonuses and premiums	Decentralized matrix structure	Differentialist; several subcultures with a single dominant culture. Subcultures • Patriots: retirees and elder managers hired by the THA to manage companies or serve on the supervisory boards of companies • Self-interested patriots: young, successful managers lent to the THA for a short period of time by western firms • Profiteers: eager young people, just out of college with business or law degrees from West German universities • Easterners: East Germans who filled the lower ranks of the agency
RTC	Personnel • FDIC employees and managers borrowed for a short period of time • Private sector hires on limited term contracts • Private contractors Compensation • Decoupled from government grade system • Pay-for-performance system for executives and lower-level employees • Asset managers paid for sale and management of contracts	Decentralized	Differentialist; several subcultures at work. Subcultures • Respected bureaucrats: FDIC employees who served their time at the RTC • Discredited Regulators: FSLIC employees • Discredited S&L managers • Private contractors

added emphasis, however, on establishing a stable pattern of obedience by ensuring that personnel share a strong belief in the legitimacy of the system of authority—what Max Weber termed "rational-legal authority." Such authority is accomplished through establishing rational norms "in such a manner that the legitimacy of the authority becomes the legality of the general rule, which is purposely thought out, enacted and announced with formal correctness" (Gerth and Mills 1958, 299). Such a system ensures that employees' allegiance is not tied to an individual but to the "impersonal order," and that values of employees coincide with values of the organization.

Both models reconcile public demands for efficiency and accountability by embracing specialization and enabling policymakers to "rationalize" the executive branch of government. At the same time, hierarchic structures maintain accountability to managers, legislators, and the public. The political power of both models and their widespread appeal rest in their apolitical, almost mechanistic approach to public problems.

Although they shared some aspects of the classical and bureaucratic elements, the RTC and THA diverged significantly from both traditional models in a number of important ways. The RTC and the THA broke with the classical model by adopting highly decentralized structures in which clear lines of authority and hierarchy were not well established. Moreover, in contrast to the Weberian idea of "government of laws and not men," the RTC and THA represented a government of individuals and firms. That is not to say there were no rules or norms. Much of how the agencies defined and implemented privatization, however, was left to the discretion of the individuals and firms hired by the RTC and THA.

In addition, rather than rely on socialization and training, the agencies purchased expertise in short-term doses from other government agencies or the private sector. As a result they depended heavily on contracts to ensure that the values of the individual were aligned with those of the organization. Both agencies also faced the challenge of mediating several different subcultures with differing and sometimes competing values.

In short, the RTC and THA administrative characteristics differed significantly from traditional models of public administration.

Furthermore, the breaks with tradition affected the agencies in two ways. First, administrative features shaped the organizations' *capacity* to achieve certain bureaucratic outputs while reducing the capacity to achieve other outputs. Second, administrative factors affected the way in which the agencies interpreted the public purposes assigned to them.

The following sections compare the content of each of the administrative characteristics.

PERSONNEL POLICIES

Personnel policies and practices define what is distinctive about the public sector. The professionalization of the civil service in the nineteenth century in the United States and elsewhere included a unique mix of hiring standards, ethics, training and recruitment practices, employment guarantees, and compensation. These practices were the most efficient and effective means for achieving public goods. At the same time, they were viewed as crucial for developing and maintaining the legitimacy of the democratic governments.

Out of necessity, design, or both, the RTC and THA were set up as buyers of services and expertise and as the managers and arrangers of the private implementation of government policy on a vast scale. Table 3.2 presents a summary comparison of the THA and RTC personnel practices and the challenges they were designed to meet.

Personnel Challenges

Both the THA and RTC faced a number of similar personnel challenges. Both agencies were initially mere shells. During the summer of 1990 the THA was little more than a notary bureau with several hundred employees distributed among the central office in Berlin and fifteen regional offices scattered throughout East Germany. Even in the first month after unification, only 653 employees worked for the THA. Only sixty-eight of these employees had any training in business or market-related areas such as accounting, bookkeeping, or marketing. As an agency charged with the privatization and restructuring of the largest state holding in the western

78

Table 3.2

THA and RTC Personnel Practices and Challenges

Practice and Challenges	RTC	THA
Personnel Challenges	Hiring Challenges • Required to "hit the ground running" with little preparation; find staff for a new bureaucracy and management for 750 ailing Savings and Loans • Need for competent and "clean" managers to manage conservatorships, thrifts taken over by the government Recruitment Challenges • Temporary and public agency • Little time to process applicants	Hiring Challenges • Required to "hit the ground running" with little preparation; find staff for a new bureaucracy and management for 8,000 industrial firms • Need for competent managers who were not part of the communist elite Recruitment Challenges • A temporary and public agency • Organizational insecurity • East German location • Little time to process applicants
Hiring and Recruitment Practices	Extensive use of private sector limited-term employees, many hired from failed thrifts FDIC personnel fill management positions FSLIC employees Heavy dependence on contractors	Extensive use of private sector limited-term employees from three groups: • Retired managers from the west • Managers on loan from private West German firms • Recent business and law school graduates with little experience Heavy dependence on contractors
Compensation	Decoupled from government grade system High salaries especially for managing agents Executive level bonuses	Decoupled from government grade system Higher level employees paid an annual salary, performance bonus, and an exit bonus East-West pay differential
Socialization and Training	Minimal	Minimal

capitalist world, it was an organization that still had to be con-structed (Seibel 1997; Seibel and Kapferer 1996; Seibel 1992).

The RTC was also an agency that had to be constructed, though not completely from scratch. From a personnel standpoint, the RTC was largely an empty shell. All RTC employees fell under the auspices of the FDIC and were legally FDIC employees. The RTC manage-ment consisted of FDIC managers assigned, often unwillingly, to the RTC.[3] Despite the ready pool of FDIC employees capable of filling the managerial ranks, the RTC still needed 4,000–5,000 employees to staff its central office, four regional offices, and fifteen field offices scattered throughout the United States. Ironically, drawing managers from the FDIC created a bottleneck in the agency's hiring practices.

FDIC managers had experience implementing the FDIC's model of bank resolution, namely whole bank sales. This resolution model is relatively clean since the investor purchases all the assets and lia-bilities of the troubled financial institution. However, the complete failure to sell thrifts in their entirety meant the RTC suddenly required a cadre of employees with new types of expertise and know-how in a variety of areas for which the FDIC staff had never been responsible.[4] Richard Fogel, assistant comptroller general at the Gen-eral Account Office, testified before the Senate that this was a major problem, particularly in the area of contracting (U.S. Senate 1990). Fogel said, "One of the problems . . . is that the RTC has got to hire a fair number of people who really have to be able to understand how to monitor contracts. And FDIC's culture . . . really was not one steeped in contract monitoring. . . . So there was not a reservoir of deep talent in FDIC that they could bring over" (U.S. Senate 1990, 18). The RTC consequently lost valuable time in hiring new employ-ees with the expertise to take on the new challenges.

In addition to building an organization, personnel managers in both agencies needed managers and staff to manage the failing enterprises and to prepare them for closure or sale. The RTC needed hundreds of thrift managers to run 750 failed thrifts that had fallen into the government's hand. The agency also needed operation and loan specialists who could handle the operations and portfolios of, in some cases, multibillion dollar operations.[5]

The problem was particularly severe in Germany, where the THA needed not just firm managers but also personnel for the administrative boards overseeing the firms. The East German conglomerates were run by people who lacked adequate qualifications and skills to handle the challenges of a market economy. Many of these managers were part of the *nomenclatura*, former communist leaders with close ties to the East German regime, in particular its secret police.[6] Detlev Rohwedder, the THA's second president, described the sheer magnitude of the problem: "We have a problem of colossal quantitative proportions . . . if I just begin with the assumption that 5,000 of our firms require two competent first-rate managers, free from political liabilities, then I need 10,000 managers from the West. If I add to that the need for just a small administrative committee of six members, then I need 30,000 managers to serve on administrative committees. We have a lot of experienced people from the West, but this is not going to solve our problem" (Kampe and Wallraf 1991, 58).

Recruitment presented the THA and RTC with a number of challenges. The temporary and public status of both agencies made it difficult to hire competent individuals away from secure positions in the private sector where salaries were typically much higher than those in the public sector. As a West German auditor put it, "If you were really good, why would you leave a high-paying position in West Germany to go work on a temporary assignment for a government agency? . . . Only those without a job or without experience would want to work for a temporary government agency." Uncertainty over each agency's mission, its purpose, and its organizational framework added to the risk new employees were being asked to take. In addition, both agencies needed personnel immediately and could not give potential employees time to consider their decisions or prepare for the transition. The immediacy of the personnel problem reduced the flexibility of the positions and thereby lowered the pool of willing and qualified candidates.[7]

A final recruitment problem for the THA was the lack of appeal of the work location. Few West Germans were interested in moving eastward. Dieter Rickert, a personnel consultant to the THA, stated in response to the question of whether life in the east discouraged recruits: "That is in fact our primary problem. There are no homes in the East that are comparable with western German living standards. It is missing the entire cultural infrastructure. And who wants to send their kids to school there?" (*Der Spiegel* 1991).

Personnel Practices: Hiring and Recruitment

To fill their ranks quickly the RTC and the THA employed two strategies that deviated significantly from traditional hiring polices. First, they hired experienced private sector individuals on short-term contracts. Second, they relied extensively on private sector contractors. Both strategies deviated from the traditional model in several ways. In contrast to the life-tenure model, the majority of employees were on very short-term contracts. Contractors were used for only a finite period. Instead of the accepted view that public employees should be motivated to provide a public good or public value, the majority of employees and contractors were expected to be motivated by a very private sense of their own benefit. The essence of the personnel policies in both cases was a strategy that attempted to align the private interests of employees with the legislative mandate to provide a public good. A statement by a THA personnel manager captures the sentiments expressed by personnel managers in both agencies: "We had to hire private sector people. No one else could have done the job. This was not like a government agency. If you were good and we wanted you, then you could start immediately. It was extremely unbureaucratic. In fact in many ways it operated like a business."[8]

Whereas the THA completely transformed itself in to a quasi-private entity soon after unification, the RTC moved more slowly in replacing FDIC managers with private sector hires. The contrast is evident at the highest echelons of both agencies. Over the course of its first year of operation, reorganization in the two most important governing committees in the THA—the supervisory committee and the executive committee[9]—as well as the top management in all fifteen regional offices led to the dominance of western corporate executives.[10] The RTC, by contrast, was governed initially by an oversight board consisting of several agency heads including the chairman of the Federal Reserve. The two most important operational committees—the RTC board and the executive board—along with the leadership in the field and regional offices were also filled with FDIC management, though most were experienced bankers and lawyers from the private sector. Over time these positions were filled with private sector individuals, including Albert Casey, the former CEO of American Airlines, who became CEO of the RTC in 1992.

Line and staff positions in both agencies were dominated by private sector hires. The THA, for example, relied on a combination of human resource firms, personal contacts, and various national initiatives to recruit employees from the private sector. Under the slogan "Professionals for the DDR!—an initiative of the Treuhand Berlin" the THA launched a major campaign to recruit experienced western managers. In his testimony before the German parliament committee, Peter Wild, an original member of the THA's executive committee, said, "One tried, through personnel consulting companies, to recruit individuals with a business-type personality into the top positions; individuals who had business experience . . . but also a sense and understanding for medium-size firms" (Treuhandanstalt 1994a, 608). In a somewhat more clever campaign to hire younger executives, the same company that brought Herman Wagner to the THA also ran an advertising campaign with a picture of the notorious former East German President, Erich Honecker. Beneath Honecker's photo was the statement, "Unfortunately we had to let him go. When will you start?" The statement was then signed by dozens of the largest and most prominent western corporations. The campaign produced thousands of applications.

After sorting through the applications, two groups of qualified applicants emerged: recent (less than five years since degree) university graduates and older managers close to retirement.[11] The young grads were placed as *Referenten* in the lowest-level executive positions while many of the older managers were sent to the firms to manage or oversee the supervisory committees. Younger employees viewed the THA as a springboard to the higher ranks of private corporations. For example, a young man in his early thirties, who was hired by the THA soon after he completed his law degree, became a consultant for one of the largest managerial consulting companies in Germany. He recalled, "Many of us were quite young and inexperienced. The Treuhand was an incredible opportunity for us to immediately put into practice what we had just learned in school. Most of us intended to work in the private sector, and this experience was a great preparation and great advantage."

The THA also launched campaigns to lure skilled and experienced managers working in western firms. During a meeting with corporate executives and union leaders from the largest German corporations, Chancellor Helmut Kohl called upon the group to provide 100 experienced managers to aid the country in transforming the East. These so-called "one-dollar men" were loaned to the THA from western corporations, typically for six months. And finally, one of the largest business associations organized an initiative entitled "Manager-Transfer für die Treuhand," which produced 106 managers in only a few weeks. The effort centered on giving younger managers with some experience an opportunity to take on greater responsibilities in firms in the East. Firms agreed to this short-term transfer because of the intense applied training their employees received. *The Economist* reported that 70 percent of the western managers were hired under consulting or short-term contracts (*The Economist* staff 1992, 71). Again, like the young executives, these experienced managers did not intend to remain in government but to return to their firms following their public sector sabbatical.

While the U.S. Congress suggested that the RTC make greater use of the Senior Executive Service (SES), in practice the agency rarely considered civil servant alternatives to the FDIC. In response to a senator's question of whether the SES had been called on to help the RTC, Charles Bowsher, comptroller general of the U.S. General Accounting Office, responded, "I think that is what is needed, and I don't think it has been called on too much. That is something we ought to look at" (U.S. Senate 1990, 19).

The RTC targeted private sector candidates with experience in various legal and financial areas. Known as "Limited Grade" employees (LG),[12] the private sector hires were distinct from Government Grade (GG) employees brought in from other government agencies, notably the FDIC and the Federal Savings and Loan Insurance Corporation (FSLIC). The RTC's first annual report articulated the agency's strong commitment toward hiring from the private sector: "Because the term of RTC's existence is limited, the agency has tried to . . . hire temporary staff whenever possible. Over 60 percent of the field staff at year-end were temporary employees" (Resolution Trust Corporation 1991). Three years later, during a hearing before the House Banking Committee, RTC CEO Albert Casey testified that three-quarters of the RTC's staff of 5,000 were limited term employees hired from the private sector to work in the THA (U.S. House 1993, 19).[13] A year later in 1994, there were 6,371 employees of whom 4,382 were temporary private hires. A securitization specialist with the RTC, who identified himself as a private sector person, described the transition from FDIC to private sector control:

Initially most of the senior management positions were FDIC people. . . .
They came in and hired people like myself shortly after FIRREA was
approved. Then over the next eighteen months those from the FDIC
phased back into the FDIC. By January 1992 most of the FDIC people had
gone back to the FDIC. What you had now were no FDIC people in the
management and field positions. So there was a transition from the FDIC
to bringing in the private sector people and then taking over the management positions.

Regional and field offices were set up in depressed areas of the
country hardest hit by the recession. These areas also contained the
greatest concentration of unemployed thrift and bank employees,
real estate auditors, and lawyers. This worked to the RTC's advantage.
A contracting manager hired by the RTC in 1989 was typical of the
agency's hires. A former real estate and lending manager at Norwest
Bank, who had retired just before the RTC went into business, said
that most of his new colleagues in the RTC were from the lending
community: "Employees came from various sources. Many had been
in the S&L industry and were now looking for something to do. The
trouble was that they had little experience in managing contractors.
Most of their experience was in loans." He added that the employees
that were hired had no intention of staying; they saw their time at the
RTC as a holding station until something better came along. An
example is an employee who worked three years for the RTC after
she was laid off by a failed thrift. She said, "It was just not uncommon
for folks to take a couple years and work for the RTC and wait until
the market turned around."

Managers of thrift conservatorships and German industrial firms
comprised perhaps the most important subgroup of private employees recruited heavily by both agencies. These were important positions because of the enormous authority ceded to them. Their close
proximity to the enterprises and the importance of transforming
them into something that could be sold made these positions linch-
pins in the entire process.

While initially staffed by FDIC agents, the troubled conservatorship operations were quickly filled with managing agents, operations
specialists, and loan specialists hired primarily from the banking sector. These individuals, many of whom were near retirement, possessed

years of experience running large and complex financial institutions. Of the fifteen managing agents interviewed for this study, only one was from the FDIC, and he was replaced by a private banker within a year after the RTC started.

As noted earlier, the THA's challenge was far more daunting in that it had to find managers for its enterprises as well as individuals to serve on the supervisory boards of its largest firms.[14] The THA's strategy was to locate a manager from one of the top West German firms to serve as the chair of the supervisory board. Phyllis Dininio notes that in the largest firms, the agency appointed its own senior staff as well as representatives from the federal Economics and Finance Ministries. Members of the agency's managing and administrative boards, THA directors sat on boards of a few dozen of the very largest firms (Dininio 1999, 53). The chair of the supervisor board would not only recruit other committee members, but would also directly manage the company. It is important to note that under Germany's corporate law, supervisory boards are prohibited from taking an active role in the direct management of a firm's operation. In the THA's case, this rule was largely ignored. The supervisory boards, particularly in the very largest firms, took an active management role. A senior THA official, whose job it was to find qualified managers for East German firms in the heavy machinery sectors, said, "The THA's administrative boards were like no other in West Germany. We were not looking for people interested in meeting only a couple of times a year. You have to remember that, in contrast to West German companies, all of these firms were bankrupt. This was not a normal situation. The administrative committees were expected to play a major role in the transformation of the companies." The official added that the circumstances put special pressure on managers, "You had to be extremely innovative. I not only called upon the contacts I had, but I also went to the best personnel consulting firms in Western Europe. You simply had to operate in a very private sector fashion in order to ensure the best talent."

The THA did not begin a concerted effort to hire western managers until mid-1991. At that point, the agency was replacing eastern firm managers at the rate of fifteen to twenty per week. Even at this rate, however, only a fraction of firms could be reached, leaving eastern managers in charge of most of the THA's firms (Dininio 1999, 53).

In short, the recruitment of private sector individuals was extensive in both the RTC and THA and provided rapid relief to both agencies, which were under enormous pressure from external actors and the public at large. These efforts, however, were not enough to complete the agencies' enormous number of tasks. Fortunately for personnel managers in both agencies, it was not the intent of the U.S. Congress or the German Bundestag that all the activities involved in both agencies be done in-house. The legislative mandates encouraged the agencies to use private sector contractors when it was deemed necessary or efficient.

At the peak of the THA's privatization activity in 1991–92, nearly half of the positions at the executive level and above were occupied by private sector contractors on three-month contracts.[15] The agency spent nearly 30 percent more on contractor salaries than on the salaries for the entire agency combined. In some years it was much higher (see Tables 3.3 and 3.4). Table 3.3 shows that in 1991 the THA spent nearly $209 million on contractors and $108 million on agency employees. What is particularly remarkable about the amount is that for every full-time contractor there were at least four and sometimes five agency employees.

Both tables illustrate how important private contractors were to the implementation of THA policies. Despite the fact that they comprised only about 20 percent of the total agency employees, the total paid was nearly 30 percent more than the total paid to all regular employees. In addition, the majority of the remaining management

Table 3.3

THA Salary Expenditures, 1990–95 (in $ thousands)

Year	Totals for Contractors	Totals for THA Employees
1990	10,938	8,299
1991	209,143	108,622
1992	232,174	168,792
1993	204,014	187,772
1994	190,800	177,052

Source: THA. Dollars are converted from German marks: DM1 = $.60.

Table 3.4

Development of THA Employment, 1990–94

Year	Total No. of Employees	No. of Full-time Functional Contractors and Case Workers (*Funktionalberater und Sachverständige auf Vollzeitbasis*)[a]
1990	1,231	NA
1991	3,410	800
1992	3,614	714
1993	3,593	684
1994	2,795	627

Source: THA Office for Contractor Oversight.

[a]The total number of contractors was significantly higher because contractors often did not work full time but were paid on an hourly basis. The number translates total contractor workforce into full-time positions to make it comparable with full-time THA employees. The head of contract oversight estimated that at various points contractors comprised 80 percent of the total leadership.

and executive positions at the top not filled by contractors were occupied by the elite of West Germany's corporate world. Next came recent West German university graduates and experienced corporate managers near retirement or on loan from western companies.[16]

The THA director of the regional branch offices said that contractors were incorporated into the agency's hierarchy. Callers to the agency had no idea whether the person who answered was a contractor or a THA employee. The director said, "The external contractors hired by the regional offices were incorporated directly into the line functions of the organization. From outside, you would not have been able to tell whether the person was a contractor or a department employee." A former privatization agent, who later became a contractor, affirmed the point: "In the THA there was little distinction between the contractors and the THA employees in terms of the work. We [THA employees] did the same things they did, and we often worked together. The main difference was, of course, pay. Contractors made a lot more than we did."

According to the RTC's own estimates, the American agency spent four times more on the salaries of external contractors than on

Table 3.5

RTC Administrative Expense Budget, Third Quarter 1990 (in $ thousands)

Type of Expense	Amount
Noncontract Salaries and Benefits[a]	64,071
Contracted Services—Legal	32,915
Contracted Services—Asset Management	139,647
Contracted Services—Other	32,583
Total Contract Costs	205,145

Source: U.S. Senate 1993.

[a]Expenses include amount for FDIC support in legal services, accounting, personnel, and equal opportunity.

its own employees. CEO Albert Casey testified to Congress that his goal was to contract out 80 percent of the RTC's activities. The agency entered into more than 100,000 contracts for a variety of services but primarily in the same areas that the THA hired contractors: legal, auditing and appraisal, and management consulting.

Table 3.5 illustrates the extensive role contractors played in the RTC. The table compares expenditures on contractors with expenditures on RTC employee salaries for the third quarter of 1990, when the RTC was nearly a year into its operation and had finally geared up its staffing.

The figures listed are estimates for a single quarter, and although the amounts changed over time, the proportion spent on contractors versus staff remained fairly constant. The agency spent approximately $800 million a year in contracting services, roughly four times what it spent on its own staff. According to the RTC's legal information system, the agency approved for payment approximately $1 billion in contracting fees and expenses for legal issues alone from 1992 to 1995.[17] The RTC spent over $500 million in 1990 on outside legal support alone.

While the hiring and recruitment practices of the THA and RTC were clear breaks with tradition, the set of incentives new hires faced was also a long way from the visions of Max Weber and Woodrow Wilson.

Compensation Systems

Both the RTC and THA were decoupled from the government grade and compensation systems. Leaders in both agencies argued vehemently that the government's wage system was sorely inadequate to be able to recruit the necessary talented staff quickly. In particular, public sector salaries were considered too low, the governmental grade systems were inadequate to offer talented individuals an incentive to apply, and the governmental pay structures offered little incentive to do the job quickly and efficiently. Recall again that the traditional model of public personnel in both countries included a lower level of compensation in exchange for life-time employment, compensation typically deferred until after a long probationary period, and promotions and compensation levels based on a grade system, within which salaries were relatively equal. Whereas the general structure of a grade system was applied in both cases, salary levels were highly differentiated, significantly higher than in other public agencies, paid up front, and included a performance-based bonus system for all levels in both agencies.[18]

The THA rewarded employees financially in three ways: an annual salary, a performance bonus, and an exit bonus. Table 3.6 reports on the annual base salaries paid to employees in 1993.

As Table 3.6 illustrates, the traditional notion of a standardized pay system was ignored in the THA. There is a significant variation in the pay between easterners and westerners, reflecting the agency's demand for West German recruits. At the level of department head, westerners earned nearly 100 percent more than their eastern counterparts. Moreover, the pay itself was extraordinarily high, even at the lowest executive level. Given that the average age of western executives was about thirty-two, it was quite remarkable for them to earn close to DM100,000 (approximately $70,000) just out of school, with little practical experience. Citing estimates from the German federal auditor, the German newsmagazine *Der Spiegel* (26 September 1994, 40–51) reported that salaries for the new THA employees were up to 160 percent higher than what their previous positions paid.

Table 3.6
Average Salaries of THA Employees

Positions	Average Salary ($)
Directors/Executive Com. Members	178,114
Department Head (West)	114,300
Department Head (East)	58,291
Executive Leader (West)	84,547
Executive Leader (East)	53,230
Executive (West)	56,599
Executive (East)	34,432
Case Worker (West)	31,154
Case Worker (East)	22,018
Secretary (West)	32,926
Secretary (East)	19,879

Source: BMF (1994).

Salaries for managerial recruits hired to run the state-owned enterprises were targeted at 50 to 60 percent of West German commercial standards. According to the Ministry of Finance report, this worked out to between DM200,000 and DM300,000 (BMF 1991). East German managers, however, were paid significantly less.

In addition to their annual salary, employees below the level of department head received a premium, while those in higher tiers of leadership received sizable bonuses.[19] According to the Ministry of Finance report, the maximum premium an employee received was 20 percent of his or her monthly salary. However, reports from employees place the figure much higher. And those who worked in the regional offices also stated that regional office directors would offer bonuses to individuals or teams who succeeded in achieving a certain level of performance, typically measured in terms of the amount the office divested. At the higher levels of leadership (above the department head level) the agency paid maximum bonuses of 25 percent of annual salaries. In 1992 the average bonuses were the following: directors, DM76,000; regional office managers DM88,000;

department heads DM57,000; and regional office directors DM74,000 (Treuhandanstalt 1994a, 631).

West Germans also received compensation for being separated from their families. This compensation typically included a free furnished apartment in the East or hotel expenses if no apartment was available. The agency also paid for monthly flights back to the West as well as complete moving costs. The THA managers also received an automobile, which they were encouraged to use for private as well as professional affairs (BMF 1994). Finally, many THA employees were paid exit bonuses. The exact amount is difficult to determine since, according to the internal auditing division (Revision 1993), data prior to 1993 was not systematically collected on employees who left the agency. In a report published in October 1993, the internal auditing division reported that in 1993, DM526,000 were paid in exit bonuses to twenty-one workers, seven of whom worked in the central office. The report did not include employees in the leadership positions (Revision 1993).[20]

The RTC's system of compensation resembled that of the THA in a number of ways. Unlike most federal agencies in the United States, the RTC was given the authority to set the compensation of its employees without regard to the basic rates of pay set forth in Title 5 of the United States Code. In addition, the agency was exempt from the Office of Personnel Management regulations governing the award of bonuses to executives. An unusual provision of FIRREA made all RTC employees into employees of the FDIC, a government corporation that has had the authority to set its compensation levels since 1933. As a result, employees in the RTC were paid significantly more than public employees in other agencies.

The agency was given the freedom to hire private sector short-term employees at market rates. Furthermore, FDIC employees transferred to the RTC received a salary premium of approximately 25 percent of their annual salary. Forty-two executives in the agency earned more than $100,000 per year, with the top salaries earned by Lamar Kelly, senior vice president for asset management ($150,000), and William Rolle, senior vice president for institutional operations (also $150,000) (U.S. House 1993, 918–19).

Like the THA, the RTC also made extensive use of a pay-for-performance system for executives and lower level employees. Albert

Casey estimated that the RTC spent nearly $1 million on bonuses in 1992 and $440,000 in 1991.[21] The GAO reported that in 1990, 88 percent of RTC executives were awarded bonuses. In 1991 and 1992 the figure was 70 and 71 percent, respectively. The maximum bonus for executives in 1990 and 1992 was $25,000. In 1991 the maximum was lowered to $15,000.[22]

As in the German case, the RTC often had to rely on the current management of thrifts when the government took them over. To ensure that thrift employees did not become government employees (and receive government benefits), the RTC's policy was to dismiss all employees and then rehire them through a temporary agency. An FDIC employee of thirty-three years, who later transferred to the RTC and worked as a managing agent, explained:

> When we took over an institution, we explained to the individuals that the institution would close down. . . . They were then rehired through a temporary agency, not by the government. If we'd hired them directly, they'd have gotten all sorts of benefits, but through a temp agency you could avoid all that. This was standard operating procedure . . . even if they made 85K a year. The temp agency would tack on their 30 percent but we'd have paid more than that in benefits anyway and more importantly, it would have been harder to close the institutions.

In certain cases the agency took steps to lower the salaries of top executives in the firms. At the end of 1990, the RTC was paying seventeen thrift executives in excess of $300,000, including David Paul, chairman and CEO of Centrust Federal Savings Bank of Miami. With a salary of more than a $1 million per year, Paul was perhaps one of the highest paid public sector employees in the country. The practice became highly controversial when it was reported that management in government-owned conservatorships was earning over $300,000 (U.S. House 1990a, 31). Following a number of press accounts that the RTC was continuing to pay savings and loan executives and managers their high salaries and bonuses, Michael Martinelli, director of the Central Regional RTC Office, testified before an extremely hostile RTC Special Task Force. His statements capture the problem the agency faced:

> When FIRREA was enacted, don't forget we were all of a sudden thrust into this thing. We had to pick ourselves up and run into it and get as

much help as we could. Until we could get people hired to fill these positions . . . we had to continue to hire these people [S&L executives] for a
few months. Then we were able to hire people, get on board, and get the
best quality people that we could to run the institution. . . . When we were
getting started a year ago . . . we didn't have that many people on board
(U.S. House 1990a).

David Cooke, CEO of the RTC, testified before the same hostile committee: "Basically what we do is we get somebody in the institution to
try to oversee the institution. I can't emphasize enough how complicated some of these institutions are. Believe me, I am a career civil
servant. . . . But you could not get up and train a career person to
take over an institution like Franklin or Centrust or some of these.
You have got to get experienced people" (U.S. House 1990a). The
tension between the demands for a skilled managerial staff and
ensuring that the firm managers were untainted by their prior
involvement in the savings and loan crisis was something that RTC
and THA personnel managers had to grapple with consistently.

Training

The training of personnel and socialization in the THA and the
RTC were similar in a number of important respects and contrasted
sharply with the traditional model of civil servants in their respective
countries. Training within the public sector is designed to give
employees important skills that enhance their job performance.
Given the crisis situation both agencies confronted at their birth, neither the THA nor the RTC spent a great deal of effort on training or
socializing agents into the organization. Personnel managers in the
THA said that training was a luxury that early on they could not
afford. But they had two expectations: first, that employees were competent the day they were hired; and second, the situation was so
unusual and unprecedented that it would have been difficult to structure any type of training system. Policy statements, manuals, and
handbooks were approved by the executive and administrative
boards on a variety of topics. The majority of the guidelines, however,
were passed and published after a significant period of time had
elapsed and most of the privatization had been completed. Moreover,

privatization and control agents indicated that they had spent little time studying or using the manuals. One employee who worked in the Dresden regional office before being transferred to internal auditing in the central office in Berlin said in a bitter tone, "Every other week there was another special action or reorganization called for by the central office. It was ridiculous. We didn't spend a lot of time reading manuals. Most of the learning came from different experiences."

In the RTC, training was formally more a part of the organization. In practice, however, it was kept to a minimum. According to Cooke, the agency sponsored three types of training: (1) training mandated for certain positions by federal law, such as equal opportunity counseling; (2) job essential training requested by a principal supervisor on an individual basis for a subordinate when such training was essential to the job; and (3) career development training for employees who wished to be promoted (U.S. House 1990a). Cooke also noted that training responsibilities were decentralized, handled in the four regional offices. During the same hearing Carmen Sullivan, director of the Southwest regional office, testified that training for employees consisted of a one-day orientation period followed by monthly meetings with staff at the regional office, updating organizational goals and objectives.

Sullivan's comments are consistent with responses from interviewees at the central office and two of the field offices in Dallas, Texas, and Newport Beach, California. Both FDIC and private sector employees working in the RTC stated that an implicit assumption among employees and the RTC was that "you were expected to perform the day you were hired." Even though many of the employees from the private sector had never worked in a public agency (nor thought of themselves as public sector employees), they received only minimal preparation and instruction. An employee at the National Sales Center in Washington, who had worked for a savings and loan institution that failed prior to being hired by the RTC, described the training in the following way: "The expectation that came along with being paid a private sector salary was that you could do the job. What you didn't know you quickly learned. The norm was OJT— on-the-job-training."

ORGANIZATIONAL STRUCTURE

Organizational structure refers to the ways in which discretion, authority, and responsibility within an agency are configured and delegated. While their internal architecture differed from one another, the RTC and THA's organizational structures shared two features that contrasted sharply with classic or bureaucratic models of administration. These features had a significant impact in shaping their bureaucratic outcomes. First, responsibility and authority were highly decentralized in the two organizations, giving agents closest to the assets an unusually high level of responsibility and authority. Second, the lines of accountability and authority remained blurred throughout most of their operation, thereby increasing bureaucratic discretion while weakening coordination and oversight.

Decentralized Operations

The RTC and the THA allocated authority and responsibility to three separate levels: (1) a central administration, responsible for governing the agency and privatizing and/or resolving the largest and most politically sensitive firms and thrifts; (2) a set of regional and/or field offices, overseeing and implementing the majority of privatizations; and (3) the THA-owned firms and RTC-owned thrifts, where much of the reorganization, downsizing, and sale of assets occurred. Though much of the governance and planning occurred at the top of the organization, the lion's share of responsibility and authority was ceded to the field offices and to the firms and thrifts.

In the THA 3,826 companies were placed under the control of the central office and 6,718 state-owned enterprises were made the responsibility of one of fifteen "mini-Treuhands" following the passage of the Allocation Act in January 1991.[23] The branches were separate and independent, and they adopted policies that varied depending on the preferences and backgrounds of their leadership. In contrast to the central office, which integrated operational and functional responsibilities, the branch offices were organized strictly along functional lines. Each office was headed by a branch manager who oversaw four directorates, including (1) privatization, the directorate responsible for selling of firms; (2) firm accompaniment, the directorate responsible for reviewing and approving requests for liquidity by firms and overseeing the restructuring of firms; (3) finance, the directorate charged with ensuring budgetary and contract supervision as well as the liquidation of firms; and (4) personnel, the directorate charged with personnel issues, administration, information management, and social issues.[24] Of the four divisions, privatization received the greatest staffing. Its employees were mostly private contractors (who were the highest paid employees in the THA), and it was considered by those in the branches as the most prestigious and most desired area in which to work.

The THA's policy guidelines stated that "branch offices are to exercise their functions independently." In practice, according to scholars and interviews with branch employees, this meant that branch managers were transformed into small kings. Each branch manager was limited by a complicated delegation of authority that required approval from the central office for decisions concerning firms of a particular size or the extension of credit of a certain amount.[25] THA employees noted that these delegations of authority still left branches with wide discretionary authority. Even in cases where additional authorization was needed, branches still controlled much of the decision-making process since they collected and provided the information on which decisions were made.

Seibel and Kapferer (1996) write, "Branch managers had 'enormous power' during their initial period in office. In formal terms, this was expressed in their financial freedom of decision, with an upper limit of DM30 million. However, it was the factual relationships that caused those of them who were later questioned to describe their position in feudalistic metaphors: 'miniature king,' 'guru,' or 'oriental potentate" (124). In testimony before a parliamentary committee President Breuel defended the decentralized organizational structure:

[Decentralization] was for the Treuhand an indispensable necessity given the massive and varied number of tasks it was given. . . . What do I mean by decentralization? For example, allocating high levels of responsibility and authority to the branch offices . . . who really had the mass of the THA's business to take care of. Such an undertaking was only possible by allowing them to rely on their own competence and discretion. . . . The alternative would have been a centralized, so to speak, "bureaucracy" which would have had to be perfectly organized, in order to give the

impression of a mistake-free organization, even though no such agency
could possibly exist (Treuhandanstalt 1994b, 593).

President Breuel makes clear in her testimony that the THA deliberately sought to develop an alternative to the traditional bureaucratic
model and that a core element was the decentralization of responsibilities and discretion to the branch offices.

Branch office power was further strengthened by the fact that
branch jurisdictions did not coincide with any governmental jurisdictions. Branches were created to overlap with East Germany's fifteen governing district boundaries. The unified Germany, however,
replaced East Germany's district system with four large states and one
city-state, Berlin. THA branch offices thus overlapped these political
jurisdictions and further weakened the ability of state politicians to
place constraints on the branches or their managers.[26]

The independence enjoyed by the branches filtered down to the
level of individual agents. Privatization agents in the branch offices
report being given enormous discretion. An important reason for
this is that early on, agents were completely overwhelmed with the
number of firms for which they were responsible. A contractor in the
Dresden office compared the situation with a private firm: "In the private sector I might be responsible for four or five firms and I'd have
a competent staff to help me manage and sell them. When I started
working at the THA it wasn't unusual for me to have a portfolio of
fifty or sixty firms and with very little staff. We had a lot of discretion."

While the THA's branch offices were the "kings" of privatization,
it was the management and supervisory boards in the firms themselves that were ceded the most difficult challenges: downsizing and
passively restructuring firms. Neither the THA's central nor their
branch offices were in a position to enact the politically difficult
changes necessary to transform 8,000 firms into attractive investments. The agency was barely capable of hiring enough staff to
oversee the privatization process. Developing and enacting a restructuring strategy, laying off thousands of workers, and separating out
the valuable parts of firms required expertise, supervision, and
skilled management on site, not in a state office far away.

The agency's solution was to keep firms an arm's length from the
agency, legally and organizationally, cede to them freedom to downsize
the firms, and shield them from external pressures that might jeopar-

dize their work. A young THA executive was hired in 1991 to work in the Dresden branch office to oversee the restructuring of as many as fifty firms at one time. He said, "The primary work of restructuring was clearly placed into the hands of the firm managers on site. . . . One wasn't allowed to take on the work of the firm managers. The managers were charged with carrying out the business of the firm in a very normal fashion . . . to implement the restructuring concept." A former manager hired by the THA to oversee a large electrical manufacturing company in Berlin described his role:

> The situation was fairly grim when I took over. The company had 7,000 employees and many held non-firm-related positions that were completely unnecessary to production. . . . After I took over I developed a business plan. We reduced the work force to 2,000 and carved out many of the subsidiaries that detracted from the value of the core business. I had to work to find buyers and investors. In the first two years I had a lot of freedom and was constrained only by the financial situation. I had the freedom an entire executive committee would have in western Germany except that the THA was unwilling to invest in turning the company around through new investments. We could have sold the company's real estate and reinvested it into new machinery, but the Treuhand wanted none of it. The agency was concerned primarily with reducing the size of the workforce to make it easy for investors.

The manager's comment suggests that discretion was not unlimited. Autonomy was ceded to the firm's managing committees in cases where employees were fired. In instances where capital investments were needed, though, approval was required from the executive committee and the THA. The manager noted:

> In the firm you had an executive committee, manager, and owner. However, the owner, the THA, also sat on the executive committee. There was therefore a clear line of information going to the central office (THA). Moreover the executive committee did not operate like a normal executive committee since the owner's influence was great. The agency began to play a greater and greater role in the functioning of the firm.

This indirect arrangement allowed the THA to remain a comfortable distance from the difficult decisions and consequences of the firm without losing control. The THA could, as one auditor bluntly put it, "blame the company's management for the firm's poor performance while also saddling the management with the difficult task of reducing the workforce."

As in the case of the THA, responsibilities and authority in the RTC were shared among several hubs within the agency. The bulk of the work, however, was conducted in the field offices and thrifts. Institutions with liabilities in excess of $500 million were assigned to the national office in Washington, D.C. Institutions with less than $500 million were assigned to one of four regional offices which, in turn, oversaw the operations of fourteen field offices.[27] Since the RTC did not opt to close and sell off all institutions at once, the institutions themselves (and in particular their new management) were also ceded a great deal of responsibility and authority not only to sell assets but to transform the institutions or "shops" into salable entities.[28]

The division of labor did not follow an exact blueprint. In general, national and regional offices were assigned to oversee the management, operation, and resolution of the conservatorships, with the national office being assigned the larger institutions. In addition, the national office was assigned to set the RTC's policies and, along with the regional offices, ensure that oversight structures were in place. Field offices were primarily responsible for the management and sale of assets after resolution had occurred. Beginning in 1991 the national office became heavily involved in the sale of large bundles of assets. A director of loan sales hired in 1990 by the RTC said, "In 1990–91 things were very regional-office driven. The goals and strategies were set by the regions. It was only later on that you started seeing the central office play more of a role. But in the early stages it was all regions." More than 90 percent of resolutions were conducted in the field, with the remainder conducted in Washington (U.S. House 1990b).

The fourteen consolidated field offices were located in areas with a high concentration of thrifts and holdings since they were closely involved with the sale and management of the assets held by the thrifts (U.S. House 1990a). Much like the THA's branch offices, the RTC's consolidated offices were ceded a great deal of authority. An RTC manager charged with organizing and running loan auctions spent much of her time coordinating with the regional offices. She said, "At one point all the regions were responsible for whatever assets were taken down out of their S&Ls, regardless of where they were. . . . Each of the field and regional offices worked on their own and there was little effort to put things together. . . . All tried to function autonomously." An RTC official at the national sales office stressed how independent each consolidated office was, stating, "At the national sales office we had to go begging to these regional offices to get these people to give us assets to sell."

The organizational structure of the fourteen consolidated field offices centered mainly around asset management and disposition.[29] In describing the role of the field office in the larger RTC structure, the GAO (1991c) reported, "The field offices function as service centers for RTC's assets and real estate management activities." A former director of a consolidated office described the responsibilities of the field: "We were in the asset sales business. The primary goal of the consolidated office was the management and disposition of assets. Once a conservatorship ended and the institution was sold or in receivership, the field offices would get the assets." Field offices were equipped with sizeable marketing teams and asset specialists whose primary responsibility was managing and selling assets.[30] Initially the agency continued to use on a temporary basis the contractors that had been employed by the conservatorship through interim service agreements. Once the field offices became more established, assets were typically placed with asset managers using Standard Asset Management Disposition Agreements (SAMDAs). Finally, just as the managers of THA-owned firms were critical to the process, the RTC depended heavily on the managers hired to run conservatorship operations.

The relationship between the thrifts and the RTC was similar to the relationship the THA had to its firms. The conservatorship/receivership construct allowed the RTC to couple itself loosely to the institutions. As conservator, the RTC was appointed to operate or dispose of the association as a going concern and was specifically empowered to take any necessary steps to put the association in a sound and solvent condition, to carry on the business of the association, and to preserve and conserve the assets and property of the association.[31] The agency was connected in the sense that it provided managerial expertise and financial support and imposed constraints on borrowing, while at the same time it treated the thrift institutions as separate nongovernmental private entities. The new managers placed in the thrift institutions by the RTC were given many of the same responsibilities, faced many of the same challenges, and enjoyed much of the same power and authority as managers of THA-owned firms. The responsibility of the managing team was to reduce the association to its core deposits, fixed assets, and cash or cash equivalents with an eye toward selling the institution. The GAO (1991c) noted in its report on the policies and procedures of the agency, "RTC's policies state that orderly downsizing, or selling of assets, is the major thrust of the conservatorship; management of a conservatorship should not result in growth. Managing agents are supposed to try work out or reduce non-performing assets. . . . Managing agents are required to devise a downsizing plan" (2–4). The RTC's Conservatorship Manual provides a more formal list of tasks that parallel the responsibilities of German managers in THA-owned firms.[32]

New managers typically confronted a failing business, an extremely hostile and skeptical labor force, and a documentation and record-keeping nightmare.[33] The challenge for the manager was, therefore, to treat the institution as a going thrift enterprise while taking steps to downsize the operation, reduce staff, and sell off parts of the firm. And managing agents were given broad and sweeping powers to carry out their responsibilities, the most important of which was the ability to repudiate leases and contracts.[34] Section 212(e) of FIRREA provides authority to conservators and receivers to repudiate any contract or lease to which a failed association was party. The agreements the thrift had made with creditors—whether it was the rental contract to the building that housed the thrift or a multimillion dollar agreement to fund a shopping mall—were reassessed and, if determined detrimental to minimizing the cost of the operation, were repudiated. The managing agent at one of the largest RTC-run thrifts in the country described the power he had as a managing agent: "You're in a unique position when you can call somebody up and say, 'Hey, we have a billion dollar a year lease with you and we're sending you notice.' Like hundreds of years ago, it was like having the power of the king."

In short, the THA and RTC organizations were characterized by an extraordinarily high level of decentralization of power and responsibility. While such a structure is unusual for a public organization, it is not unheard of. Indeed, many managerial reformers often stress the importance of decentralization in the public sector (Osborne and Gaebler 1992; Peters 1996). What truly sets these two agencies apart, however, is a second organizational feature they shared, namely the lack of clear lines of authority.

Lack of Clear Lines of Authority

What failed to develop in the organizational structures of the RTC and THA were clear lines of accountability and authority. As RTC Chairman William Seidman put it, the agency's structure "defied all rules of organization: strategic planning and decision making were completely separated from operations, and everything conspired to cut the channels of communication from boss to line worker. Any ex-business school dean should have been appalled, and this one certainly was" (Seidman 1993, 201).

What did emerge in place of clear lines of authority in both agencies was confusion. Relations between central and branch offices were initially quite tense and soon became worse. In the fall of 1990, THA President Breuel, who at the time was serving as the executive committee member in charge of branch offices, replaced each of the fifteen East German branch managers with West German managers, most of whom were businessmen in their fifties with experience primarily in small and medium-sized firms.[35] Given that the employees in the branches were almost all East Germans, the move caused some hostilities. The allocation of firms caused further tension. According to guidelines set by the executive committee, firms with fewer than 1,500 employees were to be assigned to the branch in whose district the firm was located. While theoretically a clean division of labor, the large number of exceptions in the guidelines coupled with the geographic complexity of firms, contributed to a great deal of confusion and animosity between regional and central offices.[36] Seibel and Kapferer (1996) write, "Until the allocation was complete . . . there was nothing but confusion in the branches and in the central office industrial directorates. . . . In view of the unclear allocation of companies there was no avoiding cases in which companies during this period of time were sold twice: once by the central office and once by the regionally responsible branch" (126). Georg Cadel adds that constant personnel and responsibility changes in the executive committee contributed to a sense in the branches that no one in the central office was responsible for their oversight. Confirming Seibel and Kapferer's observations, Cadel (1994) writes, "The lack of cooperation between the branches and central offices led to situations in which branches would negotiate with investors that had been dropped by the central office because of financial problems" (73).

In a similar vein, contractors were also able to take advantage of the split and lack of coordination between central and branch offices. Private contractors were sometimes successful in playing the central office and branches off one another to increase their fees.[37]

Confusion also reigned in the RTC. Responsibilities and tasks overlapped vertically and horizontally within the organization. RTC Chairman Seidman (1993) captures the sense of confusion in an editorial:[38]

> Who is the Chief Executive Officer of the S&L cleanup? Please answer from the following list: (1) Nicholas Brady, Secretary of the Treasury; (2) John Robson, Deputy Secretary of the Treasury; (3) Peter Monroe, President of the Oversight Board; (4) David Cooke, Executive Director of the RTC; (5) William Seidman, Chairman of the RTC and FDIC; (6) Philip Searle, head of the Advisory Committee of the RTC; (7) None of the Above. The correct answer is No. 7, 'None of the above.' . . . No one is in charge of the RTC (222).

In the RTC there was a mismatch between the structure that was set and the structure that was required to fulfill the mandates of FIR-REA. In an interesting comparison, the problems that prompted the THA to abandon its functional framework in favor of a more sectoral-based one were problems that the RTC faced at the national and regional levels. The resolution division, for example, was involved in asset sales whenever assets were included in the sale of an institution, as in the case of a purchase and assumption. The operations group, which formally provided support and oversight to conservatorships, was also involved in approving and overseeing the sale of more than $150 billion in assets. An RTC official in one of the regional offices emphasized the point saying, "The organizational split between asset management and resolutions was completely artificial and created enormous difficulty at times. A lot of what happened during the course of resolutions was selling assets and placing them with contractors. Therefore, the division between asset sales and resolutions contributed to a great deal of confusion." A GAO auditor said, "The RTC's structure mattered a lot. What happened was the RTC was originally set up under the management theory that headquarters would set down policies and field would go implement. The head didn't need to do oversight, no evaluation and refinement component as in a textbook management cycle. No back end of the loop." When asked why, the auditor laughed and said, "Because they didn't know what they were doing and because they wanted to go out there and sell, sell, sell. There were no clear lines of authority. People in the field thought they were out there running their own thing and to hell with Washington."

The resolution of City Savings, a New Jersey institution with nearly $10 billion in assets, illustrates the confusion caused by the organizational structure. City Savings was placed under the RTC's control in December 1989.[39] Following an attempt to sell City Savings as a whole entity, the RTC offered the institution for sale a second time with an option to purchase a number of high quality assets not connected to the institution. The RTC believed the option would increase bidder interest and provide the RTC a chance to test the previously untried option-as-asset disposition method. In January 1991 about $2.5 billion in insured deposits were sold to First Fidelity along with an option to purchase $3 billion in high quality loans. First Fidelity assigned the option to Goldman Sachs investment company.[40] The deal was structured by the national sales center (located within the asset sales division) and the resolution division.[41] Soon afterwards the agency ran into difficulty locating and delivering all the assets required by the option. Between May and July 1991, RTC officials scrambled to find qualifying assets. They were largely unsuccessful in part because of an increase in securitizations (done by the finance and administration division), which were taking away many of the assets from sales and resolution.[42] In July 1991, RTC agreed to fulfill $1 billion of the option by delivering $1.2 billion worth of loans from Florida Federal Savings, an institution scheduled to be resolved in August 1991. That still left $2 billion outstanding. After the RTC and Goldman Sachs failed to reach an agreement to purchase additional loans, the agency agreed instead to make the investment company the lead managing underwriter for two securitization transactions involving $2 billion in assets, netting Goldman Sachs between $8 million and $12 million in underwriting fees. In the case of City Savings, each division played a role in the transaction and nearly every group within each division had a hand in the resolution. The coordination difficulties were sizeable. As late as March 1992, the RTC continued to operate without a corporate-wide system to manage and sell loans and other assets (GAO 1992i). In the case of City Savings, the RTC struck a deal to sell $3 billion in high quality loans, assets it was unaware it had and did not know how to deliver.

In summary, the organizational structures of the RTC and the THA are somewhat deceptive. With three levels extending outward from a central office, they both suggest a hierarchical internal architecture with responsibility clearly delegated to different levels. In practice, each unit within the organizations, including the firms and thrifts, operated with a great deal of independence and discretion. Lines of accountability often overlapped between and within levels of the organizations. The organizational structures of both agencies more closely resembled independent hubs than hierarchical levels.

The result was that organizational structure (1) formally ceded agents working closest to the assets more formal power and discretion for handling the assets; (2) increased the difficulties in developing agency-wide accountability structures; and (3) increased the difficulty for political principals and legislators to alter the agencies' course.

ORGANIZATIONAL CULTURES

Organizational culture refers to the shared assumptions and beliefs within a single group or set of subgroups within an organization.[43] The RTC and THA were initially composed of a collection of subcultures with consistent, yet distinct sets of beliefs and assumptions. In many cases these differences contributed to a great deal of tension within the two organizations. During the course of privatization, however, the challenges confronted by employees, along with symbolic actions taken by leadership, led to the development of a more singular and unifying dominant culture.

The dominant culture held a "private sector" or "neoliberal" view that assumed the RTC and THA were private entities in the business of limiting the state's involvement in markets through divestiture, divesting assets as quickly as possible, and resisting strategies that might prolong the tenure of the agencies or force them to stray from the narrow path of rapid privatization. These beliefs were the result of a combination of (1) cultural forms, such as internal and external architecture, dress codes, the crisis atmosphere, and the animosity directed toward the agency from outside; (2) formal and informal practices, such as the lack of standard operating procedures, the reward system, the publication of annual reports and agency-wide newsletters highlighting important accomplishments; and (3) the common threads of what is considered important, which were espoused by agency leaders to internal and external audiences (Martin 1992).

Organizational culture is typically seen as the glue that binds individuals to an organization's purpose, making the organization, in turn, more efficient (Ouchi 1981; Schein 1985; Blau 1955). Herbert Kaufman's 1960 classic account of the U.S. Forest Service found that socialization into a single culture was a key ingredient to controlling the "centrifugal forces that might be expected to fragment" the agency (Kaufman 1960, 4). At the same time, scholars provide examples in which issues within an organization are decoupled, allowing conflict to form around certain types of organizational behavior and consensus and coordinated action around others. Such a "differentiation" approach is akin to John Kingdon's (1984) view of the policy process, in that it accepts inconsistencies in the themes, practices, and forms in the organization, reflecting various subgroupings. This view also recognizes the possibility of consensus within subcultural boundaries, either over particular actions or within particular groups.[44] The argument that follows is that the RTC and THA were combinations of subgroup cultures that each developed a singular dominant culture which, as a result of a combination of factors connected to the task and actions taken by leadership, embraced neoliberal ideas of markets and governments.

Multiple Cultures

Three distinct cultural units comprised the RTC. One group was composed of FDIC employees who were transferred to the RTC to staff the management. These were civil servants who had undergone extensive training and socialization in the FDIC model of bank regulation.[45] FDIC employees received special upgrades in their salaries as an incentive to participate in the RTC. In the beginning they occupied most of the managerial positions in central, regional, and field offices. A long-time FDIC employee who later worked for the RTC board described the FDIC culture as a military type organization:

> The FDIC has more military discipline than the military. What they've got is an inculcated discipline. They don't allow outside interference. Didn't allow non-examiners into agency. If you weren't an FDIC examiner, you didn't get a lot of respect. Once you left supervision, don't expect to come back. Once you were an examiner, they didn't want you to go to another division at FDIC. Once you came to Washington, they didn't want you back in the field.

A managing agent's description of the FDIC behavior was similar to the classical view of bureaucracy:

> A legacy of the FDIC is that we had to write up cases for decisions that were laborious and bureaucratic. We had to justify everything we did in the form of a case report which included a presentation of sale, reason for the sale, and the quality of the buyers. . . . The FDIC folks were more interested in following the law and the regulations.

A second distinct group was composed of former Federal Savings and Loan Insurance Corporation employees, a hundred or so of whom were reassigned to the RTC after their agency was dissolved under FIRREA. "The FSLIC people were younger and more innovative," said an FDIC senior level manager. "FSLIC had been a very small agency. In the early 1980s you had an interest rate environment that was very difficult. In the 1980s you also got a whole lot of people who weren't wedded to the status quo. They were new. They came and had to deal with very substantial problems. They didn't have time to sit back. So in the mid-1980s they had to get real innovative without having the financial resources." The experience of being responsible for the regulation and resolution of thrifts during the 1980s, added the FDIC executive, contributed to their low status within the agency: "They came to RTC with scarlet letters. The FDIC employees treated them like dirt because of what happened in the '80s and the private sector people didn't respect them because they were public sector employees." Thus the group with the greatest governmental experience directly managing and selling conservatorships was also the group least respected in the organization.

A third cultural group consisted of those hired from the private sector, who very much understood themselves as distinct from their public-sector colleagues. This statement by the manager of real estate sales in a field office is representative:

> This was a marriage between the private sector and the government. In the private sector, we're accustomed to quickly cutting a deal and getting out. In government they're more concerned about constituents. We in the private sector care about the customers we're dealing with, not about constituents, and in the case of the RTC, the customer is the taxpayer. The FDIC people were a bit more cumbersome. They were more interested in making sure that regulations were followed. . . . Fortunately that didn't kick in until 1992–93.

Without prompting, the sales director identified himself as a private sector person. He defined private sector as not letting regulations get in the way of efficient business transactions. Later in the interview, however, he shifted to a public sector analogy:

> We came from the private sector. We did our mission and now we're going back. The war is over. It's like the army. What drove people was a feeling of patriotism. For many of the people here there was the expectation that you're going to go back out there, so you want to make sure that what you do at the RTC will be recognized. There was a real work ethic akin to the military.

A managing agent from Phoenix, Arizona, who had worked in the RTC for four years, also emphasized that the central differences between public and private had to do with concern for rules versus interest in quick sales:

> Look, the mission of the RTC was to grab hold of the institution and maximize the cash flows. Casey was good because he brought an aura of the private sector to the RTC. . . . The private sector folks were more business. They were interested in just getting the job done.

The RTC was thus an amalgam of different cultures: FDIC, FSLIC, and the private sector. Similarly, the THA was made up of a mixture of different cultures.

Wolfgang Seibel, a public administration expert at the University of Konstanz, is one of the few scholars who surveyed THA personnel. His research found that top managers in the THA were motivated by patriotism and by the opportunity to take on a major challenge in the closing phase of their career. For young executives Seibel noted, "It can be assumed that the attraction in joining the THA . . . was the high level of responsibility in relation to their age and the pioneering aspects of the THA's work which they probably regarded as enhancing their careers" (Seibel and Kapferer 1996, 142). Seibel's findings support the observations described in an article titled "Treuhand-anstalt Gives Young Staff Passport to the Business Fast Track," published in the *Wall Street Journal* (Durr 1993). The report noted that the THA offered young and inexperienced West Germans, hoping to make it quickly in the business world, an unusual opportunity. The article stated:

> In a country that can't boast of an Old Boy network, the Treuhand and its mandate to privatize eastern German industries have produced a unique opportunity for aspiring young managers. By chance or choice, many of Germany's would-be movers and shakers—as well as a generous helping of native nobility—have been drawn to the agency, where they've enjoyed uncommon access to the country's top private-sector management and ministry officials. . . . The Treuhand has come under fire in recent months over allegations that investors have plundered the assets or real estate of companies they bought from the agency . . . but long before the experts have finished assessing the agency's successes and shortcomings, many of its younger employees will have used their CV-fattening stint there as a big career stepping-stone (1).

In addition to the differences between old and young westerners, there was also a significant group of East German employees that comprised a separate cultural grouping. In fact, the majority of the THA's workforce was East German. The eastern German employees contrasted sharply with their western counterparts. While westerners were extremely arrogant and confident, easterners were insecure and uncertain about their own skills and position in a market economy that they had only read about. While western executives were quite young and had little work experience, their eastern counterparts were often a generation older with a great deal of work experience. Perhaps the greatest difference between the two groups was the skepticism easterners felt toward the THA's brand of narrow privatization. One privatization agent's comments capture the sentiment:

> The belief that the THA was composed of a pile of gangsters was something that East German workers had to carry inside themselves. . . . They of course experienced great frustration personally and in their homes

where they would be harassed for working in the agency. Most had been committed socialists. They had been in high positions; they had to be committed socialists . . . and that these were the very same people that would now work in the worst example of capitalism, the Treuhand, was of course a terrible thing for many easterners. And the eastern workers themselves did not trust themselves to do anything. In this sense the easterners indirectly aided in the rapid privatization because by not doing anything or taking a stand they let the western workers, who in many cases really weren't qualified, easily privatize.

A young agent from Dresden, responsible for providing assistance to fifty firms, put the matter in less abstract terms: "The differences between easterners and westerners could be seen in where they placed their priority between sales price, investment guarantee, and employment guarantee. Whereas the East Germans were predisposed to placing greater emphasis on investment and job guarantees, westerners were more concerned about price."

The diversity of cultures, the dependence on private-sector hires, and the decentralized structures of the organization contributed to internal tension and conflict in the RTC and THA. A comment by a former employee of the RTC's national sales center captures several of the tensions in the American agency:

There were big-time conflicts between offices. . . . Competition was fierce because what you've basically got is a bunch of salespeople who were there for a year or so. Now, you're hiring private sector people where what counts is, "What did you do for me today?" meaning sales. As a result, competition over sales accomplishments was unbelievable."

She recounted the difficulty in constructing larger portfolios for sale because field offices and conservatorship institutions were often unwilling to release what they perceived to be their assets. An FDIC examiner, who later worked in the RTC, described the differences and tensions at the RTC. He focused on the public versus private split in the agency:

You had the corporate culture of the S&L people. . . . S&L people were used to a lot more independence than they had with RTC. When they wanted to sell, initially they would just say, "What will you give me?" and sell it. Well, you can't do that in a public agency. You need to have bids to protect against the public saying "You just gave that away." So there was a lot of getting the savings and loan people used to the government. They were less cognizant of oversight and accountability. The guys in middle and high management were used to having a secretary doing everything for them. They didn't know how to use a computer. Our [FDIC] culture is, you type it up yourself. Initially there were some clashes. It was an undercurrent of cliques, where S&L people would talk amongst themselves, former FDIC people would talk amongst themselves. Took a lot of work to make the S&L people realize, you're not in the outside world anymore, you're in a government agency, and this is the way we do it.

Several agency employees described it as kind of "proprietorship." The same FDIC agents stated that the agency "got compartmentalized as it went along. People started saying this is my job, I'll do my job. They should have paid attention to how it affected other areas. Became competitive. Some of that's healthy, I think. Collections were reported internally each month, and different regions would compete. Upper management paid attention to it. Meant more to them than to us. We just did our job."

The tensions were exacerbated by the fact that government grade employees occupied the managerial positions in the organization (typically in one of four regional offices and RTC headquarters in Washington) while private sector hires were overwhelmingly in the fifteen field offices, closest to the institutions and their assets. Much of the animosity and hostility between field and regional offices was thus transformed into generalizations about private and public employees.

A senior GAO auditor assigned to the RTC in Dallas, Texas, captures the sentiment:

> The relationship between the LGs and the FDIC was not good. They couldn't stand one another. Everything in the RTC, for example, required "case" write-up. The case lays out a strategy for selling the property which is then presented to a committee. These [private sector hires] were not guys that were interested in writing up cases and making presentations. They knew the market, they would have a buyer and they didn't understand why any of the bureaucratic steps had to occur.

The "cases" referred to by the auditor typically had to be sent to one of four regional offices or the central office for approval, depending on the size of the transaction. Requiring justifications for decisions contributed to the sense among private sector hires that their expertise was being questioned by individuals they considered incompetent bureaucrats.

Conflicts were particularly severe within the conservatorships where managing agents—many of whom exhibited little tolerance for government employees—viewed any action by the field offices as an intrusion on their turf. A former director of the largest consolidated office stated that the biggest challenge he faced was trying to improve cooperation between the field offices and the managing agents, "The managing agents had very small staffs, and they needed our help but didn't asked for it often enough. The cooperation was vital in the RTC, but we just didn't get it as often as we would have liked."

The THA also experienced significant tension. A statement by a privatization agent captures the sentiment expressed by most employees with whom I spoke: "Everyone knew that the western workers earned a great deal more money. The eastern workers were extremely angry that they made so much more money particularly since the easterners were often much older and had occupied much higher positions. . . . Suddenly they found themselves in fairly subordinate positions." Several East Germans promoted to management in the RTC agreed with the privatization agent's general assessment about east/west tensions but argued that the tensions diminished over time and were largely overstated. One of the few East German department heads was placed in charge of privatizing mining companies. An elderly man nearing retirement, he had served in East Germany's Council of Ministries for more than twenty-five years. He said, "Yes, there were many East Germans who worked for the Treuhand that were extremely bitter. My wife and I lost a number of good friends as my responsibilities in the agency grew. Remember that the Treuhand was originally an East German agency, and all its employees were from the former East Germany. There were a lot who were committed to the ideals of communism and opposed to capitalism. However, over time, those most bitter left the Treuhand, and the others realized the opportunity they had to learn about the capitalist system from the inside."

A number of privatization agents reported tension between central and regional offices and among individuals. For example, although the THA's stated policy was that all contracts and decisions were to be reviewed by at least two people (the so-called "four eyes principle"), privatization agents report that it was not uncommon for executives in the field to work on their own. As one privatization agent said, "A number of agents wanted to make sure they worked alone. They didn't want others to look into their cards." When asked why, given the absence of any direct commission, the agent responded, "I don't want to impose any assumption on anyone, but I think it was often an issue of insecurity. I can think of a number of cases where individuals just didn't want to admit that they lacked competence." Agents report that because the central office exercised very little control over the directors of the regional offices, the regional managers became akin to "small emperors" in the agency.

Integration of Cultures

Despite the various cultures imported into both agencies, a dominant singular perspective emerged among RTC and THA employees. The culture reflected a private or neoliberal view that (1) valued rapid privatization over other goals; (2) believed secondary goals to be "political" and detracting from the agencies' central apolitical purpose of rapid divestiture; and (3) viewed internal controls and bureaucratic procedures often as undermining the agencies' purpose. A number of factors contributed to the development of this dominant culture.

Among the factors, the time line set by the legislatures in both countries stands out in its symbolic importance. The legislative deadline was mentioned by every RTC and THA official as an important part of their calculus in determining how they did their job.[46] Reminders were constantly circulated throughout the agencies through press releases, quarterly and monthly reports detailing the sales progress, and annual reports.[47]

An RTC managing agent who worked in several of the larger conservatorships for years described the phenomenon: "When Congress set up the RTC it said, 'you will go out of business in six years.' That meant there was no leeway. You were to sell the stuff. You weren't supposed to sit around and wait for the market to change. We were to get rid of the real estate and the loans and close the shop as quickly as possible, period."[48] The sense of urgency exacerbated the chaos that already existed in the work environment that was crisis-driven by the lack of adequate personnel, the growing inventory, and widespread public attacks on both agencies. Wolfgang Seibel describes the THA's early years:

> The outward manifestations of this chaos included overcrowded offices, unclear and constantly changing lines of responsibility, no proper internal telephone directories or organizational charts, and no secretaries or other assistants. . . . Sales discussions went on in every corner of every large room. Company decisions of wide-ranging importance were made on the landing. . . . The atmosphere was topped off in every respect by the shabby interior (Seibel and Kapferer 1996, 122–23).

RTC and THA officials commonly described their efforts in terms of "fighting a war or battle," "constantly putting out fires," and "blowing out inventory."

Names and titles were also important. The RTC, for example, was headed by a chief executive officer. Later it hired a chief financial officer. Similarly, the THA was led by a president and changed the names of its regional offices to "Niederlassungen" or branches, a term normally used to describe satellite offices in private corporations rather than a public agency.

The architecture that housed both agencies further reinforced a sense that neither agency would be around for very long. The RTC was barely recognizable in Washington, D.C., within eyesight of the FDIC building. A plain office building with three small letters "R-T-C" attached to the front gave the only indication of what was inside. As noted above, the THA initially filled the floors of the socialist-style office building "House of the Electrical Industry" on Alexander Platz. Following unification it was moved to the infamous building that had housed the Air Ministry during the Second World War and, later, East Germany's House of Ministries. Only a small temporary sign with the THA's name revealed the contents.

In addition, many formal and informal practices of both agencies helped to institutionalize a private-sector culture. The dependence upon private sector hires and contractors, the lack of many formal standard operating procedures, the differential compensation and pay-for-performance schemes all helped to blur the line between public and private.

Hierarchy and leadership also made a difference. The leadership positions in both the RTC and THA were filled by corporate leaders.

Secondary goals such as affordable housing and the MWOB program lacked the organizational prominence of resolutions or asset sales, the twin pillars around which the entire RTC agency was organized.[49] Similarly, the THA's final executive hierarchy lacked a separate division or functional responsibility for restructuring or economic development. The informal hierarchy in both agencies placed employees charged with secondary goals and auditors at the bottom of the prestige ladder.[50]

Compensation practices also mattered. Private sector hires and contractors earned more than government employees. And, while not the official policy, employees in both agencies reported that bonuses and financial rewards came from rapid privatization. Dieter Kampe, correspondent for *Der Spiegel* (a German news magazine) quotes Sylvia Birkhold, a lawyer working in the THA's satellite office in the city of Halle:

> There was enormous pressure to privatize rapidly and to sign a contract with the investor as quickly as possible. In Halle the management wanted to be done with the privatization by September 30, 1992. As an incentive to speed up the process, there were premiums paid to everyone. The premium for the director was DM80,000, for the division head it was DM40,000 and for the executives, a month's salary. In addition, all who worked in privatization were offered a trip to Turkey as an additional incentive. The oversight and control files sat on my desk. When I would determine that a contract could not be approved . . . I immediately experienced massive pressure from all sides: 'Mrs. Birkhold is responsible for our not being able to take a trip to Turkey' cried the executives. They claimed to have done such a good job, it couldn't have been done any other way. . . . And on top of that you had the pressure from above. Berlin asked twice a month how many firms were still there. Why were so few firms privatized this month? (Kampe 1994, 127).

Kampe's account is confirmed by a large study done by political scientists at the Free University in Berlin who note the strong opposition by branch managers to efforts taken in 1992 to hold branches more accountable. Up to that point, branches enjoyed nearly absolute discretion in privatizing and reporting (Cadel 1994, 17). RTC and THA officials talked about a reward system outside the agency where it was believed that future private sector employers would reward employees based on the experience they had gained and the deals they had closed while in the agency.

Finally, perhaps the most important factor that contributed to a distinct private sector identity was the rhetoric of leadership. Pronouncements by leaders to the public and their staff identified what was important and valued by the organization. Leaders in both agencies stressed the deadline. President Breuel emphasized the deadline during major management and staff meetings. She said in a keynote to employees: "Time is certainly the scarcest resource available to us. Or to put it more exactly, not usually available to us. We are therefore compelled to use factual knowledge, intelligence, idealism, motivation, and dynamism at record speed" (Seibel and Kapferer 1996). In the RTC, the story of Chairman L. William Seidman working out the pace of privatization on the back of an envelope was retold to me by a number of officials. Seidman himself retells the story in his autobiography:

> In mid-March 1990, while preparing for testimony on the RTC operations, I did some back-of-the envelope calculations. If the RTC sold $1 million in assets a day every day of the year, it would sell $365 million per year. At that rate it would take about three years to sell $1 billion of its assets. But the RTC had an inventory of about $40 billion in difficult assets—commercial mortgages, nonstandard home mortgages, problem real estate, and so on. So even at sales of $1 million a day, it would take more than 120 years to clear our inventory, and it was still growing. The obvious conclusion of this little bit of arithmetic was that only by selling large pools of assets would the RTC complete its job in its legal lifetime (Seidman 1993, 218).

Leaders in both agencies emphasized their organization's private-sector or corporate identity. In media interviews President Birgit Breuel consistently described the THA as the "largest holding company in the world." As the THA's director for personnel, Alexander Koch said, "For God's sake we're not a bureaucracy. We are the largest corporation in the world with four and half million employees. But unlike a normal corporation, we have the colossal job of becoming the smallest firm in the world and making ourselves redundant" (*Die Presse* 1991). Bill Rolle, the RTC's vice president for operation and resolutions and one of the three most important executives in the RTC, called the agency a "real estate sales corporation" and compared it to Citibank and BankAmerica. A senior evaluator in the GAO described the phenomena in terms of a story about an RTC director he had interviewed during an evaluation of the agency's subcontracting procedures. The GAO auditor said:

> I met an RTC office director—a guy who ran an entire district office— who looked at me and said, "You know the RTC is the private sector— we're not the government," and I looked back and said "Excuse me? RTC is a mixed ownership government corporation. Look at who signs your paycheck." He had no idea that he was really running a mixed ownership government corporation, not a federal agency under the law. He had absolutely no conception of that. He didn't understand that.

In summary, the organizational cultures in the RTC and the THA were initially amalgams of several separate cultures that were imported into the organizations. Over time a more singular culture took hold. While the more unified culture did not end the tensions in the agencies, it did allow for a very narrow definition of divestiture to dominate throughout the organizations, one that valued rapid privatization above all else, including secondary goals and oversight.

CONCLUSION

The extraordinary bureaucratic outcomes produced by the THA and the RTC are direct results of the agencies themselves: their personnel policies, organizational structures, and organizational culture. Tapping into the private sector for agency employees and using private contractors to fill the remaining personnel deficit allowed the RTC and the THA not only to construct their organizations quickly but to staff them with trained individuals who were often well connected to the very markets the agencies were engaging. It would have been impossible for any government employee to take over and manage the kinds of economic enterprises placed in the THA and RTC's jurisdiction, much less attempt to transform them into something investors might find appealing. Such a task requires more than just knowledge about a particular firm. It requires expertise about an entire industry, which few public or private sector employees possess. High compensation, differential wage systems, and pay-for-performance structures made it easier to overcome the recruitment obstacles faced by both agencies.

In addition to expertise, staffing practices and a decentralized organizational structure gave both agencies flexibility, a capacity to respond to changing environments, and most important, the capacity to learn from experience and incorporate new knowledge quickly into practice. This last characteristic—the learning curve—was particularly crucial as most assumptions concerning the viability of firms and the value of the assets turned out to be wildly overstated. The unfulfilled expectations forced both agencies to transform themselves from sales agencies into management and restructuring bureaus. One observes this in numerous examples in both agencies: the RTC's revision of the asset management contracts; the THA's shift to an active marketing and sales strategy; the RTC's move to various purchase and assumption resolution techniques; and the THA's varied restructuring initiatives. Had these been traditional agencies, such flexibility would have been difficult if not impossible.

Given the temporary nature of their employment and their private sector background, many employees demonstrated not only an ability but a willingness to take risks and be innovative selling assets. The decentralized structure gave agents the freedom to take those risks. In the RTC, the development of a securitization program for its vast pool of nonperforming loans was something that had not been done in the private sector. The program was designed by private sector hires from the large investment companies and is now emulated by the private sector. Similarly, the THA attempted various public-private experiments such as the Management KGs, which created intermediary organizations located between government and firms awaiting restructuring. Scholars note that the THA was a "trial ground for developing new company forms" (Kern and Sabel 1996).

While the impact of the administrative characteristics was similar in both cases, they were more pronounced in Germany, in part because bureaucratic discretion was so much greater in Germany than the United States. The RTC's extensive system for checking and keeping track of contractors, the random selection process to ensure evenhandedness, and the preference built into the contract award system were features absent from the German agency. The capacity to privatize rapidly was enhanced significantly by the hiring and compensation practices of both agencies.

The organizational culture nurtured by the leadership in both agencies further reinforced innovation and risk behavior by instilling a strong crisis-like sense that time was running out. The private or corporate set of values also meant that success became a function of what agents perceived as measures of success for employees in the private sector. This phenomenon was similar in the RTC and the THA and included concepts as vague as simply "making the biggest deal" to more specific measures such as reaching certain goals, particularly sales goals, or consolidating and downsizing aspects of the agency by a certain date. The young agents in the organizations viewed their achievements as directly translatable to greener pastures in the private sector. And among the older employees—those hired close to retirement—these were also the accomplishments with which they could most readily identify.

At the same time that they increased both organizations' capacities to privatize, administrative characteristics also created an organizational bias within the THA and the RTC toward rapid privatization over alternative goals, including oversight and accountability. Under the traditional model of public personnel there is typically a long probationary period before an individual receives his or her maximum salary. This allows agencies to compensate for some of the imbalances in qualifications they face when first hiring an unknown. It also imposes a longer time horizon on the employee and contributes to his or her socialization into the culture of the agency. By front-loading the benefits and paying high salaries immediately, the THA and the RTC not only reduced the incentive to take a long-term approach but increased the attractiveness of pursuing policies that provided short-term results. Meeting sales goals, either individually or as part of a team, offered the most immediate recognition of effort and consequently the strongest evidence that money paid up front was well spent. Goals that took longer to develop, such as successful restructuring in Germany or the implementation of a successful affordable housing program and minority- and women-owned contracting system in the United States, did not offer nearly the attractive recognition or rewards. Working to ensure that oversight and accountability measures were effectively and correctly implemented also lacked the appeal of rapid sales. In fact, to the extent that these other goals and oversight measures detracted from the ability to garner recognition for sales work, they were—from the perspective of employees—performance liabilities.

Organizational culture instilled the belief that goals that did not coincide with those in the private sector were "political" and the result of interest group pressure. An RTC director of sales complained bitterly over what he referred to as "the RTC's quota system for minorities and women" and the costly delays in sale of real estate because of the affordable housing program. A managing agent was extremely outspoken concerning the agency's MWOB program. He said, "There were some congressional hearings that pushed the [MWOB] program. It just really went crazy. They hired this lady to report directly to the board. And they really just cost the taxpayer millions. . . . The question is whether it is a goal or a quota. Until 1992 there was a goal. Afterward it was a quota which cost the taxpayer money. . . . That kind of politics you would not see in the private sector."

Bonus and premium systems also played a role in creating a bias. Personnel managers in both agencies were quick to note that bonuses were not based on sales indicators alone. However, the GAO in the United States and the Bundesrechungshof in Germany both found that there were no specific objective criteria for granting bonuses. Rather, awards were based on the arbitrary evaluation of a supervisor in the organization. The GAO found that no objective indicators were set forth in advance and that measures used such as leadership and motivation were vague. The Bundesrechnungshof was even more critical of the THA's policies, arguing that it contributed not only to shortsighted behavior but left the agency open to potential abuse and fraud. Since the assessments of supervisors were based largely on meeting sales quotas, the bonuses and premiums they controlled added to the attractiveness of rapid privatization.

Short-term contracts also reduced the time line agents faced in the organizations. To ensure that their contracts were renewed, employees in both organizations were more likely to pursue policies that provided immediate recognition of their worth within the organization. In addition, the short-term contracts contributed to the turnover. Few employees in either agency intended to remain in the public sector, thus when more attractive jobs in the private sector became available, the short-term contracts encouraged employees to take advantage of the opportunity. In the case of the THA, employees were often hired by contracting firms. To give the agency more flexibility, it frequently switched an employee into a contractor. Again, goals that were more long-term or that required greater coordination and teamwork were less likely to generate the rewards of the big sale. The effect of the high fluctuation weakened the knowledge base of both agencies.

Finally, the adoption of differential wage policies, decentralization, and the absence of clear lines of accountability reduced both agencies' organizational capacity to pursue policies that required high levels of coordination and instead favored those policies such as rapid privatization that typically required very little coordination between different parts of the agency. Merit pay and wage differentials undermined alternatives that required more complex patterns of interdependence in public organizations by altering the individual's attachment to the organization and creating conflicts or inequities within the organization.[51] Both were evident in the RTC and the THA: employees had little attachment to their organizations and intra-agency conflict was high.

Similarly, decentralization and the lack of clear lines of authority weakened the ability of agencies to develop policies that required a great deal of intraorganizational cooperation. In the RTC case, this included, in particular, affordable housing programs and minority- and women-owned contracting programs. In the German case, actively restructuring and investing in firms also required greater levels of coordination as the experiences with the Management KGs and the Atlas Program suggest. However, the area that was weakened most by the lack of coordination was oversight and the ability to develop and implement information management systems effectively. To oversee the activities of such major undertakings required information management systems capable of keeping track of a diverse set of assets, standardized systems for recording information effectively, and an enforcement system to check and ensure that procedures were followed. All of these require strong coordination, clear lines of accountability, and personnel practices along with a culture that places a value on oversight. All of these were absent in the RTC and THA.

In summary, administrative features mattered. They were, however, only part of the explanation. Administrative characteristics were partly caused by the political principals who structured the agencies. The next section considers the politics that structured the RTC and THA administrative choices.

NOTES

1. For a good summary of the difference between the two see chapter 3 in Fesler and Kettl (1996).

2. The classical model was most clearly articulated by Luther Gulick (1937) in the 1930s while he chaired the Brownlow Committee, which advised President Franklin Roosevelt on the reorganization of the executive branch.

3. John Ryan, deputy and acting CEO of the RTC in 1995, stated before a House Banking subcommittee, "The RTC was not allowed a leisurely start-up. The day it was created, 262 institutions were placed under its control to be resolved. Many FDIC employees—entire offices, in fact—were reassigned involuntarily to the RTC overnight with little more than the 'wave of the wand'" (U.S. House 1995, 126).

4. The new tasks were associated with managing and disposing of assets as well as managing conservatorships for a longer period of time than expected and implementing various purchase and assumption deals.

5. HomeFed Bank in San Diego, for example, held nearly $13 billion in assets at the time the government took it over.

6. In describing the quality of the leadership in East Germany's enterprises, Detlev Rohwedder said, "I do not wish to broadly condemn them out of hand. However, I must say, that it has been extremely difficult for managers in the east used to fulfilling the punctual and quantitative exceptions associated with a planned economy, to become used to business-economic categories" (Kampe and Wallraf 1991, 58). Alexander Koch, the personnel director of the THA, was far less polite. In an interview in 1991 he stated that keeping so many East German managers was "a mistake from which we're still suffering today. We should have just sent every firm manager and member of the administrative committee home" (Sirleschtov 1991, 3). For a description of the differences between West and East German managers see Myritz (1992) and Henkel (1991).

7. For an account of the RTC's personnel challenges, particularly in the area of contracting, see RTC Inspector General John Adair's testimony before the Senate Subcommittee on Federal Services, Post Office, and Civil Service (U.S. Senate 1990).

8. The THA's first personnel director, Herman Wagner, has a story that typifies the hiring practices of the agency. In the summer of 1990 Wagner was introduced to Detlev Rohwedder. After an hour's conversation in an airport, Rohwedder asked if he had an interest in the job of THA personnel director. Several days later, Wagner was on a plane to Berlin to meet the THA's executive committee. According to Wagner, "This was not your classic interview, since each of the four executive committee members were relieved to quickly have a personnel director with business experience." Wagner was hired immediately, without even a contract.

9. All executive committee members and directors of regional offices were private sector hires.

10. The importance of the private sector is reflected in the selection of Detlev Rohwedder to head the agency. The chairman of Hoesch, a large steel company in Düsseldorf, Rohwedder developed a strong reputation for having transformed the company into a profit-making entity through significant downsizing and restructuring. In addition, as a member of the conservative wing of the Social Democratic Party, Rohwedder had served as state secretary for East German relations in the federal economics ministry under Helmut Schmidt (SPD) and Otto Graf Lambsdorff (FDP) until 1979. Rohwedder served as chair of the administrative committee until August 1990, when he took over as chair of the THA's executive committee. Jens Odewald, the CEO of one of West Germany's largest department store holdings, Kaufhof AG, replaced Rohwedder and served as the chair of the administrative committee for two and a half years, until April 1993.

11. The THA's most important personnel consultant, Dieter Rickert, said, "Our success in hiring occurs primarily with West German managers who don't have the job that matches their skills and who cannot move up in the company because of seniority . . . our target group for the export of personnel into the East are young people, to age 40, and older individuals, from 50 to retirement. With people in their forties who enjoy a great career here in the west, we don't even bother" (*Der Spiegel* 1991).

12. A contracting manager for the RTC, hired in 1989, gave a tongue-in-cheek laugh when he gave an alternative definition: "I was classified as an LG, which means "let go.""

13. In 1993, there were 6,705 employees of which 4,720 were temporary hires from the private sector.

14. The THA was legally obligated to install supervisory boards in all enterprises employing more than 500 employees. The THA director of personnel estimated that in 1991 the agencies still needed more than 13,000 managers for the firms with less than 500 employees (Marissal 1993, 51).

15. Most decision making in the organization occurs at these levels. They are broken down into three job categories: directors and department heads (1.4 percent), senior directors (3.7 percent), and executives (54.17 percent). Below these categories are case workers (23.25 percent), secretaries (14.79 percent), and other workers (2.62 percent) (Treuhandanstalt 1994b, 217).

16. A survey conducted by Wolfgang Seibel found that while East Germans made up the majority of THA employees (nearly 70 percent), no directors, only 19 percent of the department heads, and 43 percent of those who filled out the survey identified themselves as East German. The questionnaire was sent to all directors, department heads, and a random sample of 170 executives. The response rate was 45.6 percent for directors, 34.3 percent for department heads, and 61.7 percent for executives. Seibel notes that the percentage of actual easterners in leadership position is likely to be exaggerated by the findings since questionnaires were more likely to be completed by East Germans than West Germans (Seibel and Kapferer 1996).

17. The RTC's Legal Information (RLIS) reported payment for legal fees and expenses for 1992-95 of $984 million.

18. Both agencies placed agents into grades, although this was primarily an administrative device. Not only did the grades used by the agencies not conform to any federal grade system but there was great variation within the grades themselves. Employees, particularly those with a high level of responsibility, were by and large paid more than the prescribed salary for their grade.

19. Herman Wagner, the THA's first personnel director, testified before a parliamentary committee that the reason the THA adopted a bonus system in 1991 was to ensure that privatization would be conducted in a rapid manner. After meeting with the managers of regional offices, he said there was a concern that those most responsible for privatization might begin taking their time, being too careful and becoming perfectionists. This type of behavior threatened the pace of privatization. A system that rewarded individuals based on performance goals was considered a solution to the problem. That is how the bonus system began, he said (Treuhandanstalt 1994a, 635).

20. Following a number of critical assessments of the THA's bonus system, the agencies put out a press release justifying the use of a bonus system (20 June 1993). Numerous German newspaper accounts described the bonus system (for a sampling see *Frankfurter Allgemeine Zeitung* [28 February 1992, 15] and *Wirtschafts-Woche* [28 February 1992, 32]). For two representative critical accounts see stories in the *Tagesspiegel* (1 March 1995, 1) and *Frankfurter Rundschau* (28 February 1995, 1).

21. In defense of the RTC's bonus system Casey told House members: "I have dealt with bonuses all my business life. We have specific goals, sales goals, resolutions goal, timing goals. . . . Once we were able to get this new form of governance, if you will, and I was able to give these people and many others authority and so forth, they saved hundreds of millions of dollars in their new innovative ways, in moving assets out and downsizing their operations" (U.S. House 1993, 15).

22. William Taylor, chairman of the RTC/FDIC, thought it was unseemly for the agency to grant large bonuses at a time when the FDIC-administered Bank Insurance Fund was nearing insolvency (GAO 1993a).

23. On this point, see especially Seibel and Kapferer (1996).

24. These included working out the severance packages received by laid-off workers of THA-owned firms.

25. Roughly speaking, branch managers were required to seek approval for deals affecting firms with more than 500 employees, receipts of more than DM75 million or an outstanding balance with the Treuhand of more than DM50 million. The extension of credit was initially limited to DM30 million but was later reduced. For a more detailed account see "Genehmigungserfordernisse der Treuhandanstalt," in Treuhandanstalt (1994b, 619-25).

26. Branches were located in the former capitals of the districts: Berlin, Chemnitz, Cottbus, Dresden, Erfurt, Frankfurt/Oder, Gera, Halle, Leipzig, Magdeburg, Neubrandenburg, Potsdam, Rostock, Schwerin, and Suhl.

27. Offices were in established in Dallas, Atlanta, Denver, and Kansas City.

28. From 1989 through 1995 conservatorships accounted for over $110 billion worth of assets sold by the agency (RTC 1996).

29. Carmen Sullivan, former director for the Southwest Regional Office testified before Congress that "the regional office is responsible for thrift resolutions under $500 million, managing the conservatorship program, and providing overall direction and oversight to the Region" (U.S. House 1990b, 114). In practice that meant many of the same tasks as the national office,

including hiring conservatorship managers. Asset management and sales responsibilities were left to the field offices.

30. The larger field offices (sites with more than $15 billion in assets) were headed by a director and three deputy directors and were responsible for: (1) asset disposition of real estate and affordable housing; (2) asset disposition of loans and asset marketing; and (3) investigations, claims, contracting, finance/ budget, and administration (GAO 1991c).

31. See Conference Report from the U.S. House (1989), 336.

32. The manual was issued on July 6, 1990. Until it was issued, managing agents were guided by a series of individual policy memos and directives. The tasks listed in the manual include: establishing control and oversight of the thrift according to RTC guidelines and delegation of authority; promoting the confidence of customers and employees; implementing a no-growth policy; evaluating the thrift's financial condition and identifying losses; ensuring that the thrift is operated in a safe and sound manner by minimizing operating losses; limiting growth; eliminating any speculative activities; terminating any waste, fraud, and insider abuse; preparing a strategic plan that identifies the most viable alternatives for cost-effective resolution; managing the thrift in a manner consistent with the objectives of an approved business plan and over-all downsizing efforts; and taking all necessary actions for the smooth transition of assets and operations once final resolution occurs.

33. A managing agent said, "When the RTC took over an institution, thrift employees typically viewed the government as the enemy, as part of the problem. The difficulty was that you needed these people to help in the transition. The records in the institutions were so poor we needed the staff, especially management, to assist in figuring out what the institution had. This was one of the paradoxes the RTC had to face. In conservatorship you were losing all the talented people, but you had to figure out some way to keep some of them because they knew the files and knew what the institution had. At the same time, the RTC had a policy of not paying thrift employees more than $100,000. This meant that the salaries of management were going to be cut."

34. Under FIRREA, the conservator or receiver was granted the following general powers: merge the association with another federally insured depository institution; transfer any asset or liability of the association with, in the case of a transfer to another depository institution, the consent of appropriate regulatory authorities; disaffirm or repudiate any contract or lease to which the association is party that the conservator or receiver determines to be burdensome to the association; pay all valid obligations of the association; obtain a

stay of legal proceedings to which the association is or becomes a party for a period not to exceed forty-five days in the case of conservator and ninety in the case of receiver; litigate any appealable judgment involving the association in place of the association; and bring civil actions against the officers and directors of the association for gross negligence.

35. Breuel called a press conference on October 4, 1990, and introduced all fifteen new West German managers. Seibel and Kapferer (1996) stated that "it was in this way that in the branches, or former external offices, the actual THA era began" (124).

36. Exceptions to the rule included banks, printers, magazine and newspaper publishers, travel agents, hotel chains, the former German Film company, DEFA, scientific organizations and circuses, transport companies, energy and petroleum companies, and water and waste water collection firms. Many of the firms contained a number of subsidiaries spread through the country. According to the allocation guidelines, subsidiary firms with more than 1,500 employees were the responsibility of the central industrial directorate. Despite this rule, many regional branches in which subsidiaries were located felt very differently.

37. The chief of contractor controls stated in an interview that in cases where a contracting firm worked for a branch office and the central office and fees were worked out differently, it was not uncommon for a contractor to make the case for a fee increase based on a higher premium received in some other part of the agency. This was particularly the case in the central office where, because the firms were so large, contractors were typically paid more.

38. Seidman never submitted the piece for publication but did include it in his book.

39. Example taken from an investigation conducted by the GAO (1993b).

40. The initial terms of the option provided bidders the opportunity to buy residential mortgage assets in an amount up to 125 percent of the City Savings Deposits acquired. Residential mortgages were typically the highest quality assets owned by the RTC. The option stated that the asset may be located in a maximum of three states selected by the acquirer and that the assets would be delivered to the acquirers within six months.

41. The GAO (1993b) noted there was a significant dispute between the two divisions over what type of option to offer. The national sales office believed the package of assets should include assets of varying quality, whereas the resolutions division argued successfully for only high quality assets.

42. Securitization is the process of assembling similar assets into pools that are used to collateralize newly issued securities. The process resulted in mar-

ketable securities that enabled the RTC to convert its assets into cash. An RTC official told the GAO investigator that the increase in securitization meant that fewer residential mortgages were available to help satisfy the option (GAO 1993b).

43. The literature on organizational culture is immense. For overviews of the field, see work by Joanne Martin (1992), Hassard and Pym (1995), and Edgar Schein (1985).

44. For a contrast of differentionist views of organizational culture with other approaches, see Martin (1992).

45. For an excellent comparison of the FDIC's approach with other bank regulators, see Anne Khademian's (1996) work.

46. An RTC official who helped start the national sales program compared her agency to a real estate office stating, "You might, honest to God, think we were all getting paid billions of dollars in commissions."

47. "We knew exactly what all the other field offices were doing," said a privatization agent in Texas, "Every week or every month we'd be given an update on where we stood with respect to the others." Similarly, a German privatization agent specialist, who later became an auditor, said, "We were constantly told where we stood relative to other sales people and other offices. In the regional office where I worked we had to provide periodic reports comparing projected and actual sales numbers."

48. A managing agent at one the largest savings and loans taken over by the Office of Thrift Supervision and run by the RTC confirmed that his interactions with the national and regional offices were primarily over the pace of resolution and asset sales. Because his institution held liabilities in excess of $500 million, the agent worked mostly with the Washington, D.C., resolutions division. He recounted: "DC would say we want to move this many assets in this amount of time, and your department is responsible for, say, two and a half or three billion, and that's how it went. We had goals and if we met them we got bonuses. Goals were public information and widely understood in the institution. We knew what we had. . . . Our institution was the largest in the country. Washington left us pretty much alone to figure out what we had and how best to work with it. Then when we were in a position to liquidate, we'd talk to Washington and Denver, and at very high levels they'd make a decision."

49. The affordable housing director initially answered to an assistant director of real estate, who was responsible to the deputy director of asset dispositions, who answered to the director of asset and real estate management division. Similarly, the MWOB contracting program manager reported to the assistant

director for contract management, who answered to the deputy director of contract management and asset operations, whose boss was the director of asset and real estate management division.

50. "There is no question," said one senior GAO auditor, "that we weren't that welcomed in the agency." In the German agency, members of the internal auditing department reported enormous resentment and animosity. "Being an auditor in the Treuhand placed you at the bottom of the heap. We had very few people in our department and those we hired were inexperienced and anxious to leave."

51. For a theoretical account of this phenomenon, see James Thompson (1967) and James Perry (1986).

4

Structured Choices and Consequences

American and German policymakers argued intensely among themselves over the best way to divest large sums of public holdings and how to develop effective accountability and control mechanisms to govern the Resolution Trust Corporation (RTC) and the Treuhandanstalt (THA). These were not separate debates. It was clearly understood that oversight and outcomes were linked. The controller or overseer of the agencies' operations would leave his or her imprint on the outcome and effectively prevent others from influencing the process. In other words, while administrative characteristics contributed to bureaucratic outcomes they were not "uncaused causes" in the policy process. Administrative characteristics were themselves a function of actions taken by political principals who established mandates and adopted structures designed to promote the desired ends of the principals. This chapter explores the ways in which the RTC and THA were products of a politics of structural choice (Moe 1989; 1990).[1]

Structural choice refers here to the formal mechanisms political principals adopt to constrain the activities of executive agencies. According to Terry Moe, risk-averse legislators and executives operate in an environment of great uncertainty. They seek a balance between advocating for the interests of their constituencies and maintaining cautious distance from any crises that may cost political capital. Uncertainty, in turn, is a function of two factors—election cycles and politics. Legislators and executives are unsure whether

131

they will be elected again and whether their policies will be undone following the next election cycle. In politics, winners get to make the rules often without the consent of the losers. It is a process in which those who are able to exercise public authority can impose their will on others. "However benign and beneficial a public program might appear," writes Moe (1990) "they are essentially structures of coercion" (126). Within such an uncertain environment, the political battles center on establishing structures aimed at "protecting" the policy or organization from opponents. Paradoxically, such structures can add to inefficiencies and/or increase bureaucratic autonomy by insulating the policy or organization from the "winners" as well as the losers.

The politics of structured choice plays out in all democracies. In their comparative study, Moe and Caldwell (1994) note, "The basic forces at work are generic. In all democracies, the struggle to exercise and control public authority gives rise to political uncertainty, political compromise, and fear of the state which in turn shape the strategies of all the major players in the politics of structure" (176–77). Moe's theory offers a useful means to understand the experiences of the RTC and the THA.

The political stakes in the battle over the two agencies charged with the task of privatization were extremely high. President George Bush and Chancellor Helmut Kohl both faced national elections at the height of their respective crises. And as political winners, both leaders left their mark on four sets of structural choices that set the important parameters within which the THA and RTC could operate.

The four structures included the following:

1. **Supervisory Governance.** Executives in both countries succeeded in establishing an elaborate and complex network of controls at the national level that made little managerial sense but was politically ingenious. The supervisory structures gave executives control over the organization's central management, yet they institutionalized enough distance to allow the administration in both countries to use the agencies as scapegoats to deflect public anger over the process.

2. **Financial Accountability.** Like the supervisory institutions, the funding structures established to finance the agencies circumvented standard budgetary procedures in ways that made little

sense from a public management or organizational perspective. Politically, the finance mechanism ceded a great deal of authority to the agencies by making it extremely difficult for opponents of the administration to intervene in the agencies' activities.

3. **Legislative Mandates.** The legislative mandates passed by legislators provided one of the few opportunities for opponents to insert their preferences directly into the governing structure. However, the notable feature about the legislative mandates is less their content than their lack of specificity, clarity, and priority. Rather than help to steer the agencies, the lack of clarity and specificity freed the agencies and allowed their personnel to define the content of privatization.

4. **Legal Identity.** Finally, their hybrid legal identity, as a mixed-ownership government corporation in the RTC's case and an *Anstalt* in the case of the THA, were important structures that shaped the relationship between agency and opponent groups. The identity dictated the legal terms on which private and public actors could make claims upon the agency. As neither public nor fully private organizations, the RTC and THA experienced the best of both worlds in terms of the inability of outside actors to control them.

These structures were political choices. They were the result of enormous conflict among parties with different stakes in the organizations' impact on society. The Kohl and Bush administrations, as the political winners, shaped these structures in ways that not only allowed them to minimize political liability but to maintain control and ensure that their narrow version of privatization would prevail.

Scapegoat Governance

The oversight structures designed to govern the RTC and the THA defied managerial logic. Lines of authority were complicated and obscured by shifting responsibilities and shadow allegiances. Yet while the agencies may have failed Management 101, the governing structures of the RTC and THA were political solutions that gave administrations in the United States and Germany the ability to control the controversial agencies and criticize them at the same time. I term this "scapegoat governance."[2]

Scapegoat governance in the RTC and THA consisted of internal and external elements. Inside both organizations, oversight and control were diffuse, complicated, and often informal. Different groups and individuals were ceded control. Jurisdictional boundaries blurred and changed over time, leaving the impression that many were in charge. The result was that no single individual or group was truly accountable. Externally, both agencies were overseen by a single executive agency closely allied with the administration. In the THA's case it was the Finance Ministry, in the RTC's, the Treasury Department. Neither of these institutional placements was natural or predetermined. They served the political purpose of institutionalizing important levers of control that the Bush and Kohl administrations could use to influence the agencies' actions.

Diffuse Internal Control

The THA and RTC were multiheaded creations by design. Their governing structures lacked transparency, coherence, and clarity. Contrasts with the traditional bureaucratic or classic model of administrative organization were examined closely in chapter 3. The purpose here is to highlight the internal oversight structures that were political choices made by political principals.

The Treuhand Act established a two-tier governing structure for the THA. It resembled a German corporate structure but also deviated from the form in important ways. The structure is illustrated in Figure 4.1.

At the top was the supervisory board, modeled after a private corporation, a legacy of the East German Volkskammer's decision to transform the THA into several large private stockholding companies. Prior to German unification, the supervisory board had consisted of Jens Odewald, CEO of Kaufhof Holdings, and eight representatives from several of the largest corporations in western Europe (handpicked by THA President Detlev Rohwedder), six representatives from East German firms, and two members of the Volkskammer. The stockholding company model was eventually dropped. Yet the supervisory board remained a fixture of the THA.[3] Following unification, the supervisory board was expanded from sixteen to twenty-three members. Representatives from four of West Germany's largest labor unions, the federal Ministry of Economics and Ministry

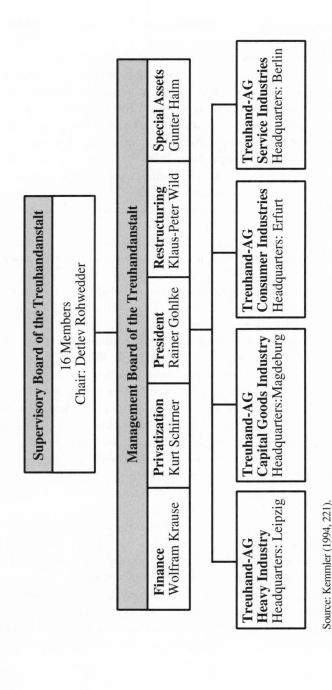

Source: Kemmler (1994, 221).

Figure 4.1 THA Governing Structure in Summer 1990

135

of Finance were added. Each of the five new eastern state governments was also given representation. Finally, two additional representatives from west European industry were added, while all but one of the East German members of the board were dropped.[4]

The supervisory committee was formally charged with overseeing an executive board, which handled the day-to-day operations of the agency. Initially the executive board was organized along functional lines—privatization, restructuring, and liquidation. The structure proved unworkable and inflexible. Prospective buyers of THA assets complained about the lack of transparency in identifying which assets were held by which divisions.

A new executive board structure adopted by the supervisory board took effect January 1, 1991, and remained in place until the end of the THA's tenure. The structure integrated functional and operational responsibilities under the direction of each executive board member. The exceptions to this structure were one division that retained pure operational responsibilities and two divisions that kept pure functional responsibilities (Dininio 1999, 49; Seibel and Kapferer 1996) (see Figure 4.2).

Combining functional and industrial assignments gave the organization a matrix character. For example, the executive for Corporate Division 2 (U2), Klaus-Peter Wild, was responsible for optical firms and firms that produced precision instruments. Wild was also responsible for drafting the rules governing restructuring. The matrix structure increased the overall degree of flexibility. Wolfgang Seibel notes that the change "brought technical knowledge and competence together effectively, as far as the industries were concerned. For these corporate groups, the whole responsibility for privatization, management of holdings, and corporate finance now lay in one pair of hands" (Seibel and Kapferer 1996, 129).

The distribution of functional assignments also led to a diffuse network of control and oversight. Seibel notes that following the change in structure, "the functional responsibilities had been made a little more opaque. . . . The areas of responsibility of previous functional Executive Boards had to be redefined and in some cases redistributed between the Divisions" (Seibel and Kapferer 1996, 130). Each executive board member was charged with some element of oversight and control. Many of these divisional functional responsibilities

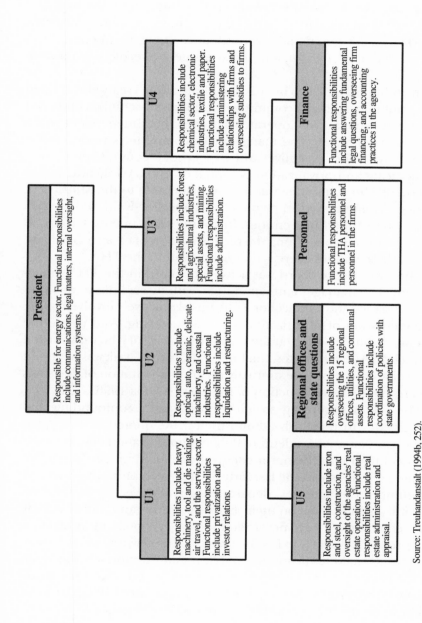

President

Responsible for energy sector. Functional responsibilities include communications, legal matters, internal oversight, and information systems.

U1

Responsibilities include heavy machinery, tool and die making, air travel, and the service sector. Functional responsibilities include privatization and investor relations.

U2

Responsibilities include optical, auto, ceramic, delicate machinery, and coastal industries. Functional responsibilities include liquidation and restructuring.

U3

Responsibilities include forest and agricultural industries, special assets, and mining. Functional responsibilities include administration.

U4

Responsibilities include chemical sector, electronic industries, textile and paper. Functional responsibilities include administering relationships with firms and overseeing subsidies to firms.

U5

Responsibilities include iron and steel, construction, and oversight of the agencies' real estate operation. Functional responsibilities include real estate administration and appraisal.

Regional offices and state questions

Responsibilities include overseeing the 15 regional offices, utilities, and communal assets. Functional responsibilities include coordination of policies with state governments.

Personnel

Functional responsibilities include THA personnel and personnel in the firms.

Finance

Functional responsibilities include answering fundamental legal questions, overseeing firm financing, and accounting practices in the agency.

Source: Treuhandanstalt (1994b, 252).

Figure 4.2 THA's Management Board Structure in January, 1991

137

overlapped one another. Division 1, for example, was responsible for overseeing the firm—monitoring, privatizing, restructuring, and evaluating business plans. These responsibilities certainly intersected with Division 5's functional responsibilities of overseeing financing, environmental protection, and the assessment of ecological damage (Kemmler 1994, 233).

In addition to the two boards, the Unification Treaty also created a separate management committee (Leitungsausschuß), composed of eighty consultants who operated alongside but independent of the executive committee. The management committee's responsibility was to advise the executive and supervisory committees on the restructuring and privatization potential of firms. While advisory to the boards, the committee was legally answerable to the Ministry of Finance. As mentioned in chapter 3, Chancellor Kohl also created several powerful ad hoc entities, including the Ludewig Group, to handle questions concerning the reconstruction of eastern Germany. Each of these entities exercised oversight within the THA.

The supervisory board was actively involved in the THA's management. The management committee, with direct links to the Ministry of Finance and Chancellor Kohl, was also actively involved in the implementation of privatization and restructuring. And where the Ludewig Group's power ended and the supervisory board's started was unclear. As Czada notes, the Ludewig Group's "task was to attend and probably to supervise mutually the implementation of decisions concerning the reconstruction of the East" (Czada 1996a, 157).

The RTC's governing structure was equally confounding and advantageous to the Bush administration. As quoted earlier, Allan Dean of the National Academy of Public Administration described the RTC's configuration before a congressional committee. He stated, "Let me say that I spent the last forty-five years in continuous work on the setting up of agencies, departments, and government corporations and advising them on their structure and organization. I will say to this committee: I have never seen such a jerry-built, unsatisfactory structure as that which exists for the RTC framework" (U.S. Senate 1991, 42). Donald Kettl, another public administration scholar, wrote that FIRREA created one of the most complicated governing structures ever conceived of for a government entity (Kettl 1991b). Figure 4.3 illustrates the internal structure created by Congress.[5]

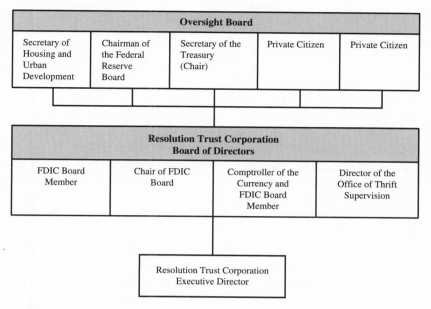

Source: RTC Annual Report (1991).

Figure 4.3 RTC Governing Structure in 1989

Like the Treuhand Act, the FIRREA mandated the creation of two boards, the Oversight Board and the Board of Directors (also known as the RTC Board) to govern the RTC. The Oversight Board was similar to the THA's Supervisory Board. It was charged with providing the RTC with broad overall policy guidance, direction, and ensuring oversight and accountability. The Oversight Board consisted of the secretary of the Treasury (who chaired the board), the secretary of Housing and Urban Development (HUD), the chair of the Federal Reserve Board, and two independent members selected by the president and confirmed by Congress.

The Board of Directors was akin to the THA's Executive Board. It was responsible for the day-to-day operations of the agency. The RTC Board was charged with approving the agency's organizational structure; approving and submitting funding requests and staffing recommendations to the Oversight Board; authorizing staff to enter into thrifts; and approving policies and guidelines for RTC operations.

The RTC Board was thus involved in overseeing the activities of the agency while it was more involved in managerial decisions than the Oversight Board. The composition of the RTC Board was identical to the Federal Deposit Insurance Corporation's (FDIC) Board of Directors, and de facto made the FDIC the primary manager of the RTC.[6] Although its personnel were the same as the FDIC Board, technically and legally the RTC Board was considered a separate entity.

In 1990 the RTC Board consisted of five members including L. William Seidman, who headed both the FDIC and RTC Boards.[7] As figure 4.3 illustrates, the lines of command were convoluted. A chief executive director was appointed by the RTC Board to implement its decisions. Thus the line of command went up from the executive director, who reported to the RTC Board that, in turn, reported to the Oversight Board.

In theory the RTC was also governed by three different sets of advisory boards. FIRREA required the oversight board to establish at least six regional advisory boards to advise the RTC on its policies and programs for the sale or other disposition of assets held in the regions. With the passage of the RTC Refinancing, Restructuring, and Improvement Act in December 1991, Congress required the RTC to create an additional advisory board known as the National Housing Advisory Board consisting of the secretary of Housing and Urban Development and the chairs of the six regional advisory boards. In the RTC Completion Act (passed in December 1993), Congress created the Affordable Housing Advisory Board (AHAB), charged with providing advice to both the RTC Oversight Board and the FDIC Board of Directors on policies and programs related to the provision of affordable housing.

The RTC's governing structure satisfied a variety of principals— Congress, the administration, various societal interest groups, and the public at large, whose patience had been worn thin by the scandals that plagued the thrift industry in the 1980s. Congress and the administration were determined to keep the RTC under careful oversight to prevent financial disasters that had occurred with the Federal Savings and Loan Insurance Corporation (FSLIC) and the Federal Asset Disposition Agency (FADA). As RTC chief executive David C. Cooke pointed out, "If I had my druthers, it wouldn't be set up that way. But I knew that coming in. I knew that if I could somehow keep all the various people that I reported to reasonably happy, I probably am not going to get into too much hot water with Congress."[8] And William Taylor, acting president and chief executive officer of the Oversight Board until May 1990, added, "As a taxpayer, I'd want some oversight. I don't defend this exact structure, but I'd want some oversight."[9]

The governing structure spread the oversight responsibilities among a number of players and prevented the emergence of a single strong manager. As in the case of the THA, the structure of managerial accountability in the agency was kept deliberately complex. It would be unreasonable to expect any program that potentially exposed the government to liabilities in the hundreds of billions of dollars to be enacted without multiple layers of protection. As Kettl (1991a) notes, "The tangled organizational framework was part of the implicit cost of maintaining that legitimacy" (105).

Yet while their internal structures were convoluted and complex, it would be a mistake to assume that the RTC and THA were out of control. An inward focus misses the important external control mechanisms that were legislated through the positioning of both agencies within the government.

External Control: Positioning Agencies within the Government

The RTC and THA's authorizing legislation placed the two agencies firmly within the legal authority and control of executive agencies closely allied with the Bush and Kohl administrations. Article 25, section 1 of Germany's Unification Treaty placed the THA under the authority of the Ministry of Finance. FIRREA placed the RTC under the jurisdiction of the U.S. Treasury Department. In both cases, the placement not only helped emphasize a neo-liberal commitment to rapid privatization as the agencies' central purpose but it also institutionalized important control levers for the administration while weakening the influence of opponents.

In Germany, the placement of the THA within the jurisdiction of the Finance Ministry was controversial and important. As Jan Priewe (1991) notes, there was nothing predetermined or natural about the choice of the Ministry of Finance. Priewe, a major critic of the agency, stated that the Treuhand was directly responsible for jobs, social expenditures, and the environmental improvement in the east. Yet, oversight responsibility for the THA was not given to the Federal Ministry for Labor (*Bundesanstalt für Arbeit*), the Federal Ministry for Work and Social Issues (*Bundesanstalt für Arbeit und Soziales*), or the Federal Ministry for the Environment (*Bundesumweltministerium*)—all agencies with an interest in the outcomes of the THA. Referring to the Ministry of Finance, Priewe notes that the Unification Treaty (signed August 1, 1990) "placed the responsibilities for the economy—whose actual legal jurisdiction rests with federal and state governments—into the hands of an extremely centralized federal agency, external to the policy process and whose democratic legitimacy is weaker than a fig leaf" (20).

The administration argued that the Finance Ministry was the natural place to house the agency since Finance was responsible for managing West German state-owned enterprises and it had helped to direct the privatization drive of the early 1980s (Dininio 1999, 66; Esser 1989). As noted in chapter 2, however, the THA was about more than privatization. Critics of the administration argued that, given its broader economic imperative to assist in the restructuring of thousands of economic enterprises, the agency would be better suited for the Economics Ministry (see especially Cadel 1994).

The placement in the Finance Ministry helped to define the THA's policy problem as a German financial and budgetary problem rather than an *East* German economic development and recovery problem. The Ministry of Finance, led by Theo Waigel, head of the conservative Christian Social Union (CSU; the Bavarian affiliate of the Christian Democratic Union), was a strong supporter and ally of the Kohl administration. The Economics Ministry, headed by the leader of the Free Democratic Party, was a far more contentious opponent to the administration's policies. Despite the broad mandate it was given by the Volkskammer on June 17, 1990, the Ministry of Finance was able to define privatization in terms of the rapid sale of assets, rather than as a policy of investment, modernization, and then sale. The agency's position within the Ministry of Finance reinforced Breuel's ability to maintain the Kohl administration's position despite hunger strikes, mass social protests, and all other evidence that it was responsible for structural politics in eastern Germany (Nägele 1994).

More important was that from the standpoint of the Kohl administration, the categorization of the THA as an arm of the Ministry of

Finance steered the type of external control structures that might be imposed on the agency. Parliamentarians note that this initial classification was crucial to the logic of interest infiltration and oversight that followed. A member of the opposition party in Parliament at the time summarized the importance of the early decision to classify the THA as a budget agency:

> We (the opposition) argued strongly that the Treuhandanstalt should be in the Ministry of Economics rather than Finance. The administration thought otherwise. The Economics Ministry is responsible for the economic development of the country. It is involved in the structural improvements of economic regions. It only makes sense that the Treuhandanstalt fall into its jurisdiction. . . . Had the THA landed in the Ministry of Economics, it would have been much more open. The agency's policies would have been discussed in terms of improving and restructuring the economy. And, you would have pulled state governments and the Bundesrat into the process because regional economic restructuring is the responsibility of state governments. If nothing else the administration would have been forced to come up with a concept for improving the east. Placing it within the Finance Ministry . . . ensured that the issues like economic development were not discussed. Rather the focus was put on money matters and the budget.

Once embedded within the Ministry of Finance, the Parliament's oversight responsibility not only fell to the busiest committee in the *Bundestag* (lower house), it also took the SPD-majority *Bundesrat* (upper house) out of the picture. The point was made clear when I asked a conservative member of parliament why the Bundesrat was not involved in the THA. He responded somewhat indignantly: "The THA was federal money. It had nothing to do with the states.[10]

As the quotation suggests, the interests of the *Länder* (state governments) were constrained partly because of the THA's federal status and partly because the Ministry of Finance is not responsible for structural politics or industrial policy, two areas for which the German Constitution gives states responsibility.[11] Nägele (1994) writes, "Because of its designation as a federal 'independent administration' the Treuhand was extremely effective at shielding itself from others, in particular from state-level influences" (46).

One area where external oversight by minority party members was institutionalized was in the area of finance. As an arm of the

Ministry of Finance, the THA was subjected to the oversight control of the Bundestag's Budget Committee that was responsible for approving the amount of credit the federal government extended to the THA during its tenure. Theoretically, the Budget Committee could have attempted to extend its control into other areas of the agency by threatening to withhold funding until information was provided or agency reforms were undertaken. Although members of parliament suggested that it would have been possible, every member of parliament interviewed, regardless of party, flatly denounced such a strategy. "While we thought about it," noted one opposition leader, "we decided not to try to blackmail the Treuhand. It would have been counterproductive. The likelihood is that they would have cut back on those things we cared a great deal about, such as restructuring programs and controls." A second reason for not using the financing of the THA as a greater control instrument was the lack of expertise and resources necessary to oversee the agency. Another opposition member put it this way, "We didn't put more pressure on the Treuhand simply because their job was so complicated and their challenge too great. Who should be the one responsible to find his way through the jungle? Certainly not the subcommittee." The placement of the agency within the Ministry of Finance was the result of the majority conservative coalition's control of the Bundestag, the transitional nature of East Germany's government, and the weakness of states and unions.

The RTC's relationship with the U.S. Treasury Department was as important as the THA's connection to the Ministry of Finance. The Bush administration sought to ensure that it had control over the RTC. It was also concerned with minimizing the RTC as a political liability—particularly in the wake of the much-publicized scandals involving thrifts. As quoted earlier, a staff member to the House Banking Committee during the drafting of FIRREA said bluntly: "The key problem of the RTC is that it was a toxic waste site. . . . What do you do with a toxic waste site? I'll tell you what you do. You stay the hell away."

The RTC's convoluted internal governing structure solved the problem. Scapegoat governance structures gave the administration indirect control while ensuring that any blame from the potential fallout could be deflected elsewhere. Seidman, the head of the FDIC and RTC, noted that the governing structure was a product of the administration and its desire to remain in control of the resolution process. He stated:

> The administration proposal defied all rules of organization: strategic planning and decision making were completely separate from operations, and everything conspired to cut the channels of communication from boss to line work. . . . The FDIC would administer and operate the cleanup, but could not participate in strategic planning or budgetary control. The administration was stuck with using our independent talents, which it had already discovered it could not fully control. So it did so through the budget process. The money to close the failed S&Ls would be supplied only with the approval of the RTC Oversight Board (Seidman 1993, 203).

A scholar who studied the beginnings of the agency noted, "Although the FDIC, HUD, and the Federal Reserve shared responsibility with the Treasury Department for oversight of RTC operations, the fact that the Office of Thrift Supervision is chaired by the Secretary of Treasury meant that the Treasury Department was 'first among equals' and thus, that a particular point of view within the Bush administration dominated the conduct of the bailout" (MacDonald 1995, 559).

The case of Daniel Kearny, an investment banker from Salomon Brothers hired as the Oversight Board's first president, illustrates the point. Kearny assumed his position to be the chief executive officer of a board that was independent of Treasury. He found out, however, that his job was that of a top staff position, and the Oversight Board was an arm of the Treasury. John Robson, a deputy in the Department of Treasury, was made secretary to the Oversight Board and given control over its daily operations. As Seidman (1993) explains, "After learning that he could do little without Secretary Robson's approval, he resigned in protest. . . . In terms of bureaucratic valor, he had thrown himself on an enemy machine-gun nest and taken it out at the cost of his job, and to some extent his reputation." In an article titled "Major official in thrifts' bailout quits," published in the *Wall Street Journal* (12 February 1990, A16), Kearny stated diplomatically upon his resignation, "After serious reflection I have concluded that the role of president and chief executive officer of the Oversight

Board does not currently afford me the authority that I believe is essential to be effective in this process."

The governing structure of the RTC ensured legitimacy by spreading oversight responsibilities among several different institutional actors. However, just as the Ministry of Finance was the central controller of the THA, the Treasury Department was "first among equals" in overseeing the RTC. The structures developed in both instances served the administrations' goal of ensuring control over the process without being fully associated with the agencies' actions.

Among the formal accountability structures established by the RTC and THA's authorizing legislation were the budgetary oversight structures. The structures that controlled the agencies' purse strings protected the agencies from external pressure and gave the agencies greater discretion.

FINANCIAL ACCOUNTABILITY

When the RTC and THA began their operations, some lawmakers in their respective countries believed that they could be self-financing. They perceived that the agencies' assets could be sold to pay off the liabilities incurred by the failed enterprises which had been taken over by the state. Such hope quickly diminished as policymakers uncovered the true economic state of the assets and the enterprises. At the point at which it became clear that these would be extraordinarily expensive agencies, lawmakers were faced with the dilemma of how to pay for the party. The question on the table was: Pay now or pay later (with interest)? As predicted by Terry Moe in his *Politics of Structural Choice* (1990), German and U.S. policymakers opted largely to defer payment (and the immediate political costs) for their agencies' activities rather than try to swallow the large pill immediately.

During the early phases of the THA's development, when self-funding hopes were high, the agency was given authority to raise DM17 billion in start-up capital.[12] The Unification Treaty raised the debt level to DM25 billion. The treaty also gave the Ministry of Finance the authority to extend the payment of the debt and the ability to exceed the limit "in the event of a major change in general conditions" (Kloepfer 1996, 57).

As the financial needs of the THA increased, the conservative-majority Bundestag passed legislation in 1992 that dramatically increased the agency's credit limits and gave the THA a great deal more flexibility in how it raised its resources. The Unification Treaty and the *Treuhand-Kreditaufnahmegesetz* (Treuhand Credit Act passed July 3, 1992) gave the THA a special-asset status akin to the national-ized train service or the postal service. The status was important because it meant that the financing of the agency was excluded from the federal budget. The effect was that parliamentary budget com-mittees were limited in their efforts to oversee the agency's actions and the Bundesrechnungshof (auditing arm of Parliament) was con-sistently blocked from auditing THA firms. The Treuhand Credit Act also allowed the agency to raise up to DM30 billion each financial year, and it gave the Ministry of Finance discretion to increase that amount by an additional DM8 billion. And finally, the THA Credit Act made it significantly easier for the THA to raise credit on capital markets by freeing it from a number of regulatory constraints (Kloepfer 1996). Phyllis Dininio (1999) writes that in terms of its finances, "THA managers faced no budgets, specific mandates, or stringent oversight in the allocation process. Indeed, the Treuhand secured its own financing on world markets which freed it from bud-getary constraints: in lieu of budgets for restructuring activities, there were merely guidelines for developing and implementing new firm concepts" (10). Funding structures thus increased the agency's oper-ating discretion while at the same time allowing lawmakers to push difficult funding priority decisions into the future.

THA officials including Birgit Breuel spent a great deal of time flying to different parts of the world to raise funds on the global cap-ital markets. The low supply of funds during this period and concern over what would happen after the THA closed, meant that the THA was forced to pay a special premium for the funds even though investors were assured bonds were safe (Cooper 1993, 55). The *Financial Times* reported in 1994 that the THA's deficit was financed through bank credits, bonds, and medium-term notes (Dempsey 1994). The final total on the THA's combined note from 1990 to 1994 was DM166 billion.

The RTC's funding structure reflected some peculiarities of the American budgetary process that made it more complicated than the

THA funding structure. The overall effect, however, was similar. The complicated financing structure that funded the RTC's activity was a compromise between Congress and the president to defer blame for increases in the deficit and to avoid responsibility for tax increases to pay for the bailout. FIRREA required that the agency maintain a sizable balance of funds on hand to resolve thrifts and pay off depositors. The RTC was also required to have funds to supply conservatorships with enough working liquidity to continue to function as going concerns while being prepared for sale. Without such working capital, institutions would not be able to meet the operating obligations, depositors would disappear, and the value of the institutions would plummet. This would increase the overall cost to the taxpayer.

The Gramm-Rudman deficit law added an additional wrinkle to the funding controversy. The law required that any new expenditure be accounted for with a cut in funding for some other program or an increase in taxes. Despite calls by liberal Democrats such as Joseph Kennedy (D-MA) to pay for the bailout up front through tax increases, the Bush administration and the majority of Republicans and Democrats in the Congress were unwilling to be placed in such a difficult position. President George Bush threatened to veto his own proposal if the money was an on-budget expenditure.

The resulting compromise was a funding structure that critics call "a Rube Goldberg scheme of quasi-governmental corporations, off-budget borrowing, and deferred payments" (Waldman 1990a, 120). The compromise authorized $50 billion in funding for the initial phase of the cleanup, based on the administration's estimates of the size of thrift losses (including the amount needed to finish paying for losses incurred by the FSLIC).[13] Of the $50 billion, $18.8 billion was to come from the Treasury Department (specifically the Federal Financing Bank) for fiscal year (FY) 1989, and $1.2 billion derived from assessments on the retained earnings of the regional Federal Home Loan Banks (FHLB). Since the Office of Management and Budget estimated that all of the $20 billion appropriated for 1989 would be spent before the end of the fiscal year, it would not affect the next round of Gramm-Rudman calculations for FY 1990. In fact, only about half of the $20 billion was actually spent during FY 1989. OMB, however, had already taken its "snapshot" of FY 1990 spending. Under the Gramm-Rudman law, adjustments are not permitted for technical re-estimates; thus funding avoided triggering Gramm-Rudman for its first year.

The remaining $30 billion was to be borrowed from a separate funding vehicle created under FIRREA known as the Resolution Funding Corporation (REFCORP), another mixed-ownership government corporation. REFCORP operated under the supervision of a directorate composed of the director of finance for the Federal Home Loan Bank Board and two presidents of regional FHLBs. It was created as a quasi-governmental corporation that raised money for the RTC by issuing long-term (forty-year) bonds to private buyers. The borrowing, in turn, transferred to the RTC.

The odd structure and method for raising funds for the bailout kept its activities off-budget, which was the goal of the administration and members of Congress. But it did far more than that. The government treated the payments by REFCORP to the RTC *as revenue*, even though the money was borrowed and the RTC was obligated to repay the funds plus interest. Legal scholar Michael Froomkin (1995) wrote, "In the case of REFCORP, the accounting problem is compounded by the way that the sham GSE uses the funds that it borrows. . . . The two federal corporations together are used to understate the true federal debt twice—once when borrowing is ignored and again when it is treated as revenue" (617).

The creative accounting practices also came at a significant price. REFCORP was forced to pay sizable fees and commissions to private investment bankers. Also, since REFCORP was not a government agency per se, the investment market considered its bonds to be inherently riskier than those sold by the Treasury Department. REFCORP therefore had to borrow its funds at approximately one-third of a percentage point higher than comparable Treasury securities—adding about $2 billion in present value costs for interest according to the Congressional Budget Office estimates. As one observer noted, "The government is paying more for the sole purpose of pretending it is spending less" (Waldman 1990a, 111).[14]

In addition to the $50 billion allocated to the agency in FIRREA, the RTC received three additional authorizations to cover its losses. All were extremely contentious battles in Congress focusing primarily on how losses would be paid for (on budget vs. off budget, current vs. future outlays), whether the agency was pursuing all its goals, and accountability problems within the agency. On March 23, 1991, the RTC Funding Act of 1991 was passed, increasing the agency's loss fund by another $30 billion. On December 12, 1991, an additional $6.7 billion was authorized. And finally on December 12, 1993, Congress enacted the RTC Completion Act that contributed another $18.3 billion. All four appropriations were paid for through borrowed funds. Congresswoman Patricia Schroeder (D-CT) commented in the *Wall Street Journal* (31 October 1991), "It makes me gag. . . . Wait till the children find out we passed the bill to them." In the same article, Jim Slattery (D-KS) stated, "This is the biggest single example of intergenerational robbery in this Congress."

In addition to the legislative loss authorizations, FIRREA and subsequent authorization bills also allowed the RTC to borrow up to $125 billion (later increased to $160 billion) from the Federal Financing Bank.[15] These funds, referred to as "working capital," gave the agency enormous budgetary freedom from Congress, the president, and interest groups. Working capital was used by the RTC to maintain the thrifts during their conservatorship operations, fund the administration of the agency, and pay for the maintenance of assets (typically managed by contractors) that were not sold as part of the resolution.[16] Working capital was not intended to cover failed thrift losses because the funds were borrowed and were expected to be repaid with interest (one-third of a quarter of a percent above the thirteen-week treasury rate). More important for lawmakers, working capital was also not included in the budget deficit figures. It was assumed that the money borrowed would simply be matched by the assets proceeding from the subsequent sale of assets in receivership.

Legislative Mandates

Legislative mandates are the most explicit forms of structured choice. In the classic model of bureaucracy, politics expresses and conveys the "will of the state" to an administration charged with implementation (Goodnow 1900; Wilson 1887). Yet as numerous public administration scholars have pointed out, such a separation between politics and administration is rarely so neat. Legislative mandates—expressions of the state will—are often ambiguous, contradictory and, in some instances, impossible to achieve.

While mandates provide a clear mechanism of legislative control, their purpose is often to promote a legislator's particular interests and only secondarily to give the administration clear operating instructions. Nowhere is this more apparent than in mandates given to the THA and RTC. Political principals asked both agencies to pursue broad and often conflicting outcomes. While such actions undermine classic notions of administration, they fit well within a "politics of structured choice."

The selection of mandated goals is the result of compromises made among competing principals. Majority and minority interests are reflected in both sets of goals. The views of the political winners—the Kohl and Bush administrations—ultimately prevailed precisely because the goals are so broad and contradictory. The agencies are given greater discretion to fill in the details while groups (including the winning administrations) are given ample cause, when it is politically advantageous, to criticize the agencies for not adequately meeting their goals. First consider the case of the RTC.

Among the many policies introduced by FIRREA, the RTC was created to dispose of insolvent thrifts and their assets. In line with America's brand of interest-group pluralism and open policymaking process, hearings were held before six different Senate and House committees. Individuals representing varied groups were given the chance to influence how the RTC should proceed with the cleanup. The participants represented bankers, realtors and brokers, affordable housing advocacy groups, environmental groups, women and minority contractors, local government, and inner-city development banks. The final version of FIRREA required the RTC to pursue the following:

- Manage and prepare thrift institutions for resolution expeditiously.
- Maximize the net present return from the sale of troubled thrifts and their assets.
- Minimize the impact of these transactions on local real estate and financial markets by not selling assets below 95 percent of their book value.
- Minimize the losses of these transactions to the government.
- Maximize the availability and affordability of homes for low- and moderate-income individuals.

- Maximize the opportunity for minority- and women-owned businesses (MWOBs) to participate as contractors, buyers of institutions, and purchasers of assets.
- Make efficient use of the funds allocated by Congress.

FIRREA also ensured that interest groups would be given plenty of opportunity to shape the agency's mandates even after the legislation passed. The legislation called upon the RTC to solicit additional public input in crafting the agency's strategic plan in the months following FIRREA's passage. Eighty-five individuals and groups responded to the request including public interest groups; municipalities; national, state, and local housing organizations; realtors; professional and trade associations; asset managers; and investment bankers. To ensure the continued input from interest groups, FIRREA called for the creation of six regional advisory boards and one national advisory board to advise the RTC on its policies and programs.[17] The regional and national advisory boards met a total of 164 times from 1990 to 1995 in cities throughout the United States. Later legislation increased interest group involvement by adding two more advisory boards: the National Housing Advisory Board, created in 1991 to provide the RTC with advice on policies and programs specifically related to the provision of affordable housing, and the Affordable Housing Advisory Board, created in 1993 to "provide advice to both the Thrift Depositor Protection Oversight Board and the Board of Directors of the FDIC on policies and programs related to the provision of affordable housing, including the operation of affordable housing programs" (Thrift Depositor Protection Oversight Board 1995, 6).

FIRREA was clearly the product of compromise among diverse sets of interests. It also contained a range of goals that were clearly in conflict with one another. How does one maximize returns on sales while simultaneously pursuing strategies to divest holdings as rapidly as possible? Compounding the problem for the agency was the fact that Congress neglected to fill in the details on how the agency should carry out its goals or what priority should be given to the goals. As William Seidman, chair of the FDIC and the first person to head the RTC, wrote, "The goals set for the RTC would be forever in conflict, but Congress went away happy" (Seidman 1993, 199).

Two real estate experts who closely examined the RTC's activities added that "the potential conflict inherent in this mandate . . . points out the political tightrope the RTC will constantly be walking. On the one hand, asset sales must be sufficiently rapid to provide Congress evidence of the progressing resolution of the thrift problems. On the other hand, if there is any indication in local markets of asset dumping or any of its impacts, congressional scrutiny will encourage a slowing of the disposition process" (Vandell and Riddiough 1991, 50). A securitizations specialist who worked in the RTC during most of its existence put the matter far more bluntly: "I didn't think you could ever reconcile the different goals stated in FIRREA. I have a theological background and this is what is called "intenity", where you have an apparent conflict that cannot be resolved. It was absolutely crazy." A GAO examiner who had worked on the RTC investigations agreed: "The problem with FIRREA was that no one knew its intent. And no one was ever willing to deal with the difficult problem of spelling out its main purpose. It is legislation that tries to please everyone."

Notwithstanding these conflicts, the legislative mandate opened up the opportunity for a significant range of possible ways institutions and assets could be transformed and transferred to the private sector. Despite the numerous advisory boards and hearings, the legislation—with its lack of priorities and specifics—largely empowered the agency to determine the nature of privatization. The THA's mandates served a similar purpose.

In March 1990 the *Volkskammer*, East Germany's Parliament, established the Anstalt zur treuhänderischen Verwaltung des Volkseigentums (Institute for the Trustee Administration of State Property) or Treuhand, for short. The resolution created the Treuhandanstalt and placed state-owned enterprises under the agency's jurisdiction. Throughout that turbulent first year the agency and its mission evolved substantially.

Following passage of the first resolution on March 1, 1990, the "original THA" took effect on March 15, 1990, under the watch of the GDR's last communist government headed by Hans Modrow (Fischer and Schröter 1996). The agency's primary tasks included: (1) converting the large state-owned enterprises into private legal structures;[18] (2) restructuring and dividing large state-owned enterprises into smaller and more efficient entities that were easier to privatize; (3) overseeing the process of privatization; and (4) providing some accountability and control to ensure that illegal sales did not occur.[19] The original THA was directed to use the proceeds from the sale of

153

assets to fund the restructuring of the national budget, provide start-up capital to firms, and contribute in general terms to monetary union.[20] Privatization was ill-defined and its priority was left ambiguous. The primary emphasis was on taking stock of the state-owned enterprises and ensuring that West Germans did not take advantage of East Germany's vulnerable position (Fischer and Schröter 1996).

On March 18, 1990, roughly two weeks after the first THA resolution, East Germany held its first and last free election. The conservative Alliance Party for Germany, led by Lothar de Maizière (and strongly supported by the Kohl administration), emerged as the victor. Over three-fourths of East Germans voted for parties committed to a speedy unification.[21] Under the new government the THA's goals and structure could be clearly retargeted toward privatization. The de Maizière government drafted a new Treuhand Act on June 17, 1990.

Under the new law the THA was charged with the following responsibilities[22]:

- Administration of state-owned firms according to the principles of a social market economy; disengagement of company structures and promotion of marketable firms and efficient economic structures; assistance in preparing opening balance sheets on a Deutschmark basis and organizing firms according to western laws.

- Transfer of whole or parts of companies to the private sector as quickly as possible. Transfer means selling to the private sector—even at "negative prices"—returning firms to former owners who lost them before 1972 or restoring public ownership by communities.[23]

- Reorganization of firms that could be reconstructed into competitive companies and then privatized. Reconstruction was intended to be achieved by splitting up firms into marketable units, downsizing the remaining companies, and rearranging local economic networks.[24]

- Closing firms not capable of being restructured and subsequently selling firm assets in bankruptcy proceedings.[25]

This list of tasks was later incorporated into Article 25 of the Unification Treaty.

As this list suggests, the THA's mandate under the Treuhand Act was a compromise among several different agendas (Nägele 1994; Lichtblau 1993; Priewe 1991; Spoerr 1993; Schuppert 1992). One observer noted that "the law itself does not set any priority among the various tasks assigned the Treuhandanstalt. Hence, because of the wide area of possible tasks, it was clear from the very beginning that the THA would be subject to continued criticism from all sides" (Schatz 1996, 156). For example, the first subclause of the Treuhand Act's preamble expresses the legislature's commitment to privatization, stating that privatization should occur as swiftly as possible. However, as Michael Kloepfer notes, the definition of privatization included the sale, restructuring, and closing down of companies; the creation of more efficient economic structures in line with the social market economy; and the preservation and creation of employment.[26] Others like Kuepper and Mayr, as well as the THA's longest serving president, Birgit Breuel, argued that although the legislation was quite broad, the agency's central mission was to carry out its task as rapidly as possible (Kuepper and Mayr 1996, 318; Breuel 1993b).

The broad range of the THA's mandate reflected the larger debate in society over how the THA should operate, and it recognized that this was a public entity with enormous power to influence the shape of markets in East and West Germany. Chancellor Helmut Kohl's administration, with strong support and encouragement from West German business groups, sought to ensure that assets were transferred to the private sector as rapidly as possible. Delays in privatization, they argued, threatened to destabilize already weak markets. Conservatives feared that the Treuhand was vulnerable to capture by its own firms, opposition political parties, and organized groups, particularly unions, all of whom in one way or another sought to extend the government's involvement in restructuring.[27] Deviation from the singular goal of selling assets as rapidly as possible would not only increase the cost of unification but would excessively politicize the process. The market mantra echoed in Bonn and in the West German business community was "Privatization is the best form of reconstruction."[28]

Opposition party members, unions, and representatives from eastern German states countered that, as the most important actor shaping regional economic structures, the Treuhand had a responsibility to pursue regional economic and industrial goals. They believed the agency had a responsibility to develop strategies for improving regional economies rather than strategies centered around individual firms. Such a regional strategy meant taking into account the importance of firms to the economic health of a geographic area and the synergistic relationships between firms and suppliers in a given region. Most important, it meant investing in the restructuring of firms to make them economically viable. The Deutscher Gewerkschaftbund, the German Trade Union Federation (DGB), opposed the Treuhand's vision of rapid privatization in favor of conducting a state-led industrial policy (DGB 1993).[29] IG Metall, the largest union within the DGB, went so far as to call for the dissolution of the THA into industrial holdings responsible for restructuring firms (IG Metall 1991; Homann 1991, 1,281). These opposition groups pointed to the Treuhand Act's mandate, requiring the agency to pursue restructuring for the purpose of preserving and maximizing employment in eastern Germany.

As in the case of the RTC, the THA's broad mandate, lack of priorities, and lack of specific instructions for implementation did several things. First, the mandate largely left to the agency the task of working out the details of privatization. This included not just determining how sales, restructuring, and closures would be implemented but what priority should be given to each option. Second, the mandate was broad enough to include the concerns of all groups. Majority and minority party members, labor and business association leaders, East and West Germans: all could point to goals in the THA's mandate that reflected their interests and preferences. Finally, the fact that the mandate was broad and included goals that conflicted with one another set the THA up to be blamed by all sides. The conflicting goals ensured that no parties would be happy with the action and reinforced the agency's role as political scapegoat.

HYBRID LEGAL IDENTITY

A final structured choice that set the boundaries within which the RTC and THA operated was their legal definition. The RTC was established as a mixed-ownership government corporation, while the THA was established as a federal trustee agency corporation (*Öffentliche Anstalt*). Legally speaking, both agencies existed deliberately at the juncture between public and private law (Kerber and Stechow 1991; Froomkin 1995). Their legal status shaped the rights and remedies of any person who had a legal or commercial relationship with them, competed with them, entered into contracts with them, was injured by them, or committed fraud upon them (Froomkin 1995). Like the structured choices noted earlier, their identities insulated the agencies from external political and societal actors, gave them greater flexibility to privatize, and limited oversight.[30]

In a mixed-ownership federal corporation like the RTC, the government may own some or none of the equity. The president appoints at least a minority of the directors even if the federal government does not own any equity. Markets assume that securities and other debt instruments carry an implicit guarantee from the U. S. Treasury.[31] Because of its status the RTC enjoyed a number of special privileges that, in a sense, allowed it to play both sides of the public/private fence.

First, federal legislative controls were far weaker than those ordinarily applied to federal agencies, and state controls were nonexistent. The agency was significantly less accountable to Congress than public agencies because (1) it enjoyed alternative funding sources such as debt or revenue from transactions; and (2) its private directors did not hold civil office and were therefore not impeachable under the Constitution. Froomkin (1995) notes that with mixed-ownership government corporations like the RTC, "congressional oversight and GAO audits are the only monitoring devices that apply. . . . These are week reeds at best. Congressional oversight is notoriously uneven; GAO audits are more predictable, but are limited to information provided by the [government corporation]. And, the audits focus on balance sheets rather than the degree to which [government corporations] are fulfilling their public purposes" (613–14).

Because of its "public" nature the RTC was exempt from many of the regulations and constraints placed on private firms. As Froomkin (1995) points out, a mixed-ownership government corporation like the RTC faced the same rules private entities face:

> Their public purpose, their links to the government, the existence of the implied guarantee, and their general uniqueness have all combined to

exclude many . . . from the same degree of federal regulation as comparable private firms. States are unable to fill the regulatory vacuum because,
absent legislation to the contrary, a federal charter gives a corporation the
same immunity from state regulation as enjoyed by the federal government
itself (Froomkin 1995, 613).

Harold Seidman, fellow at the National Academy of Public Administration and an expert on government corporations, assessed the RTC
structure by saying that entities like the RTC "are placed in a position
where they can claim whatever legal status best suits their purposes at
the moment. They are non-government entities when dealing with the
Congress and federal regulators and overseers, and federal agencies
when dealing with local taxing authorities" (U.S. Senate 1991, 75).

In short, the legal entity selected by political principals was the
least accountable of any type of domestic civilian federal government
entity. It was extremely difficult for critics of the agency's privatization
course, including legislators, to intervene because of the lack of any
constitutional, statutory, or regulatory basis. At the same time the
RTC's legal identity insulated the agency it also enhanced the RTC's
flexibility to develop its own budget, spend its resources, hire and pay
its employees, and decide on its priorities. In short, the legal identity
served as both a shield and sword for the RTC, which was precisely
what the political winners wished to accomplish. Like its American
counterpart at the time, the legal identity of the THA was extremely
important. It enhanced the German agency's flexibility and capacity
to privatize rapidly while insulating it from traditional public and private sector controls. The hybrid public/private identity gave the THA
the tools from both sectors without the controls.

During the summer of 1990 leaders in West Germany led by the
Kohl government were careful to make certain the agency's legal
character fell between the boundaries of public and private law.[32] On
the one hand, Article 25 of the Unification Treaty (31 August 1990)
placed the agency under public law. The THA was established as a
federal trustee agency with a set of mandates that were clearly public
goods designed to serve a public function, specifically the revitaliza-
tion of eastern Germany's economy.

On the other hand, the agency operated and acted as a private
"holding" company responsible for thousands of subsidiary stockholding companies and limited partnership firms. Birgit Breuel, the

158

THA's longest standing president, argued on numerous occasions that the Treuhand was not a bureaucracy but a firm. During interviews with more than a dozen "privatization agents," each one echoed Breuel's argument that the agency was not a bureaucracy but operated like a company. Even its internal managerial structure and fifteen regional offices (*Niederlassungen*) resembled the structure of a German stockholding company.[33] Moreover, the agency's relationship to buyers of assets was sanctioned not with public agreements but with private contracts and included clauses that very much resembled deals that private brokers make.

And finally, the Unification Treaty and the *Treuhand-Kreditaufnahmegesetz* (3 July 1992) gave the THA a special-asset status (*Sondervermögen*) akin to the nationalized train service or post office. The status was important because it meant that the financing of the agency was excluded from the federal budget. The effect was that parliamentary budget committees were limited in their efforts to oversee the agency's actions and the financial auditing arm of Parliament was consistently blocked from auditing THA firms.

To make sense of this confusion and its application to public administration, the German courts, in determining the types of appropriate oversight mechanisms, distinguished between the THA's dual tasks of, on the one hand, managing its firms and, on the other hand, selling assets to buyers outside the organization. This separation of the two responsibilities was crucial. Kerber and Stechow (1991) note that the external legal status, or *Treuhandaußenrecht*, refers to THA's legal position with respect to groups external to the agency. The legal character applies primarily to the agency's sales capacity. The internal legal status, or *Treuhandinnenrecht*, refers to the THA's identity with respect to the agency's relationship to the thousands of subsidiary firms that needed to be managed.[34]

Although the German courts initially favored the THA's public status, the higher courts eventually interpreted the agency's definition as private entity. The Chamber Court of Berlin (*Kammergericht*) ruled that the sale of assets is a public act in line with §40 I VwGO[35] and is, therefore, the jurisdiction of the administrative courts.[36] Similarly, the Administrative Court of Berlin ruled that external complaints against the THA fell within the domain of the administrative courts. The court argued the defendant was a federal agency whose task of rebuilding the economy clearly fell into the domain of the state. The court noted that "the sale of properties is done for economic as well as politically structural reasons" and was therefore—even in its sales activities—a public enterprise (Verwaltungsgericht [Administrative Court] 1991, 377).

The administrative court decision was appealed to the High Administrative Court of Berlin.[37] The high court overturned the decision of the lower court arguing that the agency was clearly acting as a private actor in its sales activities. The agency's legislative mandate was to sell properties as quickly as possible and to operate in a "business-like" fashion. The agency was therefore answerable to the laws of economics and the social market economy. Its activities were of a completely private-law nature and were thus the jurisdiction of the civil courts.

Despite its public trustee designation, the German courts determined that the Treuhand fell within the jurisdiction of private law in carrying out its privatization mandate. The impact of this determination was profound because issues regarding the THA's status with respect to external actors such as buyers, communities, and other external groups were placed in the jurisdiction of the civil courts rather than the administrative courts. At the same time, the courts found that the THA fell within the jurisdiction of public law in carrying out its managerial and fiduciary duty to its firms.

The dual legal character of the THA as both a private and public entity affected the privatization process in several ways. Its external identity as a private organization imbued the agency with enormous discretionary power by weakening the ability of judges and policymakers to oversee the agency's activities and curtailing the role of societal actors (affected by the agency's decision) in the privatization decision. At the same time, the THA's internal identity as a public rather than a corporate organization allowed the agency to exercise a type of "fire-alarm" control over the managerial and budgetary decisions affecting its firms while preserving an arms-length distance from the difficult decisions such as laying off workers.

As a public entity operating under the norms of private law—*Verwaltungsprivatrecht*—the THA is tied to various public laws but its actions are evaluated in the private courts. Its most important public constraint is Article 3 of the Constitution. Disappointed buyers, therefore, have standing in the court. In practice, however, it is extremely difficult to hold the THA accountable under Article 3 because of the vagueness of the Treuhand Act. To argue a claim under Article 3 plaintiffs must demonstrate that there were clear violations of the sales priorities written into the THA. No priorities, however, were given in the initiating legislation concerning how to privatize. Moreover, for the first two years only informal priorities were developed for determining to whom and under what terms to sell a property. As a result, very few were successful in making such a claim in the civil courts.

The implications of the high court ruling are even more significant given the procedural differences between civil and administrative courts. Civil courts in Germany are designed to adjudicate differences between two adversarial equals. The judge's role is presumed to be similar to a referee whose ability to collect evidence and ask questions is limited by the *Verhandlungsmaxime* (Marx 1985, 49). Marx describes the *Verhandlungsmaxime* as judges being required to take a "passive" position with regard to the process and, in particular, the evidentiary proceedings. Under the *Verhandlungsmaxime* judges cannot, for example, go beyond evidence presented by the parties in the court.

This stands in stark contrast to the administrative courts where the *Untersuchungsmaxime* is the norm that guides judges' behavior and evidentiary proceedings. The assumption behind administrative courts is that judges must decide between two unequals: the state and the individual party subordinate to the state. Smid notes that administrative courts are there "in order to eliminate the inequality that exists between citizen and bureaucracy which in turn derives from the subordinate legal structures" (Smid 1990, 308). The most important practical consequence of the *Untersuchungsmaxime* is that the administrative court regularly orders the files of the administrative proceedings to be produced in the courtroom (Rüsken 1995). The *Untersuchungsmaxime* thus provides judges with far greater discretion in the collection of information. For example, judges may question witnesses or collect administrative information on topics not directly raised in the pleadings. The *Untersuchungsmaxime* "gives legitimacy to the questioning of the parties by a judge in cases where the complexity of the situation makes it unlikely that the parties themselves will provide all the information necessary to reach a decision" (Smid 1990, 309).

In short, the high court's decision gave the THA the greatest room to maneuver and define for itself how it wished to create private property. The decision placed a premium on internal monitoring by the agency. Judges in civil courts were limited in their review of the procedures and decision-making processes that inform the privatization decision.[38] Moreover, while the THA affected the regional development of local economies, the bases of legal standing and action were limited to the dissemination of a private good by the state. In addition to privatization the THA was also charged with a trustee role with respect to its subsidiary firms.

THE THA'S PUBLIC IDENTITY

The German courts' decision to define the THA's relationship to its subsidiary firms as one governed by public or administrative law also generated an interesting mix of results. Had the THA's control over subsidiary firms been defined as a private relationship that followed the rules of German corporate law, the THA would have been limited in how it could exercise control over its firms. Three aspects of the privatization process were particularly affected by the decision of the courts: (1) liability to its firms; (2) control and oversight of firms; and (3) discretionary power to close and liquidate firms.

Exposure to Liability Lessened by Definition

An important issue was the agency's legal designation with respect to financing of firms and the potential liability to which the THA was exposed through its firms. The issue centered on whether the THA and its subsidiaries comprised a *qualifizierter faktischer Konzern* (qualified actual company) or whether the agency was a public bureaucracy subject to Article 34 of the German Constitution.[39] The distinction had enormous implications for the agency and the government. Under German corporate law, holding companies are financially responsible for the losses suffered by their subsidiaries. Had the courts decided that the THA and its subsidiary companies constituted a private company, the THA would have potentially been required to compensate subsidiary firms for their losses until the relationship between holding and firm ended.

Manfred Balz noted that the corporate law makes it practically impossible for a subsidiary to go bankrupt. First, as a private firm, the THA was potentially liable for the actions of its firms. Creditors filing against firms claiming compensation would have a right to attach claims on the THA and, in turn, the German government. And second, as a private corporation, the THA would be required to bring the capital reserve of subsidiaries into line with rules governing stockholding and limited partnership firms. The capital requirement for limited partnerships and stockholding companies is DM50,000 and DM100,000, respectively. Of course, firms received much more than that. However, the enormous deficits firms operated under would have meant that bringing them automatically in line with capital requirements would in practice have constituted a much greater uncontrolled transfer of public money.

The court ultimately agreed with the THA management's view that the agency was not a corporation under §312 AktG. The article assumes a relationship between two companies. Although a government corporation is capable of being considered a private actor, the THA was not a company.[40] A company pursues a private set of goals, primarily profit. The THA's goal was to redevelop and recover an entire economy: clearly a public not a private good. Vonnemann (1991, 1) noted, "The fact that the agency acts in a 'business-like' way should not make one confuse it with an actual business." The relationship between a holding company and its subsidiary firms in the private sense assumes that a holding company has the ability and interest to exercise power over its firms. Officials in the agency argued that the THA was in no position to exercise that type of control. Moreover, the control it did exercise was indirect and limited to the installation of managers and executive committees.

Control and Accountability

Despite numerous proclamations by the agency that THA firms were responsible for themselves, the THA nevertheless exerted a great deal of influence through indirect means of control.[41] In practice, managers in the THA sought out executive committee members to serve on the boards of firms. In certain cases a civil servant in the Ministry of Finance and/or the THA would also serve on the executive board.

In general the THA and the Ministry of Finance practiced a type of fire-alarm oversight (McCubbins and Schwartz 1984). A great deal of autonomy was ceded to the firm's managing committee in cases where employees were fired. Where capital investments were needed, however, the executive committee and the THA needed to give their approval.

To illustrate how this worked, consider the case of a large Berlin company that had made electrical equipment in the GDR. The former manager of the firm and head of the managing committee had been recruited and installed by the THA. Despite being hired by the THA, the manager was extremely critical of the agency's intervention into his affairs through the executive committee. Information concerning the important actions in the firm were immediately passed through to the THA. The manager noted:

> In the firm you had an executive committee, manager, and owner. However, the owner, the THA, also sat on the executive committee. There was therefore a clear line of information going to the central office. Moreover, the executive committee did not operate like a normal executive committee since the owner's influence was great. The agency began to play a greater and greater role in the functioning of the firm.[42]

This indirect arrangement allowed the THA to remain a comfortable distance from the difficult decisions and consequences of the firm without losing control. The THA could blame the company's management for the firm's poor performance while also saddling the management with the difficult task of reducing the workforce.

In terms of oversight, this arrangement placed enormous weight on the executive committee or firm management to act as the controller for the THA. THA employees and firm managers noted that this was perhaps the most vulnerable aspect of the arrangement with respect to control, since executive committees are often staffed with management of competitive industries in the West or through close personal contacts with Treuhand management.[43] Although the executive committees were put in place by the THA, interviews with THA employees suggest that the executive committees quickly shed their agent position and often became the principals of the firm management. Alternatively, a competitor serving on the board of a THA firm may have the interests of his primary employer rather than the THA firm in mind. Privatization agents often stood in opposition to executive committees who sided with firm management against the THA in debates over additional subsidies. Such an arrangement compromised the executive committee's ability to act as effective controller of THA firms.

Oversight was also supposed to be exercised through the reporting and auditing requirements associated with budgetary laws of a public agency. These statutes required that firms submit regular reports regarding their financial activity and be open to investigations by the federal auditor. As noted above, however, there was a great deal of controversy early in the THA history concerning the off-budget nature of the THA's subsidization of firms. Because the THA's funding was not part of the budget, should its activities be subject to budgetary rules? The controversy was later worked out through action taken by Parliament. THA firms were accountable for the same reporting requirement and subject to audits by the federal auditor. However, the reporting requirements were made the responsibility of the executive committee in the company or the manager. In short, the burden to report was placed on the firms. Reports included information about the internal organization of the company, balance sheets, and the production processes. The information was then passed on to the THA who in turn had to make the information available to the Federal Auditors Office.

Greater Freedom to Split and Close Firms

Finally, in fulfilling its mandate, the THA was often forced to split up large conglomerates into easier-to-sell pieces or close the operation of firms determined no longer capable of being saved.[44] In both instances the THA was treated as the majority shareholder (*Allein- oder Mehrheitsgesellschafter*), and the laws under which the agency took action to restructure or close firms fell under private law.

In the case of closure, the designation of the firm as unsalvageable was considered an administrative act that could be challenged in the administrative courts. Once the evaluation was completed, however, the THA—as the majority shareholder—could decide to liquidate the firm under private law. In this sense, the procedures illustrated the two-stage theory mentioned earlier. The restructuring or splitting up of firms by the THA was made easier by the passage of the Splitting Law in April 1991 by increasing the rights of owners of THA firms. The law essentially placed the decision to reorganize in the realm of private law. Similar to the rules on closure, the THA as majority owner of its firms could choose to restructure them if it was determined to be economically necessary by a recognized expert.

CONCLUSION

The structural choices made by U.S. and German legislators reflected the legacy of political winners who succeeded in legislating the institutional boundaries within which both the RTC and THA operated. While there were many types of legal and bureaucratic structures within which the RTC and THA had to work, four seemed particularly important: governance structures, financing mechanisms, legislative mandates, and legal identities. None of these structures was predetermined. Each was the product of politics. Together they had the effect of insulating the agencies from critics, giving the Bush and Kohl administrations important levers of control. These structures enhanced organizational capacity while they weakened oversight and ultimately placed a premium on the role that internal administrative characteristics played on outcomes.

NOTES

1. The following discussion, however, deviates in two ways from Terry Moe's work. First, Moe restricts his view of politics of structural choice to *public* agencies, explicitly contrasting the process of designing private firms. The following discussion extends Moe's view of structural choice to a *public/private* hybrid. Second, Moe's central argument is that agencies designed by politicians are designed to be ineffective. The approach taken here centers on trying to understand how concepts such as "efficiency" and "effectiveness" are in part products of institutional arrangements—in this case legal ones.

2. An article in the *United States Banker* noted, "The Resolution Trust Corporation has been a public whipping boy from the moment it began four years ago. . . . The RTC is battle-tested and battle-scarred, as scorned by employees of seized thrifts, community groups, and many in Congress" (Marshall 1993, 28). In an article in the *Financial Times*, THA President Birgit Breuel acknowledged her agency's scapegoat role: "No politician in the world could have taken our decisions. . . . This was the idea of our job—to have distance between the politicians and the Treuhand enterprises" (Dempsey 1993, 3).

3. THA President Detlev Rohwedder prevented the THA from fully transforming itself into four stock-holding companies. He succeeded in maintaining the THA as a public entity. The model of the overall organization as a private stockholding company remained, however.

4. The western business leaders included: Jens Odewald, CEO of Kaufhof AG Holdings; Otto Gellert, one of West Germany's top corporate auditors; Hans-Olaf Henkel from IBM Deutschland GmbH; Claus Koehler from Germany's central Bundesbank; Frank Niethammer from Agiv AG; Horst Pastuzek from the large coffee conglomerate Tchibo Holding AG; Klaus Piltz from the steel corporation Veba AG; Jahan van Tilburg from the mega-Dutch corporation Grundig AG; André Leyson from the Belgian camera company Agfa-Gavaert AG; Manfred Lennings of the Westdeutsche Landesbank AG; and Bethold Leibinger of Trumpf GmbH & Co. and VDMA.

5. Michael Waldman, in his book *Who Robbed America?* (1990b, 122–23), presents an even broader and far more complex diagram of the functional interrelationships enacted by FIRREA.

6. A high ranking RTC/FDIC manager described the FDIC as the RTC's "surrogate parent."

7. Other members were C. C. Hope Jr., Robert Clarke, Andrew Hove Jr., and Timothy Ryan.

8. Quoted in Kriz (1989, 2460).

9. *National Journal,* May 12, 1990, 1166 (cited in Kettl 1991b, 104).

10. States are not excluded from the process. Article 25, section 2 specifies, for example, that representatives from each of the new states be included in the Administrative Board, the committee that oversees the management of the agency.

11. The responsibility of the states to implement employment and structural policy is written in Article 91a, section 1, 104a of the German Constitution. A number of scholars argue that the THA was the most important actor in Germany's employment policy. However, because its authoritative legislation does not specifically mention employment policy or regional development, the *Bundesrat* is excluded from the decision-making process, and states are essentially kept subordinate to the federal government, in particular the Finance Ministry (see esp. Schmidt and Siegmund 1996).

12. The Treaty on Economic, Monetary, and Social Union, which took effect July 1, 1990, permitted the THA to issue debt of DM17 billion for 1990 and 1991.

13. Losses refers to the difference between the amount the government would need to fulfill its guarantee to insured depositors and the net amount it would recover from disposing of assets when the institution was resolved.

14. Froomkin (1995) concurred with Waldman's assessment. He wrote, "The accounting trick increases the program's costs in exchange for nothing more than (false) bragging rights about meeting budget targets" (617).

15. In the RTC Refinancing, Restructuring and Improvement Act of 1991, the working capital cap was raised to $160 billion.

16. Much of the money went to replace the high-cost funds, such as high-yielding Certificates of Deposit, which had matured while institutions were in conservatorship. In order to maintain liquidity these funds had to be replaced with government infusions of capital.

17. Robert Rubin, former chair of the Thrift Depositor Protection Oversight Board, stated, "Democratic government is based on citizen involvement in the decision-making process. . . . The RTC advisory boards . . . served an important function in advising the RTC. . . . The S&L crisis affected residents in virtually every state, and the advisory boards were integral in helping the RTC and the Oversight Board to address the concerns of Americans nationwide" (Thrift Depositor Protection Oversight Board 1995, 5).

18. Although the transformation was purely a formal legal action, it was viewed as an important step in transferring institutions from west to east (Schwalbach and Gless 1996).

19. The East German public was greatly concerned that West Germans intended to steal East Germany's property (Christ and Neubauer 1991; PDS 1994).

20. Report on the work of the Institute for Trustee Administration of State Property for the period from 15 March to 15 May 1990, pp. 2 and 16.

21. The Alliance Party formed a grand coalition government with the Free Democrats and the Social Democrats which governed until unification in October 1990.

22. This summary of legislative mandates is taken from Kühl (1997, 121). For a more complete discussion of the duties see Westerman (1996) and Kloepfer (1996).

23. Preamble of the THG.

24. § 2 section 6 THG. This is, however, specifically not seen by the agency or the executive as a general economic mandate or mandate to pursue regional economy policy (Wild 1991).

25. § 8 section 1 THG.

26. Kloepfer (1996) provides a good list of all of the tasks embodied in the Treuhand law. It includes at least thirteen separate and conflicting tasks (49–54). Section 2 of the Treuhand law illustrates the ambiguity noting that the THA's

mandate is: "to support the privatization of the national property according to the principles of a social market economy. It is to promote the structural adjustment of the economy to the needs of the market . . . by exerting influence on the development of enterprise worth being rehabilitated and on their privatization."

27. It is of course incorrect to generalize across all unions. There is great variation, for example, between the position taken by the hard line IG Metall, the manufacturing workers' union, and IG Chemie, the chemical workers' union. The former was far more radical and critical of the government than the latter with respect to the THA's actions. For scholarship that examines the role of unions during the unification process see Fichter (1993), Wagner (1993), and Schaub (1993).

28. "Privatisierung ist die beste Sanierung." The phrase was lifted from a letter written by Detlev Rohwedder to his THA employees on March 21, 1991. A week later on April 1, 1991, Rohwedder was gunned down and Birgit Breuel replaced him as president of the THA. The oft-quoted letter became known as the "Easter Letter."

29. The DGB is the trade union for blue-collar workers. The *Deutsche Angestelltengewerkschaft* (German Employees Union or DAG) represents white collar employees.

30. For several good reviews of government corporations see reports by Ronald Moe (1983) and the General Accounting Office (1983).

31. Contrast with: (1) a wholly owned government corporation where the government holds 100 percent of the equity and exercises 100 percent of the votes on the governing body; or (2) a private federal corporation where the government holds no stock but may have a statutory right to select members of the board of directors. One result of the implicit guarantee is that mixed-ownership federal corporations receive a lower rate on their securities than private entities but pay more than the federal government or corporations in which there is an explicit guarantee.

32. There is a substantial scholarship on the THA's legal identity. For overviews in English see the following: Cassell (2001), Kloepfer (1996), and Westerman (1996). For an excellent account of the contracting relationships by legal scholars, see Dodds and Wächter (1993). For the most extensive work in German see the work by the prolific legal scholar Robert Weimar (1990; 1993c; 1993d; 1991; 1992a; 1992b; 1993a; 1993b).

33. The offices had been called "*Geschäftsstellen*," a term more generally used to refer to offices of a bureaucracy. The name was changed to *Niederlassungen* after unification and is primarily used in the private sector to refer to branches

of a company. A notable exception was labor's equal representation in the executive committee.

34. The German judicial system is divided into civil, administrative, and criminal branches. The *Bundesverwaltungsgericht* (Federal Administrative Court) is the highest level of authority within the administrative branch followed by the *Verwaltungsgericht* (VGO) (Administrative Court), under which on the regional and district level are the *Oberlandsgericht* (OLG), *Landgericht* (LG), and *Amtsgericht* (AG). Within the branch of civil law are specific legal areas such as labor law (*Arbeitsrecht*) with a separate set of legal recourse to Labor Courts.

35. Unlike the United States, where a single Administrative Procedures Act is applied, Germany has two different laws for the administrative procedures: the VwGO, *Verwaltungsgerichtsordung* and the VwVfG, *Verwaltungsverfahrensgesetz* (both translated roughly as "administrative procedures laws"). The lower courts argued that the THA's sales activities were in line with the VwGO; however, the definition of what an administrative act is is embodied in 35 VwVfG.

36. Chamber Court decision was reached December 4, 1990, and published in *Zeitschrift für Wirtschaftsrecht* 1991, 407.

37. High Administrative Court decision was reached January 22, 1991, and published in *Zeitschrift für Wirtschaftsrecht* 1991, 198.

38. They were not, for instance, able to look into the administrative files of other bidders in order to judge the fairness of the process. THA's privatization activities are characterized as private law.

39. A *qualifizierter faktischer Konzern* is the conglomerate consisting of the controlling company and one or more controlled companies, which is treated like the conglomerate falling under §312 AktG *without being one* (see Wolter 1992 for more details).

40. A decision in the German Federal Court established the possibility that a government entity could also be considered a private company.

41. For additional examples of the THA exercising this type of indirect control, see newspaper articles in the *Frankfurter Allgemeine Zeitung* (18 Nov. 1991, 18; 3 Dec. 1991, 19; 5 May 1992, 15).

42. Interview with a former manager of a large electrical appliance firm hired by the THA. He served on the supervisory board of several other THA-owned firms.

43. According to internal control workers, the THA's policy of picking a person to head the executive committee and then leaving it up to him or her to fill the rest of the positions exacerbated this problem.

44. This was determined through an expert's certified opinion and evaluation.

5

The Impact of Task Environment on Performance

Once created by their political principals, the Treuhandanstalt (THA) and the Resolution Trust Corporation (RTC) were by no means on automatic pilot. The performance of both agencies was clearly shaped by their administrative characteristics. The bureaucratic structures established by political principals formed an outer ring of influence. Yet like all organizations, the RTC and THA's performance and behavior were dramatically influenced by the challenges associated with their particular task. Few anticipated the obstacles both organizations confronted. The sheer effort involved in transferring such vast assets from the public to the private sector generated its own powerful influence on the organizations and their behavior.

How does one think systematically about tasks and their influence on organizations? How did *what* the RTC and THA attempted to carry out influence *how* they carried out their mandates? At stake is a principal-agent issue. The task environment within which public organizations attempt to carry out their mandates can dramatically affect how well principals are able to observe the behavior of their agents.

James Q. Wilson's pathbreaking work *Bureaucracy* (1989, 158–75) offers a classification scheme that provides a starting point to understanding the issue. Organizations, Wilson argues, produce *outputs*—what bureaucrats do on a day-to-day basis—and they produce *outcomes*—those things that change in the world because of the outputs.

171

Wilson offers two primary insights: First, the ability to observe outcomes and outputs varies greatly among organizations. Outputs by environmental regulators, for example, may not be nearly as easy to observe as the delivery of mail by mail carriers. Similarly, it may be hard to determine the link between an organization's actions and its outcomes. An organization may lack a method for gathering the information about the consequences of its actions. Operators in the organization may lack a proven means to produce an outcome. Alternatively, outcomes may result from an unknown combination of operator behavior and other factors.

Wilson's second insight is to demonstrate that the ability of principals to observe the actions and outcomes of agents is a function of the agency's task environment. For example, given their remote location, it is often difficult to observe precisely what forest rangers do on a daily basis; yet we can easily observe their overall outcome. Alternatively, a military officer is well aware of the activities of his or her troops, but the overall impact of a particular military unit is less observable. And finally, as in the case of the U.S. State Department or Central Intelligence Agency, it may be impossible to observe either outputs or outcomes.

While Wilson's classification offers a useful heuristic with which to understand the principal-agent issues, economists, political scientists, and organizational sociologists offer some insights into the impact that greater dependence on external actors can have upon organizational behavior.

Kenneth Meier (1980) concludes in his study of public bureaucracies that an agency's power increases with the complexity of the task. He found that bureaucracies are designed to meet needs for expertise and fast, decisive actions. As the nature of tasks changes or shifts in response to unexpected circumstances, the discretionary power of the agency increases because it holds a "quasi-monopoly" on tools to meet the new challenges (Meier 1980, 53). By contrast, tasks that are routine and highly stable give political principals greater capacity to oversee implementation and erode the discretionary power of the agency.

Building on the work of William Dill (1958, 410), James Thompson argues that bureaucratic power may decline in proportion to the organization's dependence on political or technical resources outside the agency. This dependency increases with the growth of task complexity (Thompson 1967, 30; Emerson 1962). In this sense the task environment constrains an organization's capacity by limiting the set of feasible alternatives. An organization may also be constrained by the capacity and character of supporting external organizations.

Dietmar Braun's (1993) study of federal research funding organizations in Great Britain and the United States concluded that bureaucratic agents were significantly dependent upon third parties (scientists, in the case of research funding) to provide bureaucratic agents with the needed expertise to meet the changing expectations of the agencies' political principals. As discussed in chapter 3, dependence on external actors need not be viewed as a constraint. Both the RTC and THA increased their capacities through the availability of external contractors, particularly those with experience in business, law, and accounting. Proponents of contracting point out that external actors offer organizations greater flexibility by allowing managers to tailor a variety of capacities to the specific needs of the organization. Osborne and Gaebler's (1992) famous work *Reinventing Government* points to many successful cases of government "steering rather than rowing." Notwithstanding the possibility for greater capacity, high levels of dependence on external actors can alter or help to shape what James Thompson describes as a "domain consensus" (Thompson 1967, 28–29).

In the same way internal administrative characteristics contribute to a set of beliefs about an organization's primary purpose, task environments present a similar effect among organizations that face high levels of external dependence. Thompson defines domain consensus as "a set of expectations, both for members of an organization and for others with whom they interact, about what the organization will and will not do. It provides . . . an image of the organization's role in the larger system, which in turn serves as a guide for the ordering of action in a certain direction and not in others" (Thompson 1967, 29). Dietmar Braun's work provides a useful empirical application within the public choice tradition.

Principal-agent literature typically argues that bureaucratic shirking is broadly a function of an agent's desires (i.e., to maximize budgets) and opportunities due to poor oversight (Niskanen 1971;

Borcherding 1977; Buchanan 1977). Braun's study, however, concludes that bureaucratic shirking in some agencies is largely a function of third parties' ability to control the definition of the mission and often steer the agency away from the goals of legislative principals. The unique position of third parties resulting from more difficult and complex tasks gives them a "secret defining power" regarding the choices made by agents. In short, there appears to be a clear connection between an organization's task, with its task environment, and an organization's performance and behavior.

The experience of the RTC and the THA offers a window on this complicated dynamic. The legislatures that created the RTC and THA had very different organizations in mind than the ones that arose. As noted in the preceding chapter, legislators sought to keep the agencies at arm's length while also hoping to create organizations that were transparent, where the outputs were easily identifiable. Despite expectations of legislators, the RTC and THA developed into very different organizations. Outputs in both agencies became difficult to observe largely as a result of circumstances beyond their control. The RTC and THA became overwhelmed by their challenge and quickly evolved into agencies in which organizational outputs were obscured.

Both agencies were charged with divesting an unprecedented volume of public assets in a short period of time. Many of the assets were of poor quality. Both agencies carried out their divestment in markets that were weak at best and nonexistent at worst. The early flood of assets into the agencies left little room for strategic planning and assessment. These factors—inherited by both agencies—contributed to a strong dependence on external actors and institutions for assistance and strained the ability of legislators and other actors outside the agency to fully observe actions of the RTC and THA.

RTC: Struggling to Cope

The U.S. Congress and the president deliberately sought to avoid the pitfalls of a coping organization. The distressing efforts by two agencies—the Federal Savings and Loan Insurance Corporation (FSLIC) and the Federal Asset Disposition Agency (FADA)—to manage the savings and loan crisis taught American legislators that an alternative was badly needed. FADA, in particular, was an influential marker that legislators clearly wanted to avoid.[1]

FADA was a pilot project created in 1985 by the savings and loan regulator, the Federal Home Loan Bank Board (FHLBB), to give the board a more direct role in the management and disposition of insolvent thrifts. Much like its successor, FADA was charged with managing and disposing of assets using private sector actors who, in the words of FADA's founding father, W. F. McKenna, would "provide a private sector approach to a public sector problem" by efficiently liquidating the assets of failed savings and loan associations (Rom 1996). In practice FADA disposed of very few assets, preferring instead to manage them.[2] It embodied central elements of Wilson's coping organization: neither managers nor political principals knew what the operators were doing, and the outcomes of the agency's actions were equally ambiguous. Its private sector employees also proved to be extremely costly employees whose "private sector approach" left many in Congress feeling as if the taxpayer had been taken to the cleaners. A report issued in March 1991 by a special Congressional Task Force on the RTC stated, "FADA's failings are a lesson and a warning for its successor in interest, the RTC" (U.S. House 1991, 2). Both FADA and FSLIC were important reminders to Congress that the federal government needed a different model of bureaucratic organization, one that was more accountable.

The organizational model Congress and the president had in mind was the Federal Deposit Insurance Corporation (FDIC). It was a natural choice. The FDIC had a strong reputation in the political and financial world. It was known for its military-like culture, rigorous standard operating procedures, hierarchy, independent decision making, and high degree of professionalism. Most important, the relatively low number of bank failures (particularly in comparison to savings and loans) was perceived to be a function of the FDIC's conservative and prudent oversight throughout the 1980s.

When President George Bush unveiled to the public on February 6, 1989, his proposal to reform the savings and loan industry and create a new system to resolve problem thrifts, the organizational model Congress and the president had in mind was the FDIC. FIRREA took effect the following August, and the RTC was placed under the guardianship of the FDIC. The RTC Oversight Board was the FDIC

Oversight Board. FDIC managers became RTC managers. And all employees in the RTC were official FDIC personnel. Several RTC executives interviewed used the metaphor of a parent and adopted child in describing the relationship between the FDIC and the RTC. The executives were quick to note, however, that in a very short time the familial relationship deteriorated. The FDIC's "parenting style" no longer worked.

The RTC's initial strategy was to sell and market thrifts as complete entities or "whole banks." As one FDIC executive who worked in the RTC explained, "This is how we had always done it." Under this arrangement, entire institutions—all assets and liabilities—are transferred to the investor. This was the FDIC's standard operating procedure for resolving banks. The short-term costs of such a strategy are immense, largely because the buyer typically demands a steep discount on the assets of the institution. The government is immediately forced to pay the full value of the deposit liabilities and take a discount on the institution's assets. The reason for the model's popularity among bank regulators and the private sector generally is that it minimizes the time assets and liabilities sit in government hands. The underlying belief is that the less government is involved in the ownership of the institutions the more likely the institution is to survive and the lower will be the ultimate cost to the taxpayer. It is important to note that under the whole bank model, FIRREA's alternatives to rapid privatization were largely circumvented. The problems of oversight were also reduced since government's overall role was minimized.

Whole bank sales, however, proved unsuccessful. As William Rolle, RTC's manager of resolutions, testified, "there [is] not a great deal of interest for many institutions even when they are in attractive markets and even when the deposit liabilities are to be transferred without the bad assets" (U.S. House 1991, 19). Despite its efforts the agency was unable to sell as "whole banks" any of the 262 institutions that had immediately been placed under the RTC's control. Even more troubling was the pace at which the RTC's inventory was growing. During the fall of 1989 the agency was taking over thrifts at the rate of one or two a day. By the close of its first year, 318 institutions were placed in conservatorship with assets in excess of $141 billion. Only 37 institutions had been resolved.

As inventory grew, so did the number of assets such as loans, real estate, and securities. Traditionally, the FDIC did not have to manage or care for these types of assets for very long because its standard operating procedure was to sell the entire institution as quickly as possible, regardless of the cost. Yet the slow pace of institutional sales meant the FDIC was suddenly burdened with an extraordinarily large number of assets that required servicing and management, tasks that were not part of the FDIC standard operating procedure.

Several factors over which the RTC/FDIC had little control contributed to the breakdown of the organization. The sheer mass, diversity, and above all, poor quality of assets made the RTC's enterprise extraordinarily difficult. The agency was charged with selling $161.9 billion in cash and investment securities, $188.8 billion in mortgages, $34.8 billion in miscellaneous loans, $30.7 in commercial and residential real estate, and $38.6 billion in other types of assets. About half of the assets, according to William Seidman, consisted of good securities and solid loans that yielded regular interest payments (Seidman 1993, 198). The assets in the other half, however, were a serious problem. These assets included land that was often worth only about 10 percent of the money loaned on it and subperforming and nonperforming loans whose value was at most 60–70 percent of the book value. The fact that in many cases no market existed for them added to the difficulty and the need for expert understanding of specialized markets. Such a challenge would be difficult for a large private financial corporation to handle, let alone a new government agency staffed with new employees.

Since not all assets could be sold at once, the RTC needed a management system that could preserve the value of assets before they were sold. In practice this meant locating and hiring private contractors to service loans and manage and maintain properties. The use of contractors created an additional need to construct systems of accountability.

Poor economic conditions compounded the agency's problems. The recession that began in 1989 and continued through most of the RTC's tenure increased default rates, thereby turning "good" loans into difficult loans at the very moment the agency was attempting to sell them. Markets for real estate and other difficult assets were particularly weakened by the poor economic conditions. As one research institute noted in reference to the agency's real estate component, "Launched in the teeth of the nation's worst real estate deflation in 60 years, RTC's asset sale program has remained the agency's most difficult undertaking" (Southern Finance Project 1992a, 3).

Unlike resolutions, assets had to be disposed of in ways that fulfilled FIRREA's other goals: protecting markets, maximizing opportunities for minority- and women-owned buyers and contractors, and maximizing the availability of affordable housing. One of the advantages from the perspective of the RTC officials was that selling whole thrifts placed these other goals in the background. However, once the agency became an asset sales entity, its lack of progress on these other fronts became more visible. An auditor with the GAO put it this way: "When the RTC realized that they couldn't sell whole banks, there was a light bulb that went off. This was an incredible revelation because they then had to figure out what to do with stuff they didn't sell quickly. . . . More importantly, they had to figure out how to sell bad assets."

FDIC managers had experience implementing the FDIC's model of bank resolution—whole bank sales. This resolution model is relatively clean because the investor purchases all the assets and liabilities of the troubled financial institution. The agency's role centers on ensuring that enough bidders are at the table to make the process competitive and to make certain that buyers are not paying too little for the institution. Since the RTC's top management consisted of FDIC members, it is not surprising that the RTC attempted to implement the FDIC's resolution model. The agency struggled and was not prepared when it turned out that few investors were interested in purchasing the tainted thrifts. "The FDIC is like the military," said an RTC sales director: "Not only does it have a hard time admitting it's wrong, but change is also not easy." The failure of whole-bank sales in the RTC meant that the agency suddenly required a cadre of employees with new types of expertise and know-how in a variety of areas for which the FDIC staff had never been responsible.[3]

At the same time leaders of the agency and the administration made it clear to Congress that the $50 billion that had been approved for the S&L rescue less than two months earlier would not be nearly enough. New estimates placed the figure at closer to $100 billion. This particularly infuriated members of the House and Senate banking committees because the agency had shown little progress.[4] Bruce Vento (D-MN), chair of the RTC Task Force, charged that four months after Congress passed FIRREA the RTC was doing nothing. He complained vigorously that the RTC's bias for concentrating on whole S&Ls was detracting from other areas. For example, the agency had not issued any rules or guidelines to help buyers who might want to purchase individual branches or portions of thrifts (Rosenblatt 1989). Phil Gramm (R-TX), senior member on the Senate Banking Committee stated, "My fear is that the federal government will manage these assets in perpetuity" (Rosenblatt 1990).

James Q. Wilson's assertion that craft-based organizations struggle with crises that fall outside their standard operating procedures clearly played out with the FDIC (Wilson 1989). In the wake of the congressional pressure, the RTC shifted its strategy. An RTC official explained the change: "In the beginning we naturally followed the FDIC model of trying to sell entire institutions whole. That turned out to be a huge flop, and the agency was put under intense criticism for moving too slowly. By early 1990 we had 300 conservatorships, and Congress saw that not much had been done. So Congress said, in effect, 'get on the stick.' And that meant selling them quickly. Either find a buyer for the S&L or pay off the depositors and close it down. But however you do it, wipe it off the face of the earth." A number of new policies were adopted that—while radically increasing the number of resolutions—created new sets of challenges both for managers in the organization and principals outside the organization overseeing the RTC's activities.

THA Is Forced to Cope

Policymakers in Germany initially intended the THA to be a production agency. It would be responsible for selling East Germany's vast wealth of industrial holdings, a clear and observable set of outputs. And the agency would then handle the dissemination of the net proceeds to East Germans, also a clear and observable outcome.

In hindsight such assumptions appear naïve. Yet during this early period in 1990 a great deal of optimism surrounded the THA regarding its ability to serve as the motor for a successful unification. The expectation among politicians and citizens alike was that the THA's primary challenge would be to disburse fairly the enormous revenues that would flow from the sale of economic enterprises in much the same way that previous privatizations, such as VW and Lufthansa, had reaped significant windfalls to the West German federal government. The foreign press compared the scene with 1948, when West Germany experienced its "first economic miracle." In December 1990, less than three months after unification, *Fortune* magazine wrote: "Make no mistake, Germany's eastern third is set to imitate the economic miracle that the West began with the Marshall Plan and Ludwig Erhard's currency reform of 1948" (Demaree 1990, 147).

In one of the classic have-your-cake-and-eat-it-too speeches, West German Chancellor Helmut Kohl predicted that East Germany would soon become a blossoming, productive landscape. He argued on national television that East Germany's assets would pay for much of unification, fuel the growth of the east's economic recovery, and relieve West Germans of additional tax burdens. An editor of the widely read economics periodical *Wirtschaftswoche* wrote at the time: "The [West German] citizens can be relieved. They need not fear higher interest rates, tax or inflation rates. The GDR will pay for unification . . . from her own pocket" (Cadel 1994, 15). Even members of the East German parliament (*Volkskammer*), who were arguably in the best position to know the poor state of their country's industrial structure, initially expressed their strongest concern with how revenues generated from the sale of assets would be spent.

They had two reasons for optimism: first, there was a general overestimation of the value of East Germany's economic assets; and second, there had been an apparently successful merger of West and East Germany's financial systems even before the THA's activities were under way.[5]

Policymakers in East and West Germany severely overvalued East German assets and underassessed the ecological and financial problems of East German industrial sectors, particularly manufacturing, shipbuilding, and chemicals—three areas with high levels of employment. Table 5.1 shows that the original estimate of the worth of East German firms was seventeen times their actual worth.

In early 1990 the administration of East Germany's president Hans Modrow estimated the value of East German firms to be approximately DM1,365 billion. The estimate was recalibrated by THA president Detlev Rohwedder at DM600 billion. In 1992, when

Table 5.1

Estimated Value of THA's Original Portfolio
of Enterprises, 1990–92

Date of Estimate	Estimate (in DM billions)	Source of Estimate
Early 1990	1,365	Modrow administration of the GDR
Spring 1990	600	THA President Detlev Rohwedder
October 1992	81[a]	Opening balance sheet of the THA

Source: Kuehl (1993, 1) cited in Carlin (1994).

[a]The net equity capital of enterprises is estimated at DM81 billion; the cost of privatizing, restructuring, and closing them is DM215 billion.

the opening balance sheets of firms were released, they indicated a value of DM81 billion. However, because the cost of restructuring and closing firms was not factored in, the actual value of East German assets turned out to be significantly *negative*.

In an interview several years after unification, de Maizière acknowledged the gross miscalculation:

> We thought at the time we could use the money from privatization to restructure the firms and even contribute to the federal budget. . . . This privatization thought was based on a fundamental miscalculation of the value of the public property. It was only because we thought privatization would provide the funds necessary to restructure firms that we placed so much value on privatization (Kampe 1994, 110).

The great folly of these overly optimistic assessments was later recognized, but not before the Kohl administration and the THA had committed themselves to a production-based organizational model along with a program of rapid privatization and minimal active restructuring.

Banks have historically played the central role in Germany's economic development, and the successful merger of East and West Germany's banks was a particular cause of optimism in 1990.[6] The capacity of banks to support economic prosperity is explained by two factors. One is their dominant role as the provider of long-term debt. Germany does not have a well-developed equity market, and firms typically go to banks for new capital. The second factor is the role banks play in overseeing the management of firms. Banks contribute significantly to decisions about how loaned funds are managed. These two roles contribute to the long-term, future-oriented relationship between banks and firms that has encouraged industrial development in Germany. At the same time, the ability of banks to rescue industry and initiate difficult industrial restructuring rests on their representation in firm supervisory boards, their collected industrial expertise, and their depoliticized position within Germany's policymaking system (Griffin 1992). As Kenneth Dyson (1986) notes in describing how banks work in Germany's organized economy, "Banks acted as major initiators and organizers of industrial activity so that industrial policy remained somewhat screened from the general arena of politics" (51). In short, banks play the central role in ensuring that capital is allocated efficiently among private corporations, that restructuring is carried out in the long-term interests of the firm, and that monitoring and oversight occur free from political tugs-of-war. It is this "political screening" in particular that led policymakers to view banks as important institutions in brokering the privatization process.

In 1990 the outlook for West German banks was extremely good. Not only was the banking structure changing but the firms themselves were being significantly restructured in line with a more western model. In March 1990 the East German Parliament passed the Law to Change the Legal Governance of the State Bank of the GDR (*Gesetz über die Änderung des Gesetzes über die Staatsbank der DDR*) that replaced the east's one-tier banking system with a two-tier organization compatible with the west. Three months later the passage of the German Economic, Monetary, and Social Union (GEMSU) furthered the process by committing East and West Germany to uphold contract, economic, occupational, and competitive freedoms. GEMSU also committed both countries to the goal of unification of all laws and rules governing these freedoms. The Unification Treaty that took effect in October 1990 solidified the system by placing all five GDR states under the same federal legal code and constitution or Basic Law.

At the same time, East Germany's banks were undergoing extensive restructuring (Griffin 1992, 17). In March 1990 the *Staatsbank* spun off two major corporations, the Deutsche Kredit Bank AG

(DKB) and the Berliner Stadtbank AG (BSB), which received approximately DM123 billion of old industrial credits to GDR conglomerates. At the behest of the state, the DKB entered into two joint ventures in July 1990—one with the Deutsche Bank and one with the Dresdner Bank. Besides taking over all of the DKB's regional offices and most of its personnel, both joint ventures were given the task of administering the old debt credits. In December 1990 the DKB sold its shares in the joint venture with the Deutsche Bank to the Deutsche Bank. And in June 1991 the DKB sold its shares in its joint venture with the Dresdner Bank to the Dresdner Bank. Although the old credits (*Altkredite*) remained with the Staatsbank, their administration and all subsequent new financing of firms were completely handed over to the two largest West German universal banks.

The intrusion by western banks was so extensive by the time the Unification Treaty was signed that economists and German politicians believed the scene was set for a speedy and efficient privatization process. In the popular press West German bankers bragged of their future role in the privatization process, and many economists predicted a strong recovery in the new states as a result of the solid installation of western legal and financial frameworks.[7]

The optimism of 1990 concerning the ease of unification and the "flowering economic landscape" of the east predicted by Helmut Kohl was the result of the rapid privatization of East Germany's banking system coupled with an overvaluation of East Germany's economic structure. The optimism, however, soon evaporated in the wake of several factors over which the THA had little control.

Despite expectations that East Germany would experience an economic boom, the ride toward privatization did not go so smoothly. Marc Fisher, the Bonn bureau chief for the *Washington Post,* noted in early 1991: "From every corner comes the same accusation: It's going too slowly" (Fisher 1991, H1). During the summer of 1990 Detlev Rohwedder, president of the THA, remarked, "Only the Germans believe that the transformation of a communist centrally planned economy to a global market economy can occur in six to eight months or a year" (Freese 1995, 48).

Optimism and the pace of privatization were dampened by a number of factors that the THA could not control: (1) the passage of social, economic, and monetary union; (2) the reluctance of banks to extend financing; (3) the collapse of eastern markets; (4) restitution of property to former owners; (5) wage parity agreements between labor and business associations; and (6) environmental problems.

When GEMSU took effect on July 1, 1990, it pushed most East German firms immediately into the red.[8] Except for a limited amount of personal wealth, the exchange rate between East and West German Marks was set at 2:1, a rate that valued the East German Mark many times above the market rate.[9] For firms that almost always had extensive debt, the new exchange rate was devastating. Lutz Hoffmann (1993, 29), president of the German Institute for Economic Research, wrote:

> The vengeful reduction in productivity and employment in East Germany is not, as is typically claimed, solely the result of socialism . . . but rather the result of a currency unification that adopted a price-cost relationship by which no production was capable of covering its costs.

The old debts (*Altlasten*) on the books of the Staatsbank were now recognized as legitimate notes owned by West German banks. The new exchange rate immediately increased the cost of those notes (just as it gave GDR consumers an enormous subsidy) and, when applied to the corporate balance sheets of firms, meant that most were technically bankrupt overnight.[10] Sinn and Sinn (1992, 276) note that the total debt of GDR firms was 260.4 billion East Marks, converted at the 2:1 rate. East German firms were also notoriously top-heavy with employees—a result of the GDR's policy of full employment. The new exchange rate suddenly raised the already costly burden of company payrolls.

A second challenge that faced the agency was the reluctance of banks to extend credit to firms without guarantees from the THA. In nearly every case where eastern firms borrowed capital, it was underwritten by the federal government. As a result, German banks received enormous subsidies indirectly through the loan guarantees made by the THA. As Peter Lee (1992, 40), a writer for the magazine *Euromoney*, noted in 1992:

> In little over a year the three major German banks have made massive inroads into east Germany. . . . By the middle of last year over DM30 billion had been deposited into the eager hands of Dresdner Bank, Deutsche Bank, and Commerzbank. . . . A portion of the deposits has

gone into interbank market and some to west Germany. Meanwhile loans made to east German companies have mostly been guaranteed by the Treuhand. In addition, Deutsche and Dresdner have received fees for administering the old loans of the Staatsbank customers, which they inherited together with its branches in 1990. This is a risk-free business.

Policymakers in East and West Germany initially believed that in exchange for their extremely lucrative agreements in the takeover of East Germany's banks, the Deutsche Bank and Dresdner Bank would play a central role in financing the restructuring activity in the east. These expectations went largely unfilled, and banks became the targets of intense criticism from all political sides, including the THA.[11]

Scholars are quick to note that the enormous uncertainty surrounding the viability of firms and markets made it difficult for banks to extend credit without government guarantees (Griffin 1994). But the unwillingness of banks to free up investment resources led to a huge shortage of capital and a severe constraint on the recovery of eastern firms. And as it became difficult for firms to recover, the THA's task of selling became even more of a challenge.

A third challenge took the form of the collapse of the Council for Mutual Economic Assistance (COMECON), the Eastern European trade bloc. When COMECON was formally disbanded on June 28, 1991, the attractiveness of East Germany's firms to investors was significantly hurt both by the decline in productivity of the economic entities and by the decline in strategic market importance of East German firms to western investors. Exports had made up 40 percent of East Germany's gross domestic product, and half those goods were sold to eastern European countries, particularly the Soviet Union. Researchers estimate that up to 900,000 jobs were directly or indirectly dependent on exports to the Soviet Union.[12] As economies began to collapse, eastern Europeans struggled to purchase products made in East Germany. Within the first quarter of 1991, exports to the east by East German firms fell by 50 percent (Flassbeck and Scheremet 1992, 289). A further complication was that imports of production supplies from East Bloc countries also dropped by about two thirds from the end of 1989 to the end of 1991. This was triggered partly by a crisis caused by currency conversion and partly by the drop in value of the "transferable ruble" to the deutsch mark that fell nearly 50 percent after conversion. Since

East Germany imported large amounts of production supplies, the effect of the decline was like a collapsing house of cards. Eastern suppliers were going bankrupt, making it difficult for East German firms to continue, which in turn exacerbated the crises in eastern European economies.

A fourth challenge faced by the THA that proved devastating was the decision by the two Germanys to allow restitution claims by groups whose land had been taken away by either the Nazi or Communist regimes.[13] Early in 1990 the East German Communist government compensated only those who stayed in the GDR. Those who illegally emigrated were not offered compensation by the GDR government. The West German government made restitution a priority early in the unification process. This was partly because many Christian Democratic Union and Christian Social Union members had fled East Germany and partly because of the CDU and CSU's anti-communist tradition. On June 15, 1990, East and West Germany issued a joint declaration giving groups the right to make claims.[14] Article 41 of the Unification Treaty transformed the declaration into a guiding legal principle. By 1992, 2.2 million claims were registered seeking restitution. More claims were filed than there were pieces of property to claim (Drost 1993; Hall and Ludwig 1993).

The effect of the law on the development of East Germany's economy was significant. Restitution laws weakened the attractiveness of enterprises to western investors because of the uncertainty that hung over any deal or contract signed by the THA. According to Rohwedder, it led to a paralyzing stranglehold on the East German economy (Sinn and Sinn 1992, 93). More important for East Germans, Article 41 meant that they entered the new Germany with limited property assets. In market economies, title to property serves as one of the important means of attaining credit from lending institutions. As one observer noted, "With titles challenged in drawn-out court cases, what are the chances that residents of East Germany would be able to pool sufficient investment capital to start a business or expand an emerging business on a scale that would allow it to survive the first years of competition?" (Hall and Ludwig 1993, 43).

A further complication to the restitution plan was that it ceded the authority to judge restitution claims to local governments, many of whom lacked the infrastructure to handle the onslaught of claims and lawyers. The situation prompted an economist to write in 1992:

> Natural restitution carried out through the municipal authorities has proved to be a complete failure. By October 1991 only about 3.3 percent of the claims had been settled; 90 percent of the decisions regarding the restitution of firms were being contested and were thus not yet legally valid. The mayor of Leipzig has expressed the fear that, under the present conditions, natural restitution will not be completed for decades (Sinn and Sinn 1992, 83).

In response to these criticisms, the German Bundestag passed the Obstacles Removal Law (*Hemmnisbeseitigungsgesetz*) that amended the Property Law by giving investors a greater set of rights.[15] For example, it gave investors priority over the former owner in the allocation of firms and real estate except in cases where the previous owner could credibly guarantee to undertake an equivalent amount of investment. The impact that the *Hemmnisbeseitigungsgesetz* had was mixed since it continued to give former owners the ability to block the allocation of properties to investors.

A fifth external factor that significantly affected the THA was a series of wage agreements following unification. The strength of West German unions made it possible for them to press for wages high above the value of the output per worker. In 1991 eastern German firms had attained 28 percent of the productivity of their western German counterparts. In 1992 and 1993 the figure had risen to 39 percent and 46 percent, respectively. In March 1991 eastern German metalworkers and managers agreed to achieve wage parity within three years.[16] Eastern German wages rose from 35 percent of western German wages in 1990 on average to more than 65 percent of western wages in 1993.[17]

The result was that the diminishing wage differential between eastern and western German workers undermined any perceived long-term advantage of having a low-wage labor market and lowered the value of firms to investors. George Akerlof and his colleagues (1991) demonstrated that the increased labor costs in firms whose productivity was only a fraction of western German firms meant that only about 8 percent of the industrial work force was employed in firms that could conceivably hold themselves above water. This dynamic made investment in the east even less attractive to potential buyers.

A final factor that influenced the initial pace of privatization was environmental pollution. Environmental liabilities caused investors to be uncertain and reluctant to purchase eastern German firms because contamination is typically extremely costly to clean up. During the summer of 1990, with the passage of the Environmental Union, West Germany's environmental regulatory framework was transferred to East Germany over objections of businesses that argued higher standards would send investors across the Oder River into Eastern Europe. In June 1990 an exemption from any liability for environmental damage occurring before July 1990 was established with the passage of the Environmental Framework Law (*Umweltrahmengesetz*).[18] The legislation allowed the owners of property to apply to state authorities for the resale of inherited liabilities. Under Germany's constitution, assessment and cleanup of contamination falls under the jurisdiction of the state governments. At this point state governments had neither the administrative resources to process applications nor the financial resources to implement a cleanup. The task was therefore delegated to the THA. The agency in turn negotiated the cleanup as part of sales negotiations, paying up to 90 percent of the cleanup costs. The cost was enormous. In 1993 the THA estimated that it had spent more than DM15 billion (roughly $9.15 billion) on environmental payoffs alone.

Like the RTC, a defining characteristic of the THA was that it was an agency designed to address a very different set of problems than the ones it ultimately was forced to confront. The principal architects of the THA expected that it would be a sales agency managed largely with the assistance of the financial institutions. The reality was that the condition of East Germany's economic structures forced the THA to become a redevelopment agency. The THA suddenly became a financing institute charged with supplying funds to more than 8,000 companies.[19] These immense, unanticipated challenges quickly transformed the THA from a production organization into a coping organization, one almost entirely dependent on external sources of expertise to carry out its mission.

IMPACTS ON THE THA AND RTC'S BEHAVIOR

The tasks confronted by the THA and RTC were independent of their administrative characteristics or the decisions made by policymakers concerning how their operations would be structured. Yet the tasks each agency faced had a significant impact on their performance and behavior. The challenges forced both agencies to become coping organizations. The question raised is: How did this shift affect their behavior?

The most dramatic impact was on the decision-making calculus of managers. The task environment faced by the two agencies did not predetermine the outcomes. It did, however, bias the types of outcomes that managers would be predisposed to pursue. The situation was not predetermined. Managers might have selected a different constellation of outputs. However, RTC and THA managers confronted a unique set of incentives that made it far more likely that managers in the American agency would favor easy-to-measure outcomes such as the number of resolutions or asset sales rather than oversight or increased opportunities for minority- and women-owned contractors.

The RTC's monthly newsletter, *RTC Review*, distributed throughout the agency, offers a reliable account of what the organization valued. Three central statistics were featured prominently in every issue: (1) the value of assets sold (during the month and since inception); (2) the recovery on asset reduction (during the month and since inception); and (3) the number of institutions closed (for the month and since inception).[20] These outcomes were the clearest and easiest to measure. Even after the RTC established more formal programs for affordable housing and minority- and women-owned businesses, statistics on the progress of these programs were often not included or mentioned only at the back of the newsletter. Oversight issues also received little attention.

In the THA a similar pattern is explained partially by the coping nature of the organization. The agency focused on what it could easily measure—the numbers of firms and assets sold; the number of jobs guaranteed by buyers; and the amount of investment commitments by buyers. Controls and restructuring received little attention. An internal auditor who had worked previously as a privatization agent in the THA stated frankly that the weak controls within the agency were largely deliberate. The auditor explained: "I believe it was deliberate because one sets priorities. And controls require a long-term plan. One cannot simply build an effective oversight system from one day to the next. And since privatization was set as the primary criteria, one had to let certain things go because of the limited amount of capacity that was possible." He added that while he had in theory a great deal of freedom, the number of firms he had to oversee in practice meant that he was capable of doing only what it took to get the assets sold.

A second insight of Wilson's typology further helps to understand the behavior of the THA and RTC. Wilson notes that coping organizations are more likely to face internal conflict because operators will be driven by the situational imperatives they face while managers are driven by the constraints they face, particularly from politically influential constituencies. Again this dynamic played out in the RTC and the THA.

A third way that tasks influence the behavior and performance of organizations is through the enormous dependence on third parties. As both agencies quickly slipped into coping organizations, their demand for external support grew dramatically. The RTC and THA became enormous consumers of contractual services. As several RTC staff members joked, "The agency became the largest jobs program for accountants and lawyers in America's history." See chapter 3 for a detailed account of the role contractors played in the two agencies.

The heavy reliance on third parties affected the two organizations in several ways. First, as noted earlier, it increased the capacities of the two organizations. Given the enormous and unexpected challenges faced by the RTC and THA, the importance of contractors was immense. Neither agency could have remotely accomplished its task without access to the external expertise. The dependence on third parties was also a constraint because not enough quality contractors were willing to work for the agencies. The market for third-party expertise constrained the agencies' actions. The more the RTC and THA became dependent on third parties for substantive assistance, the more influence third parties had in shaping the perceived purposes of the organizations.

NOTES

1. At the behest of Congress, FSLIC eschewed the up-front cost strategy of liquidation in favor of a cost-deferment plan known as "forbearance," which gave thrifts in financial trouble the opportunity to extend their troubles even deeper. The moral hazard was illustrated by the celebrated cases of Charles

Keating and Michael Milken (Pizzo, Fricker, and Muolo 1989). Forbearance grew during the 1980s. In 1980, during President Ronald Reagan's first term, thrifts shut down by the government had been insolvent for an average of five months. By 1988, during Reagan's last year in office, the FSLIC was keeping thrifts afloat for an average of three years—some as long as ten years. The Congressional Budget Office estimated that the delay in closing failed institutions roughly doubled the ultimate cost of resolving them (CBO 1991). For one of the best accounts of the policies leading up to the collapse see Mark Rom's (1996) work, *Public Spirit in the Thrift Strategy*.

2. Although the agency proclaimed that it would manage and sell $10 billion in assets, it possessed no more than $4.5 billion worth of assets through the third quarter of 1987 (nearly two years into its operation) and sold or collected on only 283 assets (out of 2,700 managed) valued at $774 million (U.S. House 1991, 3).

3. As described in chapter 3, the new tasks were associated with managing and disposing of assets as well as managing conservatorships for a longer period of time than expected and implementing various purchase and assumption deals.

4. According to Rosenblatt and Bates, "Members of Congress who helped write the savings and loan rescue legislation expressed surprise and anger over estimates that the cleanup operation will need an additional $50 or $100 billion" (1989).

5. My understanding of the transfer of financial institutions draws upon the insights and work of several authors, including Deeg (1999); Griffin (1994); Carlin and Richthofen (1995); and Sinn and Sinn (1992).

6. As early as 1910 Rudolf Hilferding developed a theory of big bank power. He argued that the concentration of power over industry in the hands of banks would lead to a capacity to steer the economy and overcome the contradictions that Marx had predicted would destroy the system. Hilferding (1910) wrote: "The bank cannot only extend more credit to a corporation than to an individual entrepreneur, but can also invest a part of its capital in shares for a longer or shorter period. . . . The bank acquires a permanent interest in the corporation, which must now be closely watched to ensure that credit is used for the appropriate purpose" (121–22). Building on Hilferding's work, Alexander Gerschenkron argued that scarce capital, distrust of industrialization, and the sheer size of investment required by late industrialization made the big banks the ideal instruments to guide Germany's rapid industrial development (Gerschenkron 1976). Andrew Shonfield would later use similar arguments to explain Germany's tremendous growth after the Second World War (Shonfield 1969).

7. The heady optimism was captured in an article published in *The Banker* (May 1990, vol. 140) titled "West Germany: Meeting of the ways." The article stated, "With reunification now seemingly inevitable, German banks are leading the way in transplanting the market economy in the east" (61).

8. See Akerlof et al. (1991) for one of the best examinations of the effects that currency union had on East German firms.

9. The number of marks that could be exchanged at a rate of 1:1 was limited to 2,000 for children under age 15, to 4,000 for adults under 60, and to 6,000 for people over 59. Most of the remainder of the money stock was exchangeable at a rate of 2:1, with the exception that money acquired for speculation in the year of unification could be exchanged at 3:1. The black market rate prior to the currency union was about 1 West German Mark to between 7 and 11 East German Marks (Sinn and Sinn 1994, 53).

10. For a good analysis of how old debt impacted East German firms, see Nick (1995).

11. For a discussion of the lack of bank investment in East Germany, see Carlin and Richthofen (1995) and Griffin (1994).

12. This estimate was cited in the journal *Wochenbericht* (21 March 1991, 127).

13. For a good account of the impact of restitution on privatization see Hall and Ludwig (1993); Feddersen (1991); Sinn and Sinn (1992, especially chapter 4). For a complete collection of all related laws and treaties governing the restoration of property from 15 June 1990 to 1991 see Fieberg and Reichenbach (1992). For a discussion of the history behind such claims, see especially Feddersen (1991).

14. See "Gemeinsame Erklärung der Regierungen der Bundesrepublik und der Deutschen Demokratischen Republic zur Regelung offener Vermögensfragen, passed 15 Juni 1990."

15. Gesetz zur Beseitigung von Hemmnissen bei der Privatisierung von Unternehmen und zur Förderung von Investitionen (Obstacle-Removal Law), passed 15 March 1991. Other laws were also passed, including: the Investment Acceleration Law passed on March 22, 1991, creating a streamlined priority procedure for investors; and the Investment Priority Law, passed on July 14, 1992, which stipulated that all restitution claims had to be registered by December 31, 1992. For a discussion see David Southern's (1993) article.

16. Two years after the wage agreement, employers canceled the contracts arguing that the wages would drive them into bankruptcy. The action was followed by a strike that was largely successful for western German unions. The unions ended up securing both significantly higher wages and a large number

of jobs. For an account of the impact of the wage increase see Sinn and Sinn (1992) or the article in the newspaper *Die Welt* (18 March 1993) titled *Deutschland als abschreckendes Beispiel* (Germany as a shocking example).

17. See statistics in appendix of Fischer, Hax, and Schneider (1996). Much of the union's bargaining strength on the issue of wages derived from the belief (held by the Kohl administration and union leadership) that wage parity was crucial to avoid the emergence of a German "Mezzorgiorno." Mezzorgiorno refers to the geographic and economic division within Italy between the more prosperous north and poorer south. For a discussion of the Mezzorgiorno argument see "Noch ein Mezzorgiorno?" *Die Zeit* (November 19, 1993, 11).

18. The legislation was later incorporated into the Unification Treaty and subsequently expanded in the Obstacles-Removal Law passed in March 1991.

19. In the first months alone, over 90 percent of all firms required some immediate form of liquidity. From an interview with Wolfgang Schöde, the THA press speaker, cited in Freese (1995).

20. The recovery on asset reductions figure represents the percentage of the book value recovered through the sale. However, as noted earlier, "book value" is not a reliable variable. Assets were reassessed a number of times after the loan (for which the asset served as collateral) was issued. Even once a thrift was taken over, officials report that assets were reappraised, lowering the book value.

6

The Impact of National Institutional Environments

The Resolution Trust Corporation (RTC) and the Treuhand-anstalt (THA) were state organizations engaged in the regulation and creation of property rights. The process involved not simply the agencies, or a set of political principals, or even their respective task environments. It also involved what Kenneth Dyson (1992) describes as "institutionalized governance arrangements," macro-level structures that determine how societies are governed.

Governance refers here to the way a state seeks to control the behavior of societal actors in order to make those actors conform to the state's policy goals (Giamo 1994, 7). States rely upon a set of regulatory institutions merged with a regulatory culture to govern.[1] While the RTC and THA shared certain administrative characteristics, they operated in different countries where the regulatory institutions and regulatory cultures associated with the state, society, and bureaucracies differed considerably. These differences matter a great deal in understanding the RTC and THA because governance arrangements mediate the impact that factors such as administrative characteristics have on policy outcomes (see Dyson 1992; Thelen, Steimo, and Longstreth 1993). It is this interactive dynamic between agencies and their environment that triggers the question at the center of this chapter: What was the impact of the institutional environment in determining the outcomes of the RTC and the THA in carrying out their mandates? This is a difficult puzzle that resists simple solutions. Comparative political economists have developed a rich understanding of how governing arrangements, such as an independent central bank, centralized unions, or a parliamentary system impact the preferences, behaviors, and incentives of policy actors who, in turn, adopt policies that yield certain outcomes (Hollingsworth, Boyer, and Streeck 1997; Iversen, Pontusson, and Soskice 2000; Iversen 1999; Crouch and Streeck 1997). Noticeably absent from the literature, however, is an examination of the role played by the administrative structures of state organizations. Bureaucracies are left unexamined. By contrast, public management and administration scholars, particularly those who work on implementation, have contributed enormously to our understanding of factors that impact a policy after the legislation is passed (Pressman and Wildavsky 1973; Ripley and Franklin 1986; Mazmanian and Sabatier 1983). Yet this literature has largely neglected the institutional environment within which agencies are embedded.

The RTC and THA present an opportunity to examine the interactive effects of administration and institutional environment on bureaucratic outcomes. Both agencies had similar administrative characteristics that, as described in chapter 3, contrasted sharply with classic or traditional public administration. These breaks with tradition, however, occurred in different institutional contexts. As a result, the impact of the market-based administrative characteristics shared by the RTC and THA turn out to be more extreme in corporatist or "cooperationist" settings like Germany than in more neo-liberal or "adversarial" settings that exist in the United States.[2]

This chapter explores why and how institutional environments matter by first articulating the differences in the U.S. and German governing environments. The next two sections describe how the THA and RTC conformed to or broke with those traditions. The chapter concludes with a brief discussion of how governance structures on a macro level help account for the agencies' outputs.

NATIONAL INSTITUTIONS THAT MATTER

Kenneth Dyson's (1992) work underscores three types of macro-governance structures important for understanding national differences in the fabric and implementation of regulation. The governance

Table 6.1
Comparison of German and U.S. Governance Structures

Governance Structure	Germany	United States
State Culture	State viewed as important in ensuring unity and order in national life Based upon the idea of *Ordnungspolitik,* a Hegelian understanding of the state	State viewed as a necessary evil Based on the idea of a Hobbesian understanding of the state
State Structures	Decentralized but interlocking	Fragmented and lacking coordination
Market/Societal Culture	Social market economy: a view of society that is free and competitive but where the state has a role in maintaining social values and ensuring competition	Markets viewed as "natural" Any state intervention in markets viewed primarily as detrimental to liberty, efficiency, and productivity
Market/Societal Structures	Neocorporatist structures	Pluralist and adversarial
Bureaucratic Culture	*Rechtstaat:* culture that rules by law	Professional, apolitical, and business-like; a product of the progressive reforms of the early 20th century
Bureaucratic Structures	Hierarchical and independent of external actors An administrative process that is structured and relatively closed	Hierarchical and dependent on governmental participants such as other agencies, Congress, and the administration Also dependent on participants outside of government such as interest groups An open and unstructured administrative process
Form of Political Control and Oversight	The product of "private-interest government"; societal governance backed by state authority	Rules-based oversight carried out by state actors

structures are historical legacies that include: the meanings and structures of the state; the meanings and structures of society and markets; and the meanings and structures of public bureaucracies. Table 6.1

presents a summary comparison across the United States and Germany for each factor and the impact each has on the nature of political control and oversight of societal actors.

Contrasting Meanings and Structures of the State

In Germany, the meaning and structure of the state are firmly rooted in the concept *Ordnungspolitik*. Although its roots are in the authoritarian *Obrigkeitsstaat* of Bismarckian Prussia, *Ordnungspolitik* refers to more than simply preserving order. It is a concept that emphasizes the interdependence of the state and society. Smyser (1993) describes it as "a heuristic concept: All things are part of a whole, and must be evaluated in terms of their effects on the whole. All elements shape the whole, and are in turn shaped by it. All depend on it, as it depends on them. This is what *Ordnung* expresses and preserves" (133). At the root of *Ordnungspolitik* is, therefore, the sense of the importance of unity and order in national life.

In addition, *Ordnungspolitik* is rooted in a particular type of active state. It was conceived in terms of a Hegelian vision of an integrated and organized civil society; "estates" firmly lodged under the paternal tutelage of the state. During the nineteenth century, *Ordungspolitik* complemented Bismarck's authoritarian and paternalistic regime in which the state preserved order by regulating civil arrangements (e.g., the iron and rye coalition) and fostering a "public-regarding" form of obligation among societal actors (determined by a state bureaucracy) that superseded parochial interests. Despite skepticism toward a strong state that followed the Second World War, Lehmbruch (1990) notes that the concept of *Ordnungspolitik* became ingrained as a state ideology early on. Regulatory culture, he writes, tended, "to petrify into ideological sediments that guide much of the interpretation of later crises and structural adaptation" (20).

The German federalist structure set up after 1945 became more decentralized and fragmented. The centralized state was replaced by a variety of power centers including political parties, independent agencies such as the Bundesbank and, most important, state governments. The nature of *Ordnungspolitik,* however, and the work of the *Ordo-liberals* in the Erhard regime contributed to an elaborate nexus of interdependent relationships that raised the level of coordination and policy coherence.

Several important changes followed from this. The federal government was reduced to a number of small ministries dependent upon other governmental and societal actors for information and expertise. Organized societal actors such as business (trade associations) and labor (unions) stepped in to fill the power vacuum left by the central state.[3] The increase in power centers increased the number of access points for influencing policy. The increase in power sources did not lead to fragmentation (as a Hobbesian conception of the state would predict). Instead, decentralization led to an elaborate system of coordination or "interlocking politics" (*Politikverflechtung*) based on consensual-managerial arrangements in which actors were made to have a strong stake in making policy work (Mayntz and Scharpf 1975).[4]

Whereas the German state was conceived in a Hegelian vision, the United States is a product of Hobbes's Leviathan. In the Hobbesian world, the state does not seek order among organized interests but preserves individual freedom by remaining outside society, allowing individuals to pursue their own interests. Although the structure of the state has evolved over time, the belief in an unobtrusive or "referee"-type state has dominated the country's regulatory culture. The battle between Madison and his notion of a minimalist state and Hamilton and his concept of a vigorous state was ultimately won by Madison.

Such a view of the state was complemented by two sets of institutional structures: the federalist system and the electoral model. Like postwar Germany, the American state has traditionally been fragmented and decentralized. Government is divided in many ways including horizontally (through divided government) and vertically (through the separation of state and federal powers). During its first 150 years, the federal government, like the postwar German government, was extremely small. Regulations were largely implemented by states. Even today, 130 years after the American Civil War and two decades after massive federal Civil Rights initiatives, state and local governments comprise nearly two-thirds of all government involvement in the economy.

America's majoritarian, single-district electoral model further complements an anti-statist regulatory culture by expanding access to the system in two ways. First, the role of elections in American democracy is to hold lawmakers individually accountable. The politician is conceived as a delegate rather than as a trustee of the public interest. Second, the lack of strong ideological political parties reinforces the centrality of the individual candidate and further increases societal access to the system. Parties in the American electoral model can assist candidates but are largely impotent to shield a candidate from a hostile electorate. This is in stark contrast to the German model where a politician like Helmut Kohl may lose his district election yet still hold the country's highest office.

The American combination of federalist and electoral structures alongside an antistatist regulatory culture produced a system extremely open and accessible to societal interests. It is a system in which societal groups with the greatest resources and concentrated constituencies are likely to receive disproportional representation; where the salience of the delegate politician, weak party structure, and accessible policy-making environment are achieved at the expense of policy coordination and effectiveness.

In addition to the structures and meaning associated with the state, national differences over the meaning and structure of society and markets are also important.

Contrasting Meanings and Structures of Society and Markets

In Germany a crucial component of the governance arrangements that emerged following the Second World War was the combination of the development of neocorporatist institutions and the normative concept of the economy based on free-market principles and social values known as "social market economy" (*Sozialmarkt-wirtschaft*). The former reflects the institutional structures, whereas the latter reflects the meaning society attributes to the economy. Combined, the two form an important synthesis within which policy coalitions function.

Corporatism in Germany incorporates societal or interest groups directly into the decision-making machinery on such issues as industrial policy, social welfare, pensions, and economic planning. It is a model of what Streeck and Schmitter (1985) call "private-interest government" in which the state plays an important role in setting the arena in which societal actors regulate themselves (Campbell and Lindberg 1991).[5] This is often highly adversarial and contentious. It is also time-consuming since traditional adversaries (e.g., labor unions and business associations) are formally institutionalized into the policy process while their ability to exit or opt out is limited. At the same time, regulations are more stable since actors (even those affected negatively by the regulation) not only share a stake in the success but are also held responsible for its failure. Moreover, rules can be more flexibly applied—what Benz and Goetz (1996) term a "negotiated order"—than in the United States.

Such flexibility is made possible by the fact that opposing societal groups regulate themselves, their participation is institutionalized and sanctioned by the state, and as a result, a higher level of trust exists between groups affected by public policies. Although animosity between groups like management and labor may be just as high in Germany as in the United States, "private-interest government" makes a more flexible governing policy possible.[6]

At the same time during the postwar era, a faction of neoliberals referred to as *Ordo-liberals* and led by Alfred Müller-Armack established the idea of a social market economy. In contrast to laissez-faire Austrian liberals such as Von Hayek, the *Ordo-liberals* conceived of an economic order based on the dynamics of a competitive market but bound by the state. They understood state regulation as necessary to ensure competition and prevent the debilitating cartels that had undermined the Weimar Republic. At the same time, given their experience with German authoritarianism, the *Ordo-liberals* favored separation and decentralization of state powers, the establishment of independent agencies such as the Bundesbank, and the regulation of broad political and societal consensus. This view contrasts sharply with the meaning and structure of society and markets that developed in the United States.

Early on in its development, the United States embraced a strong belief in the "naturalness" of markets and sought to maintain the autonomy of markets from the state. For example, Donald Kettl (1993) argues, "Americans have long had a reverence for private markets to match their dislike of public power" (1). In line with the laissez-faire teachings of Adam Smith, David Ricardo, and later neoclassical scholars, the market is treated as a natural phenomenon: the institutional embodiment of an aggregate of individual self-interests. Any suggested curtailment or modification of a "free" market is equated with preventing natural forces from operating freely. Andrew Shonfield (1969, 289) describes "the naturalness of private enterprise" in the United States as an important ideological marker for policymakers.

Of course the notion of free markets is not an inherently American concept. What is interesting about the American case, however, is that until the twentieth century the free market meant not only a separation of state and society but a lack of much private governance structure within the economy. Until the end of the nineteenth century government had neither much of a role in the market nor any "rules governing behavior among competitors" (Fligstein 1990, 12). The dominant strategy among economic actors until the late nineteenth century was to control the competition through any legal or illegal means necessary.

In response to economic crises and destructive competition among private actors, efforts were made to increase government's role and capacity to intervene in markets in limited ways. The Progressive Era from 1902 to 1914 and the New Deal from 1933 to 1938 saw the state take a more interventionist role in markets, often to preserve the competitiveness of markets.[7] In the 1960s and early 1970s social and environmental activists attempted to alter the relationship between business and the state, which resulted in a number of regulations and interventionist policies. By the 1980s and 1990s business made an impressive comeback. Jeffrey Hart (1992) notes that business power, with the exception of environmental policies of the 1970s, has dominated vis-à-vis government and labor. Public administration scholars note the growing dependence of government on business. Kettl (1993) writes: "Government's growing reliance on its partners in the private sectors means that its success . . . has come to depend in large part on how well those partners perform. . . . In its eager pursuit of competitive prescription, government has . . . too often surrendered its basic policymaking power" (14).

In addition to the meaning and structures associated with a country's society and market, a final set of macro-governance arrangements involves the structure and meaning of public bureaucracies, the executive arms of the state.

Contrasting Meanings and Structures of Bureaucracy

In Germany these cultural and structural elements are embodied in the nature of the *Rechtsstaat* and the development of bureaucratic structures after the Second World War. Developed under Bismarck's reign, the *Rechtsstaat* refers to the legal culture that defines the state in terms of its laws. It became a powerful ideology that served the interests of the administrative elite because it imbued the bureaucracy with tremendous autonomy and made it the official guardian of the public good.[8] The fact that concepts that framed the *Rechtsstaat* were rooted not in society but in the state (or its surrogate, the prince) helps explain why, despite the regime changes in 1918, 1933, and 1945, the civil service system in Germany remained largely untouched and provided a sense of stability amid political and economic chaos. The development of laws governing justice and public administration were made the domain of a cadre of experts, primarily lawyers. Thus, in the state ministries experts were the authors of the law that they and their subordinates were responsible for applying. It was this bureaucracy that Max Weber, the intellectual father of public administration, observed and described at the turn of the century in Prussia (Gerth and Mills 1958, 3–70).

Two additional factors reinforced the discretion and autonomy of civil servants. First, by the end of the nineteenth century Germany and its states had become quite large. Prussia, in particular, stretched more than 1,000 kilometers between its borders. To accommodate the enormous heterogeneity of social and economic conditions, rules had to be flexible. Seibel and Lavenex (1997) write that legal rules could be neither too specialized nor too rigid if they were to remain workable at the decentralized levels. The state of law was structured around indefinite legal concepts and general clauses. Civil servants were ceded discretion that allowed them effectively to tailor rules to particular settings.

Second, the civil service system was the model for the private business sector, which gave public organizations and their practices a high degree of legitimacy.[9] White collar employees at the turn of the twentieth century were in fact referred to as "private bureaucrats" (Tolliday and Zeitlin 1986). The reason is not difficult to understand. Not only was the public sector better organized and better trained, it had remained fairly stable during economic and political turmoil, a factor that remains in the collective memory of Germans. Bureaucratic discretion thus allowed civil servants to make the most of their expertise.

Finally, structural changes affecting the bureaucracy that occurred following the Second World War eroded bureaucratic independence. Parties could, for example, take over certain bureaucracies as the Liberal Party took control of the Ministry of Economics. The earlier meaning of strong independent bureaucracy à la Weber was thus tempered by the distribution of power to political parties. At the same time, the development of the "departmental principle"(*Ressort-prinzip*) following the war actually affirmed bureaucratic autonomy. The *Ressortprinzip*, based on Article 65 of the Basic Law, established the independence of each government ministry. It mandated that each federal minister run his or her department independent of other departments and build up in-house expertise. Ironically, under the *Ressortprinzip*, bureaucratic independence was further strengthened by the role of political parties in making certain agencies "off-limits" to other parties (Lehmbruch 1992, 37).

In contrast to Germany, America's civil service profession was born less out of a need for skilled workers than as a reaction to an executive's desire to secure a political base of support. As Stephen Skowronek (1982) put it, "The [U.S.] merit system was born a bastard in the party state" (67). Initially governed by a small social elite class in the eighteenth century, the American federal civil service by the nineteenth century under President Andrew Jackson expanded greatly to meet the needs of a country growing geographically and economically. Rather than developing a trained civil service, however, Jackson pioneered a system for solidifying his political power by filling federal positions with allies. The so-called "spoils system" exchanged political loyalty for careers in the federal government.[10] By the end of the century the spoils system had filtered down to state and municipalities. City mayors became small kings or "bosses" by expanding and filling government jobs with immigrants who had to promise only to lend their support at the next election. Bureaucratic authority was based less on expertise than on being able to solidify a base of power within the agency or the external political system through patronage. In response to the widespread use of patronage to fill the public ranks, the U.S. Congress passed the Pendleton Act in 1883, which institutionalized the present day civil service. It created an independent executive agency, the Civil Service Commission, to protect federal employees from arbitrary removal, guarantee lifetime tenure, prevent compulsory financial contributions to political parties, and screen applicants for federal jobs by administering competitive examinations.[11] Although the system was based on the British model, these protective features resembled the Prussian and later

German civil service system. Unlike in Germany, however, the public sector was not the model for the private but rather the other way around. Civil society was well developed long before the civil service became professionalized. When public administration scholars like Woodrow Wilson looked across the continent, they saw the model through very different lenses.

Certain elements akin to the Prussian system of public administration, such as a merit system, bureaucrats ruled by law, specialization, centralized hierarchies, and clear lines of authority, were embraced by the Americans. Bureaucratic discretion, however, and the political activity of bureaucrats violated the politics/administration dichotomy that Woodrow Wilson and others believed in so fervently.

In contrast to the indefinite general clauses of the *Rechtsstaat*, the code American administrators have followed is highly specific and extremely rigid, reflecting both the adversarial regulatory environment and concern about local interests superceding national ones. Weak political parties, the dominance of interest groups, skepticism toward government, and the absence of "cooperative" power-sharing arrangements have meant that government in general and public bureaucracies in particular are held accountable through rules that specify in detail bureaucratic behavior.

While Germany's civil service principles remained largely untouched, the American model of the public sector has been fiercely criticized from the time it was developed to the present. Attacks have prompted numerous reforms. Critics pointed out early on that the politics/administrative dichotomy was empirically incorrect, largely untenable, and often not particularly desirable.[12] Others argued that the classical approach was extremely undemocratic. The criticism was further fueled by Franklin Roosevelt taking control of many bureaucracies that had been in the hands of various leaders of Congress (Meriam 1939). Still others expressed strong concern about the incentives of public bureaucrats and the absence of competition or markets. Robert Merton (1940) argued that Weberian bureaucracy led to a trained incapacity among employees: excessive prudence, over-conformity to rules, and ritualized discipline. Scholars pointed out that without market mechanisms the performance indicators used by the public sector were excessively vague and difficult to assess.

In short, German and American bureaucracies embraced important "classic" or Weberian similarities such as a standardized merit system, clear hierarchies, specialization, and an emphasis on promotion through training and socialization. Yet there are important differences in the way bureaucracies are perceived and structured that affect their operations. First, in both countries, bureaucrats are expected to be professionals who reach decisions based on their expertise. In Germany this means that although individuals are expected to implement the law and make decisions based on professional norms, bureaucrats themselves are not expected to remain apolitical. As political parties came to play a more dominant role in managing bureaucracies after the Second World War, party identification among even top-level bureaucrats became common. Derlien (1996) notes that it is viewed as an advantage in developing good policy.[13] Civil servants may also join a union and bargain collectively through a union, but their right to strike is not automatically recognized. By stark contrast, the political activity of American civil servants is severely curtailed. Rules such as the Hatch Act restrict federal and state employees from participating in any political campaigns.

Second, discretion among German civil servants is far greater than among their American counterparts. Accountability in both models relies on training and socialization but in the U.S. case, standardized rules and regulations also play a significant role in holding the actions of bureaucrats in check. By contrast, Germany's corporatist system manages oversight through a different system. The development of a corporatist system of interest mediation after 1945 accomplished a more flexible system of accountability structured around the institutionalization of affected actors into the policy process. Despite their differences, these actors share a stake in the policies' outcome.

HOW THE THA CIRCUMVENTED GERMANY'S REGULATORY INSTITUTIONS

The formal and informal rules that guide West German public administration are premised on the existence of several important factors: (1) state and local governmental infrastructures developed to take over the majority of the public administrative responsibilities

(Benz 1989); (2) civil society with organized para-public institutions and intermediary associations capable of taking on the responsibilities of private governance (Streeck and Schmitter 1985); (3) a highly trained civil service (Derlien 1992; Mayntz and Derlien 1989); and (4) a well-developed political culture committed to the principles of representative democracy, social market economy, and private enterprise. None of these elements existed in the system that created the THA, nor were they present in the early period following unification.

As a result, Wolfgang Seibel writes that the process of unification carried out largely by the THA could not operate within the two institutional pillars of West Germany's policy system: federalism and corporatism. Seibel (1992) writes:

> The assets of the West German system of government—federalism and corporatism—unfortunately do not transfer to the political management of unification. They are not transferable because the state structure and the social makeup of East Germany do not provide the context in which they might flourish.
>
> Fifty-six years of totalitarianism have eliminated the intermediary organizations that prevailed in West Germany. . . . Civil society has been almost completely destroyed in East Germany. Although voluntary associations have mushroomed since the fall of 1989, they do not provide the established and extensive base required for the corporatist style of political decision making. . . . There is no culture of cooperation between business and government. The municipalities do not have appropriate mechanisms to respond to issues raised by businesses. The situation makes urban and regional development more government-centered and technocratic than it ever was in West Germany. . . . Because East Germany lacks a tradition of private enterprise, the central government must assume a dominant role in economic modernization. And it must do so without the corporatism that guides the policy making in West Germany (194).

As a product of East Germany, the THA did not correspond to West Germany's system of governance. Seibel argues that the overwhelming imperative to move quickly and flexibly after the fall of the Berlin Wall in 1989 required the new unified government to adopt unusual bureaucratic structures. In its final form, the THA was neither West nor East but a hybrid of systems. Following unification the agency incorporated elements of both governing legacies.

At the national level, the THA adopted certain aspects of West Germany's federalist and corporatist model while omitting others. As noted above, central features of the German system include overlapping federal and state jurisdiction in the policymaking process and the ceding of administrative responsibilities to state and local governments. During the initial phase of the THA's development, the Federal Republic's interlocking negotiating system was bypassed. Policymakers argued that this was partly done in order to act swiftly (Lehmbruch 1991). The newly formed eastern state governments also lacked the organization, capacity, and personnel needed to take on the important responsibilities of restructuring and privatization (Seibel 1992).

Regardless of the reasons, THA activities largely circumvented state and local governments. This action worried some who viewed it as a way for the Kohl administration to increase the power and role of the federal government at the expense of state governments. Roland Czada (1996a) writes:

> At issue here were both the political and fiscal status of the Federal government vis-à-vis what were now 16 Länder (states) and the horizontal redistribution of revenues between the old and new Länder. The THA, directly subordinate to the Federal government, played a decisive role in this respect, since it was confronted by tasks that fell under the jurisdiction of the new Länder, notably . . . regional structural development policy. . . . The situation in 1990 gave rise to concerns about the possibility of greater centralization in intergovernmental relations.

The concerns were assuaged in part by Detlev Rohwedder's public declarations of independence from the Bonn government (Czada 1996b). In addition, as eastern German states developed their infrastructure and political muscle, the THA incrementally incorporated them into the decision-making process, institutionalized agency-state coordination, and made concessions to state governments in a number of important geographic and sectoral areas. Seibel describes the process as the coopting of state governments.[14]

Despite these initiatives by the German agency, the structure of authority and responsibility in the THA deviated from Germany's traditional federalist policy system. The federal agency continued to preserve veto power over privatization and restructuring decisions.

State governments participated in the decision-making process, were kept informed of negotiations, and later participated financially in salvaging certain key industries. Policies, however, were implemented unilaterally by the THA and its surrogate private sector employees, not by state or local governments.

A similar story applies to unions. The system of elite bargaining at the national level between the federal government, business peak associations, and centralized unions was largely circumvented during the construction of the agency's initial structure. West German business elites were included in the planning and strategy that went into the West German adaptation of the THA, whereas labor was excluded.[15] The decision to jettison the stockholding company model was based largely on a desire on the part of the THA's leadership and West German administration to limit union involvement (Kemmler 1994). An article titled "A Bureaucracy Sells the East German Economy" (trans.), written by Walter Süss (1992) and published by the German political paper Das Parlament (20 March 1992, 3), noted, "The internal governing structure of the Anstalt was developed by the Munich-based consulting company, Berger. This plan was modified in only one way: the adoption of the legally mandated stockholding company structure was renounced. It would have meant among other things that, based on German law, labor would have had codetermination rights at the central level."

As national trade unions began to organize more workers in the east and increase the pressure on the government, the THA incrementally incorporated unions into the decision-making process, granting labor representatives four seats on the THA's supervisory board. The agency took steps to institutionalize greater agency-union coordination, particularly in structuring labor force reductions and job creation programs. On April 13, 1991, the THA reached an agreement with the Federation of German Trade Unions (Deutscher Gewerkschaftsbund) and the German Union for Employees (Deutsche Angstellten-Gewerkschaft) that created a framework for the allocation of severance pay. Up to that point, each firm had reached its own settlement agreement. The April 13 agreement gave the THA what it wanted—industry-wide collective bargaining. It also indirectly strengthened the fledgling eastern German employers association.[16] In July further negotiations between the federal government, the

THA, state governments, trade unions, and business associations resulted in the THA's acquiescence to union demands for job creation programs. An agreement signed on July 17, 1991, resulted in a formal framework between trade unions, employers federations, and the THA that was the basis for the creation of so-called "Companies for Job Development, Employment, and Structural Development" (*Gesellschaften zur Arbeitsförderung, Beschäftigung, und Strukturentwicklung* or ABS for short). These were temporary job maintenance "companies" funded partly by the THA, state governments, and the federal government.

A former staff person to the THA Supervisory Board and executive committee member in IG Metall said that the role of unions was limited but that there was little they could do. The influence of unions at the national level was "informal rather than functional," meaning unions could exercise leverage by releasing information about closures to external actors and by carefully choosing the battles they fought. He said:

> The influence was very limited from the beginning. The supervisory board had twenty-four members, only four of whom were trade union representatives. They were given the right to participate and vote. In other words, like the other members of the committee unions, they weren't involved in the activities documented in the files. The committee's function was largely one of accompaniment. It was promptly informed about privatizations and received the confidential documentation. Members could develop a sense of what the THA thought about the asset and what they would do. However, in the privatization operation, the unions had little to no influence.
>
> We of course voted, and in many cases we shared the interests of the state governments that were also represented on the board. This faction would often collide with the interests of capital and the federal government. However, we achieved consensus in many areas because it was a longer term process. You had to target your criticism carefully and vote carefully because you knew that you needed a majority to secure the types of policies you wanted. With the exception of certain industries, such as steel, machine building, and chemicals, there were rarely confrontations.

The union official noted that the unions were far more flexible and willing to compromise on the Supervisory Board than is common in the old Federal Republic, adding:

> Our willingness and ability to compromise was stretched to its limits. . . . We
> accepted compromises because the political situation was such that our abil-
> ity to exercise leverage, namely through strikes, was severely curtailed.
>
> The problem was of course that the influence mechanisms were strictly
> informal, not in the rules. The unions were never incorporated in the
> decision-making process. . . . The fear that another strike would break out
> was strong enough to make the THA in the large privatizations take into
> account the union's interests. But in the end, it was the THA's signature
> on the privatization deal, not the union's.

The union official readily acknowledged that the unions were
coopted into the process through a set of compromises and concessions, but he asked what the alternative would have been:

> IG Metall had three or four job maintenance projects that it wanted to
> make sure were passed. Had it not agreed to privatization deals the THA
> would not have agreed to support the union's agenda.
>
> We were of course bought off by these ABM companies. Had there been
> other buyers interested in purchasing the firms things would have been
> very different. However, you must not forget that the THA was not a cor-
> poratist institution. Formally it may have looked like a corporatist institu-
> tion but factually it was not. We were constantly faced at the firm level with
> the argument from management that we, the unions, voted for the priva-
> tization in the Supervisory Board. And then the members would say,
> "How could you vote for this?" I returned the question and asked, "What
> choice did we have?"

The pattern of initial resistance, followed by protest and finally
incremental compromise, was a THA trademark. Although it operated as a closed federal entity (a legacy of East Germany), it nevertheless begrudgingly adopted elements of West Germany's policy
system. However, the compromises never undermined the THA's
decision-making power over the privatization of firms. State governments were given greater information. Unions were extended a role
in job maintenance programs. But the decision and process of privatization remained steadfastly in the hands of a single federal agency.
This was even more apparent at the branch and firm level.

While the national office engaged in incremental and often symbolic steps to increase the involvement and participation of unions and
state governments, interviews with THA employees at the branches,
union representatives at firms, and firm managers paint a different

picture at the level where the majority of the privatizations and restructurings were implemented.

The March 15, 1991, agreement between the THA and the state governments led to a THA directive creating fifteen economic cabinets (*Treuhand Wirtschaftskabinette*), advisory boards in the branch offices that were constructed, according to the directive, to "bring about accord with the political, economic, and societal forces of the region." Czada notes that the composition of the boards differed between regions. In some branches such as Chemnitz, Cottbus, and Dresden, industry was dominant. In other offices, such as Leipzig and Frankfurt/Oder, trade unions were strong. Still other branches, such as Erfurt, had churches play a prominent role on the boards. Table 6.2 provides a breakdown of the composition of the boards.

What is interesting about the economic cabinets is how small of a role they seem to have played in the decision-making calculus of THA employees and firm managers charged with privatizing, overseeing, and implementing the restructuring proposals. When asked about the factors that influence their action, not a single employee at the branch office or central office mentioned unions or local governments. The

Table 6.2
Representation of the THA's Fifteen Regional Branch Office Advisory Boards

Organization Represented	No. Represented
Industry, chambers of commerce	45 (33%)
Local governments	28 (20%)
Trade unions	18 (13%)
State governments	14 (10%)
Churches	14 (10%)
Agriculture	9 (7%)
Citizen action groups	9 (7%)
Total	137 (100%)

Cited in Czada (1996b, 105).

The source of the data is the THA office in Bonn, appendix to the report, "Co-operation between Länder, the federal Government and the THA" (November 28, 1991).

typical response to questions about the lack of union involvement was relief. The statement by a privatization agent, who worked in the Leipzig branch office for two years before transferring to the central office, captures best the sentiments of employees in the agency:

> What role did the unions play in my privatization activities? None, thank God! In structuring deals or overseeing the restructuring plans of firms I did not pay much attention to the unions. I sometimes had fifty firms to privatize. There was no way to incorporate them into the decision-making process, nor did I see a need to. The concept used to be different. Modrow wanted the THA to be structured into several stockholding companies. And the supervisory boards of these companies would have consisted of politicians, unions, and former firms. If that had happened, the Federal Republic would now be completely broke. And we have Rohwedder to thank for the fact that he vigorously opposed this decision. He did it and then received protection from Kohl and the CDU because even they could smell danger. We would not have privatized anything. The goal of these people was to restructure, not privatize.

Three features are striking in the statement made by the privatization agent: first, his view that involving unions would have impeded privatization comes across clearly. Second, it is clear that the agent operated with a great deal of discretion. Had he wanted to, he could have incorporated unions or other actors into the decision-making process. Finally, the pressure to privatize, stemming from the large portfolio he had, also contributed to his reluctance to seek additional input from outside actors.

An assistant to Birgit Breuel during the time she was responsible for overseeing the branch offices articulated the role of unions:

> Unions were basically handed the privatization decision. But listen. If I'm the owner of a company and I want the firm to follow a particular course, then I will either hire a GF that will do this, or I'll get the *Aufsichtsrat* [supervisory board] to get rid of the guy. If I decide to sell the firm, there's nothing they have to say about it. It's my firm.

He summarized labor's influence by saying, "Labor had a de jure say in the process but de facto not. Labor decided who would get fired and how the restructuring would occur. However, the THA executive was charged with the sale of the property. To do it differently would have taken too much time." Another privatization agent made the point even more clearly:

> Politically, I'm generally opposed to the politics that unions carry out. However, the eastern unions forced me to reconsider my position. . . . They acted surprisingly pragmatic when they had to. Of course they never participated in the privatization or restructuring decisions. Never. However, we did consult with them and they played an important role in the distribution of the social plan money. . . . Of course we couldn't have included the unions in the privatization decision. We had to make decisions quickly. If the unions had been involved, the investors would have jumped ship.

Reports by THA workers were confirmed by union representatives in the THA firms as well as by branch managers. In the case of a large electrical company privatized in 1992, a union representative who served as the head of one of the works councils noted that unions could make a difference but they had to play a proactive role in ensuring their voice was heard. He said:

> The role of unions was limited, to say the least. The works council was never addressed by the THA. The THA was more than willing to talk to the works council but it never came the other way. The only time the unions were incorporated was in the case of mass layoffs. At that point, the THA would say, we'll give you a certain amount per worker and then unions, and employers could work out how it should be divided. The unions were incorporated in the design of the "*Sozial Plan.*" But the THA set the limit on what it would give, and it basically let the individual plants work out how they wanted it divided.

The union representative noted that the THA privatization agents had a great deal of freedom. They were given complete power over how to deal with a particular company. And he stressed that most agents were relatively open to unions:

> For all practical purposes, the works councils did not have any rights with respect to the privatization decision. They did, however, exert influence in the sense that they could make the THA worker aware of what was going on. They were also able to find out information. In this sense they added a level of transparency that made a difference in the privatization process.

214

A privatization agent and auditor said, "Unions were often the fire alarms. They often had a different idea about the firm than management. They could tip off the THA concerning a problem in the numbers."

A THA manager, who also served on two supervisory boards, was quite frank about the role he understood unions to have. He said that unions did not play a role either in the sale or the management of the firm. He was quite critical of the participation of national unions on the firm's supervisory board, saying that they were more interested in establishing the same labor rights in East Germany than in helping the firm. As far as management was concerned, he said unions played little or no role.

An important point raised by union representatives as well as in scholarly writings is that the lack of union involvement was not just a result of the THA's reluctance but also a factor of the underdeveloped nature of unions in the east. Although labor laws applied to eastern Germany following unification, many of the newly formed works councils did not know the laws and had no experience in their application. At the same time, unions were confronting the far more pressing problems associated with massive layoffs. The union representative said, "The kinds of layoffs we faced would have caused a crisis for any well-established West German union. Now add to that an enormous uncertainty about the future of our plant and that neither we nor the firm's management knew what the laws were." As Seibel (1992) notes, the prerequisites for an active role for unions at the firm had not yet been fully established.

Several conclusions emerge from the THA's experience. The agency clearly circumvented the traditional model of policymaking by limiting the role that unions and state and local governments played in the privatization process. This was particularly the case at the level where restructuring and privatization decisions were made. Whereas state governments and unions were given concessions and limited representation and participation at the national level, at the branch offices and firms themselves the THA operated unilaterally with a great deal of discretion. That is not to say that unions and state government did not play a role. Unions were active in negotiating for and dividing up severance pay, while state governments were often involved in establishing early warning systems that might prevent the closure of a firm. In addition, both unions and state governments were successful in preserving certain industries, notably the chemical and shipbuilding sectors. However, the traditional cooperative arrangements that ensure not just a flexible implementation of rules but also a unique form of oversight were absent.

RTC CONFORMS TO THE INSTITUTIONAL ENVIRONMENT

Whereas the THA was created by one regime and implemented by another, the RTC suffered no such institutional schizophrenia. The implementation of FIRREA was strongly imprinted with an American style of policymaking. Recall again that in contrast to Germany, the traditional form of governance in the United States includes: (1) a federal apparatus that typically plays a direct role in governing society; (2) high levels of adversarialism and confrontation reflected in the prevalent use of the courts in the policy process; and finally (3) oversight and accountability typically established through detailed rules and procedures that are applied uniformly ensuring that the Hobbesian state is kept in check. Despite administrative characteristics that deviated from the traditional public bureaucracy, the RTC conformed to an American style of governance.

First, the RTC as a federal entity operated unilaterally in shaping markets and creating assets. State and local governments played a minimal role in the implementation of the RTC's policies. Despite an enormous impact on the regional economic development of a community, RTC employees in the national, regional, and field offices, as well as managing agents, uniformly noted that they did not consult with local or state government. Some managing agents noted that local and regional governments were sometimes an annoyance. Others saw it as an accomplishment that they were able to avoid such "political" influences. The statement quoted earlier by the sales director in Dallas captures the sentiment: "I didn't solicit any advice from local governments. Today in business there's more a trend toward making decisions through committee. We elected to make our decision without the input of local government. Sometimes you just don't want ten people at the table when three will do."

Societal groups, such as real estate interests, affordable housing advocates, and representatives of minority- and women-owned businesses were represented on advisory boards. Although advisory boards were featured prominently in the organizational structure of the RTC, however, not a single RTC official with whom I spoke at any level viewed the advisory board as a relevant body in the decision and implementation process. Managing agents had no contact with the advisory boards. Those at the regional and field office level viewed them as "political bodies" and sought to distance themselves from their activities. The comments of a director of one of the consolidated offices were representative: "How effective were the advisory boards? Not very significant. They played almost no role. You needed their input, but often they felt like they were the oversight board and they weren't. They were just advisory boards." Insofar as the advisory boards were seen as pressuring the agency to develop more effective affordable housing or minority- and women-owned contracting programs, the RTC officials I spoke with were angry and resentful. The comments of a securitization specialist in Washington were indicative:

> Congress's mandate to dispose of assets quickly and get the highest return was watered down by special interests. They prevented us from having a streamlined contracting process because we had to have minority- or women-owned contractors do the work who may or may not be qualified. Or in the sense of the most recent funding bill last year, where there was a minority set-aside for branch offices and assets. The complications that come from that are just mucking up the process to where you could sell a loan and get 100 cents on the dollar or you can go through a minority preference set-aside program and sell the loan at 90 cents on the dollar. It's the same asset but because we now have a new vision of what someone in Congress wanted to accomplish from FIRREA, specifically the black congressional caucus, then it changes your mandate and how you do business. We probably had over a billion dollars in assets that didn't get sold because they were tied up in minority preference.

A former advisory board member and professor of business at Northwestern made a similar point:

> I saw it as our [the advisory board's] job to keep the agency focused on its mission, which was to blow out holdings. I've always felt that the first loss is the best loss. . . . The initial group of board members were very good. We came from various business areas, such as real estate, and from business schools. You also had to be in line with administration. These were people who said, "We're going to see this thing gets done right and

put it out of business. Put the thing out of existence. To liquidate the
agency is the single purpose of the board. . . . The bad thing about the
boards is that they picked up a lot of social baggage; low income initiatives, women, minorities. They invented a social agenda to the agency that
would never end. That was extremely troubling. The main impact of the
board was as a sounding board for the interested, concerned public.

Potential investors and contractors that could help "sell product" were often cited as important in providing input into the process at the regional and field level. A sales director for the Dallas
office, who noted his reluctance to involve local governments,
responded to the question, "What other groups played a role in
influencing your policies?" He answered, "The real estate community. We made presentations to Rotary, Kiwanis, and whoever asked
us. The presentations were helpful to us. We learned a lot about
how to sell the assets more effectively." Another RTC official said, "If
we have something to sell you, we can't tell you you got to do this,
this, and this. We have to listen to you—to see what you can do and
what you're willing to, to structure things that way, working with the
market."

In short, the RTC directly intervened in shaping markets and creating assets through its sales strategies. It selectively sought advice,
typically from the members of the business community who were
interested in selling their contractual services or purchasing "product." Although a variety of societal groups were represented on advisory boards, the impact of the boards on the calculus of those actually
involved in selling, restructuring, and closing institutions and their
assets was minimal.

In line with the U.S. "adversarial" regulatory character, the RTC's
implementation was charged with a high level of confrontation. An
RTC official in southern California commented in reference to the
role of the courts: "The RTC was the largest make-work program for
lawyers in the history of United States." If confrontation were measured in terms of legal fees, the RTC would be considered one of the
most hostile public agencies in the history of the United States.
Lawyers, litigation, and the courts played an enormous role in the
RTC's activities. Few actions taken by the RTC were not challenged by

one or another group of defendants. At the same time, the RTC, with its deep government pockets, became a favorite target for plaintiffs. In addition, RTC staff in all divisions complained bitterly about the litigious nature of their job.

The General Accounting Office published a "Fact Sheet" detailing the number and type of legal matters engaged in by the agency from October 1991 to November 1992 (GAO 1993g).[17] During that time the RTC had more than 77,000 legal matters and was adding over 3,000 legal matters each month.[18] The overwhelming majority of legal matters (69 percent) were found to be offensive actions and included things like real estate foreclosures and collections on promissory notes. In 12 percent of the cases, the RTC was engaged in a defensive legal matter in which a party had initiated a claim against the agency or a failed thrift.

Perhaps even more remarkable are the fees paid by the RTC for legal matters. Data produced from the RTC's Legal Information System (RLIS) shows that from 1992 to 1995 the agency had nearly a billion dollars in fees and expenses approved for payment (see Table 6.3). Several features about the types and costs of legal matters involving the RTC are interesting. First, the sheer volume of legal work is remarkable. In addition, the amount spent on cases against directors and former officers is also extraordinary. More than 35 percent or nearly $350 million of the agency's legal budget was spent on 2,806 professional liability matters, which included suits brought against or by former shareholders, owners, or directors of thrifts.[19]

Since RTC officials felt under time and financial pressure, they were particularly resentful of the legal actions taken by the agency, which they perceived as intervening upon their discretionary freedom, slowing the process down and detracting from the effectiveness of the agency. The director of the Phoenix consolidated office explained, "One major problem we had was legal. We had hundreds and hundreds of lawyers. It was difficult to get anything done. They definitely slowed things down." A managing agent indicated lawyers were viewed among the management of the conservatorship as a burden. He said, "Legal was a challenge through the entire four years I worked with the RTC because they marched to their own drummer. Legal imposed all kinds of restrictions. You couldn't find out the status of a case to save

Table 6.3

RTC Fees and Expenses Approved for Payment between January 1992 and July 1995

Type of Legal Matter	Total Legal Matters	Fees and Expenses Approved for Payment
Appeals	1,042 (1%)	16,590,000 (1.6%)
Bankruptcy[a]	14,610 (12%)	76,689,000 (8%)
Corporate[b]	953 (.7%)	5,488,000 (.5%)
Litigation[c]	47,861 (40%)	264,276,000 (27%)
Nonlitigation[d]	52,415 (44%)	271,207,000 (28%)
Professional liability[e]	2,806 (2%)	349,769,000 (36%)
Totals	119,687 (100%)	984,011,000 (100%)

Source: RTC's Legal Information System (RLIS).

[a]Includes legal services involving bankruptcy cases filed under chapters 7, 9, 11, 12, and 13.

[b]Includes legal services provided in connection with drafting and analysis of legislation, drafting and review of proposal regulations, drafting responses to audits and investigations, and preparation of congressional inquiry or FOIA request.

[c]Includes adversarial bankruptcy cases, any nonprofessional liability fraud action, litigation involving real property or securities, employment or labor law, or other tort actions.

[d]Includes legal services to facilitate procurement of contracts for goods and services, contract administration, asset sales, affordable housing, or environmental issues.

[e]Includes legal services involving liability claims against former directors or officers of thrifts.

your soul. They were slower than a seven-year itch. If I had to have legal approval on any kind of issue it took forever. Once I didn't have a legal department working for me, then I was lucky to get the lawyer to come over from the CO office. . . . All your legal efforts fell into a deep hole. Every managing agent was going nuts because they had their arms tied behind their backs. . . . It was a bad setup."

Finally, in contrast to Germany and the THA, the RTC clearly adopted the oversight characteristics of an American-style federal bureaucracy. Building on the FDIC model, rules and procedures were often detailed and explicit and applied uniformly throughout the agency even though field offices and regions and institutions faced different markets and held different assets. Several of the major examples of the agency setting specific rules include guidelines that were adopted specifying the price floor (initially 95 percent of book value) below which assets could not be sold. It mattered little that in many instances the market activity was so minimal that appraisals were not very meaningful. The agency specified precisely how many appraisals needed to be conducted, who could conduct them, and how often. Contractors were required to register, and their selection was an extremely complex and complicated process requiring multiple reviews. The rules were partly a response to political pressure from Congress and partly a reflection of the FDIC's legacy in the organization.

Similarly, to compensate for the lack of oversight staff, excessive reporting requirements were imposed on contractors. The GAO noted that asset management contractors were required to provide up to 27 standard reports to about 125 oversight managers in 15 consolidated field offices. Twenty of the reports were monthly, and the remaining seven were quarterly, annual, or final reports. Contractors were required to submit all of these reports for each contract they had with the RTC. Because a contractor sometimes had several contracts with one or more field offices, the volume of data was compounded. One contractor reported that his company's monthly reports averaged around 600 pages. RTC required oversight managers to monitor the submission of SAMDA reports, review them, and deliver reports to other RTC offices (GAO 1992h). The GAO found that few offices reviewed all the disclosure reports.

In response to external pressure, the RTC adopted a policy for its Minority and Women Outreach and Contracting Program in 1992 (U.S. Senate 1992b). All RTC offices were required to set a goal to allocate a minimum of 30 percent of all contracts and fees to minority- and women-owned businesses regardless of the geographic area or business sector. The division of legal services was required to set a goal of 20 percent of the budgeted fees in new assignments to minority- and women-owned law firms (MWOLFs) and 10 percent to minorities and women in non-MWOLFs.

Finally, in another example, the affordable housing program mandated that the RTC use a uniform cap of $67,000, below which all residential properties in the RTC's inventory had to be included in the affordable housing program. The agency was further mandated to offer the property for sale for a period of time (three months) at that price before turning it over to a private sector clearinghouse. No consideration was made regarding the particularities of the market in that area or how low- and moderate-income residents would get connected to the properties. As a result, many of the residential properties were not bid on because their market value was lower than their book value, and real estate developers and others made a killing.[20]

When it became clear that the FDIC model did not fit with the challenges posed by FIRREA, the RTC loosened up many of its procedures such as the price floor constraint. Agents were given greater discretion in carrying out their tasks. This occurred in 1990 and 1991 when the agency dramatically divested itself of large numbers of institutions and assets. In 1992 and 1993, Congress sought to rein in what it perceived to be an "out of control" agency by including more and more mandatory managerial changes with each reauthorization. The changes included greater accountability and adherence to specific procedures.

Macro-Governance Structures and Performance

How did these institutional differences in the way Germany and the United States regulate affect the RTC and the THA? The RTC and the THA did share a number of important administrative characteristics that affected their performance in similar ways (see chapter 3). Their organizational structures, organizational culture, and personnel policies all help to explain, in part, their performance. At the same time, national institutional differences within which they operated help account for some of the differences in outcomes. Specifically, the THA had many of the same administrative features as the RTC, yet the German agency existed in a policy environment that presumed the presence of very different structures.

While the U.S. policymaking environment mediated some of the effects that the RTC's internal practices had on the agency's output, the Federal Republic of Germany's policy system exacerbated biases. The RTC was created and implemented by an adversarial policy system characterized by a high level of skepticism toward state action, where bureaucrats are dependent on a variety of governmental (i.e., the legislature and executive branches) and nongovernmental participants (i.e., interest groups) in the policy process. The trappings of the U.S. policy system are clearly evident in the RTC.

The RTC's pace of privatization, for example, was tempered by the agency's heavy dependence on congressional funding that was often slow in coming. Business interests, particularly local real estate and financial interests, were effective in forcing the agency to adhere to FIRREA's stringent anti-dumping mandate. And with each reauthorization, interest groups were more and more successful in forcing the agency to comply with FIRREA's MWOB and affordable housing mandates, even though administrative structures were strongly biased in the direction of rapid privatization.

Finally, privatization was also slowed by rules governing the use of contractors, the structure of sales, and the requirements for appraisals. Private sector asset managers complained bitterly about the reporting requirements. Moreover, the use of the courts and the number of suits involving the RTC were astronomical, leading to further delays. The rules and reporting requirements not only slowed privatization, they also reduced the potential for insider abuses and fraud. In short, the policymaking environment mediated many of the outcome biases that occurred as a result of breaks with the traditional bureaucratic model.

The THA by contrast is a rare example of a bureaucracy created under a very different system of governance (the German Democratic Republic) than the one charged with operating and overseeing it (the German Federal Republic). This type of institutional adoption allowed THA's administrative structures and policies to largely circumvent the West German model and the macro-governance structures associated with it.

One result was that the initiative to restructure firms actively, embraced by Detlev Rohwedder before his death, was undermined largely by the marginalization of social partners normally present in decisions regarding regional economies or firms. Two aspects of restructuring help explain this outcome. First, restructuring initiatives require a great deal of coordination between societal groups and levels of government in comparison to privatization or liquidation. Because the German federal government acted unilaterally, directly intervening in society rather than through corporatist-type instruments, the ability of the THA to effectively implement restructuring initiatives was weakened. Vertical coordination (between levels of government) and horizontal coordination (between social partners and government) were not developed by the actions of the THA. Thus initiatives such the ATLAS program—which linked the THA, the state of Saxony, and societal groups to save "regionally significant" companies —initially struggled and eventually became a major problem.

Second, and more important, there is little question that unions, social democrats, and state governments shared a strong preference for active restructuring over rapid privatization. The degree to which West German business elites and the Kohl administration dominated the decision-making process weakened the agency's interest in alternatives to rapid privatization. One sees this at the national level with unions and state governments allotted only a minority of votes in the THA's supervisory board compared with West German business representatives who dominated both the executive and supervisory boards. The phenomenon was even more profound, though, at the regional level and in the firms themselves, where most of the restructuring occurred. The absence of traditional social partners from the decision-making process eroded the THA's interest and commitment to goals other than rapid privatization.

Yet at the same time that the agency circumvented many of the macro-governance features of the West German system, it failed to adopt anything resembling an American-style system of checks and constraints on bureaucrats. THA agents and their private-sector surrogates retained the freedom and discretion that German civil servants enjoy more generally. This broader discretion, however, enjoyed by German civil servants is premised on regulatory cultures and structures that were absent in the case of the THA. This mismatch had a profound impact on its performance. The speed and pace of privatization were much greater than in the American case, and the level of vulnerability to oversight problems was more profound.

NOTES

1. The term "institution" refers to the "the formal rules, compliance procedures, and standard operating practices that structure the relationship between individ-

uals in various units of the polity and economy" (Hall 1986, 13). "Regulatory culture" refers to what Gerhard Lehmbruch (1992) calls the "institutionalization of meaning." It refers to how individuals in a society perceive the institutional arrangements that govern them.

2. On the differences between cooperationist and adversarial governing models, see especially Kelman (1992).

3. For an account of these private government institutions, see Streeck and Schmitter (1985).

4. Kenneth Dyson captures this in his description of the federal system: "Competitive pressures induced by institutional pluralism were offset by a federalist culture that placed a high premium on cooperative behavior. . . . The mutual interdependence of levels of government created a powerful incentive to cooperate" (Dyson 1992, 13).

5. Arena setting includes such state actions as passing general rather than specific rules and procedures, encouraging and fostering the organization of societal groups, maintaining a judicial system to ameliorate disputes, and granting monopoly or oligopoly power to selected organized interests that regulate particular sectors of the economy.

6. Peter Katzenstein (1982) refers to these as "private governments" because governance is carried out not by a public agency but by societal groupings. Howard Wiarda (1997) notes that the primary distinction of U.S.-style pluralism is the "incorporation of these groups usually under state auspices directly into the decision-making process and their formal representation and vote (which often implies veto power) on the vast regulatory and planning apparatus of the model state" (21).

7. Firms initially grew by controlling their competitors. The Progressive Era legislation led to dominance of large manufacturing firms; the New Deal legislation triggered the growth of firms through diversification of product lines. And finally, concentration of business occurred in the 1950s and 1960s through financial mergers. Each successive concentration of business was in response to efforts to change the structure of government and the market. In each case, however, business strength grew. Vogel (1981, 173) also notes that business initiated the reform legislation of the Progressive and New Deal eras.

8. Max Weber's essays on bureaucracy were largely a response to his concern about this dangerous ideology.

9. For scholarship on the influence of the public sector on private industrial organization in Germany at the turn of the century see Kocka (1970). For Germany in comparison to other countries see Kocka (1980) and more recently Kristensen (1997).

10. For a good account of the patronage system, see Kaufman (1965) and Skowronek (1982).

11. Initially, only a small number of merit appointments were made. By 1904, twenty years after the Pendleton Act passed, only half of the total federal employment workforce was under the merit system, and most of that was in lower-level clerical positions.

12. For other examples of criticisms of the classical model, see the work of Robert Dahl (1947); Philip Selznick (1949); Norton Long (1949); Dwight Waldo (1948); and John Gaus (1950).

13. For additional information in English on the post-WWII German civil service, see also Derlien (1990), Mayntz and Derlien (1989), and the contributions to Benz and Goetz's (1996) edited book.

14. Following unification, five representatives from the newly formed eastern German states were included in the newly expanded Treuhand Supervisory Board. On March 15, 1991, states, the THA, and the federal government signed the Principles for the Cooperation of the Federal Government, New State Governments, and Trust Agency in the Economic Upturn of East Germany of March 15, 1991 ("Principles"). Among the principles adopted were an agreement by the THA to provide the state governments with all relevant information concerning enterprise closures and layoffs, contributions THA enterprises would make to job creation programs, and a disclosure of their landholding assets.

The statement on principles included the development of THA economic cabinets (*Treuhand Wirtschaftskabinette*), advisory boards for the branch offices, and direct contacts between government and administrative offices and THA industrial divisions.

15. Fischer and Schröter's (1996) account of the THA's beginning refers to the role that West German corporate interests played in the creation of the Treuhand.

16. Czada (1996b) suggests that the THA contributed a great deal to the development of employers associations in eastern Germany. He writes, "THA enterprises promoted the establishment of employers associations in the new Länder in so far as they paid their dues on time, in contrast to some privatized companies, but did not demand a strong voice in association matters. The THA also worked with the trade unions to ensure that foreign investors would maintain the employers association membership of privatized companies and did not enter into wage and pay agreements at the company level" (108).

17. Legal matter refers to any situation occurring during the conservatorship, resolution, or receivership process that requires legal services.

18. Legal matter increased from a low of 1,403 in October 1991 to a high of 4,877 in March 1992 (GAO 1993g).

19. The ratio of fees to number of litigation and non-litigation matters is smaller because they include many routine, noncontentious activities.

20. The Public Broadcasting System's television show *Frontline* produced an episode entitled "The Great American Bailout" (22 October 1991), which describes how wealthy individuals were buying RTC properties at well below the value at which they were marketed to low- and moderate-income families.

7

Strategic Bureaucracies
and Their Consequences

Because the Resolution Trust Corporation (RTC) and the Treuhandanstalt (THA) succeeded in transferring a large amount of public holdings to the private sector at a rapid pace, academics and policymakers have suggested these agencies should serve as models to other countries in similar situations. An article titled "Moral Hazard has played a part in Japan's banking disaster, too" published in *The Economist*, 27 April 1996, took the position that other nations, especially Japan, could learn from the RTC. The difficult question is: What should be learned? And what lessons do the two agencies offer? Focusing primarily on outputs can lead one to draw overly simplistic conclusions. Those who see rapid privatization as exactly what was needed following the savings and loan crisis and the collapse of East Germany also view the two agencies as models. By contrast, critics of the outputs see the RTC and THA as examples of the type of agency to avoid in the future. Such debates are unlikely to be easily resolved since they are fundamentally based in a difference of values. This analysis makes the case that regardless of how one feels about the agencies, important lessons can be drawn from understanding the factors that made such outputs possible in the first place.

The RTC and THA were strategic bureaucracies—public agencies created to accomplish specific goals, under specific time constraints, and with unusual autonomy and freedom. The two agencies managed the largest transfer of assets from the public to the private sector in history. A second American savings and loan crisis or German unification is unlikely to occur in the near future. The general appeal of such strategic bureaucracies, however, is likely to grow as policymakers and academicians continue to explore alternatives to the traditional or classical bureaucratic model.

This book began by framing the RTC and THA's experience in terms of two types of puzzles. The empirical questions centered on the performance of the two agencies. What did they do? What accounts for their performance? What accounts for the similarities and differences in their performance? A second line of inquiry centered around the theoretical implications of this study's findings. What do the RTC and THA tell us about the use of market mechanisms within the public sector? How does national context matter?

This study offers solutions to both puzzles by identifying and explaining the factors that led to the performance of the RTC and THA. Several lessons and insights flow from this analysis to other cases.

PRIVATIZATION AS A POLITICAL TASK

A widely shared belief is that the privatization of services or assets is a decision that removes politics from what is often viewed as a set of technical tasks. Proponents of privatization and market reforms go further to suggest that such utilitarian concepts as cost-efficiency be the primary guide for assessing the privatization decision. This comparison of the RTC and THA makes clear that "efficiency," "cost-effectiveness," "success," and "failure" are ambiguous and broad concepts. They apply an objective standard inappropriate to the two cases because the RTC and THA were political rather than economic entities. One's judgment of the RTC and THA depends largely on how one values their outcomes.[1] Both agencies shared a broad set of legislative mandates that reflected the range of problems that societal and governmental actors believed the agencies had an obligation to address. In the end, the RTC and THA were fundamentally about tradeoffs concerning how privatization was understood and implemented.

The RTC and THA (and the public managers who ran them) were extremely successful in divesting assets quickly from the public to the private sector. They also completed their tasks and shut down their operations, something few scholars or policy practitioners believed possible. Accomplishing their mammoth tasks would be difficult under the best of circumstances when valuable assets, strong markets, and an ample supply of trained operators were involved. Yet these agencies accomplished their tasks with little planning or preparation, without a ready pool of trained staff, and with portfolios of assets that were often of questionable quality. Furthermore, since assets could not be privatized immediately, both the RTC and THA were forced to become the short-term managers of assets.

Despite these difficulties, the RTC resolved nearly 750 savings and loan institutions with assets in excess of $465 billion in less than seven years. In less than five years, the THA privatized nearly 8,000 former state-owned enterprises that included 45,000 plants employing close to 4.1 million workers. If the RTC and THA were strictly private sales entities, the massive blowout of inventory might be the end of the story. But both agencies were more than just sales organizations. They were public entities supported with the taxpayer resources to accomplish a set of public goals, including the rapid sale of assets.

Although the RTC and THA successfully transferred assets quickly, they largely minimized important secondary goals for which there were vocal constituencies. The RTC's enabling legislation, the Financial Institutions Reform, Recovery, and Enforcement Act (FIRREA), included three specific mandates designed to channel the resources of the RTC toward particular societal groups. The goals were to maximize opportunities for minority- and women-owned contractors, increase the availability of affordable single- and multi-family housing, and protect local real estate and financial markets from asset dumping. Of the three goals, only the protection of local markets from dumping was given a great deal of attention. The agency was slow to implement minority- and women-owned business (MWOB) and affordable housing programs. Over time both these trends changed. Under pressure from Congress and after a good portion of the institutions and assets had been sold, the agency made progress in developing its MWOB and affordable housing programs. And after fears of dumping disappeared, the agency focused attention on ensuring that its sales practices were competitive.

Similarly the THA's enabling legislation required it to do more than just privatize quickly. The Treuhandanstalt Law instructed the agency to identify firms that could be saved from liquidation and to carry out a restructuring program that would make them competitive in a market system. The THA's own management committee determined that more than 85 percent of its firms had a future with the right restructuring plan and capital investment.[2] Yet with the exception of a handful of very large and politically important enterprises, restructuring was conducted in a passive manner—drastically downsizing workforces, dismantling firms into pieces, and selling off anything of value.[3] This very restrictive form of restructuring was followed despite the fact that active restructuring and investment enjoyed significant support from vocal constituencies such as labor unions.

Both the RTC and THA struggled to maintain effective oversight and accountability. Information systems were typically either poorly developed or put in place only after most of the privatization had occurred. During its short existence the THA seemed particularly vulnerable to fraud. Its internal and external auditors lacked the necessary number of employees to monitor the activities of the agency and its firms. Auditors also lacked the expertise and knowledge concerning the various industries they were expected to monitor. The federal prosecutor who headed Germany's equivalent of the Inspector General's Office within the THA remarked that the politics of the agency was to empower the buyer and treat controls as a necessary evil (Kampe 1994, 166).

The RTC also struggled to maintain effective oversight. The General Accounting Office and the Office of the Inspector General were both critical of the agency's oversight systems, particularly the inadequacy of information management systems to monitor contractors and track the progress of assets. According to the GAO, when the RTC began, it was one of the top risks for fraud in the federal government. And as late as 1994 the GAO reported that the RTC and FDIC remained vulnerable to fraud, abuse, and mismanagement (GAO 1994a). Yet despite operating under a much more open system than its German counterpart, the RTC experienced nothing like the number of cases of fraud and abuse that were raised during the Treuhand Investigative Committee hearings.

An important lesson from the RTC and THA's stories is that strategic bureaucracies are a complicated mix of trade-offs, with winners and losers. In the American case, the clear beneficiaries included first the customers of banks and other financial institutions threatened by the uncertainty associated with the unresolved savings and loan institutions and their unsold assets. Winners also included institutions, particularly banks, that purchased the majority of RTC's financial portfolio as well as the asset management companies, law firms, accounting firms, investment companies, and even the real estate community hired as contractors. Other winners were the states, primarily in the Sunbelt region, that received the largest transfers of wealth from the rest of the country (see esp. Hill 1990; Southern Finance Project 1992a, 1992b; Waldman 1990b). The losers included future generations of Americans forced to pay for the resolution of failed savings and loans, states forced to pay for the risky actions taken in other states, rural and urban areas that failed to benefit from the resolution process, and the poorest Americans who gained relatively little from the $90 billion spent by the RTC.

The beneficiaries of the THA's rapid privatization were West German firms with the capital to purchase East German companies with heavy subsidies. West German companies also managed to limit the competitive threat posed by eastern firms, either by buying and then closing them outright or by easily acquiring information about them through seats on supervisory and management committees. West German banks, in particular, were winners after taking over eastern Germany's banking system along with the billions in firm debt underwritten to a large degree by the federal government. Eastern German regional economies were the immediate losers, especially workers in those economies. With the exception of a handful of large firms taken over and modernized, eastern Germany's economy remains in a deep recession. Despite the massive capital investments directed toward Berlin and a significant migration to the West, unemployment in the former East German states increased by 38 percent between 1991 and 1996.[4] In 1996, seven years after the fall of the Berlin Wall, the five new eastern German states contributed barely 10 percent of the total Gross Domestic Product (Schaefers 1997).

The RTC and THA excelled in many respects. A number of factors came together to create two of the most flexible and dynamic public agencies in history. Yet the elements that made these agencies strategic also narrowed the definition of their mission, with serious consequences. A number of distributional goals included in their legislative mandates, as well as oversight and accountability, were undermined by the very features that made the RTC and THA flexible and dynamic. The central questions thus become not whether the RTC and THA were efficient or successful but first, What factors helped to explain the tradeoffs? and second, What can policymakers, interested in a creating a strategic bureaucracy, learn from the RTC and THA?

MULTILAYERED EXPLANATIONS

No single factor was responsible for the performance of the THA and RTC. The behavior of the two agencies was a function of a variety of factors that congealed into a set of structures that made it more likely for agency operators and managers to behave in certain ways and not others. Some factors were within the control of the agencies' operators and managers. Other factors were outside the control of the agency but still within the control of external groups such as legislators or executives. And still other contributing factors, such as chance or history, were outside the control of the public, bureaucrats, and policymakers.

To make sense of these varied factors, the approach taken here is to examine the layers: treating outcomes at the center and moving outward with each additional layer offering a separate set of insights. Administrative characteristics, the closest connection to the bureaucratic outcomes, constitute the first layer surrounding the core. A second layer is the political environment that helped create a legal framework within which agency managers and staff were forced to operate. A third layer is the task environment that developed in reaction to a set of unintended and unplanned events that directly affected the behavior of both organizations. The fourth layer is the national institutional setting of the THA and RTC. The following summarizes the insights developed from each layer of discovery.

Administrative Characteristics

Three types of administrative characteristics were particularly important in helping to explain the outcomes of the two agencies: (1)

personnel policies—the hiring, recruitment, payment, and retention policies; (2) organizational culture—the shared set of values held by agents and fostered by the leadership in the organization; and (3) organizational structure—the configurative delegation of authority and responsibility.

Their internal hierarchies were relatively flat and loosely organized. Rather than a single source of power at the top, there were numerous foci of power and authority dispersed across geographic regions and asset types. The agencies were also highly decentralized. Those closest to the assets in the field typically bore the greatest responsibility for their transfer to the private sector.

Both agencies avoided standardized hiring and compensation systems. Hiring was done largely on an ad hoc basis by the various regional offices. Compensation levels were not only individualized but bonuses and premiums were also included for performance. The THA awarded exit bonuses. Both agencies relied heavily on private employment companies and headhunting firms to locate qualified private sector personnel. Contractors were also hired into the agencies as quasigovernment employees, *quasi* in the sense that to the public there was often little difference between private contractors and public employees.

Training and socialization were minimal. New employees were expected to hit the ground running. Much of the organizational culture was imported from a diverse set of primarily private sector arenas. Rather than unified around a set of abstract public principles, agency employees were unified in their individualism, self-interest, and entrepreneurial spirit. Although they were clearly not intended as test models for reform, the RTC and the THA offer two examples of agencies in two different countries that broke with the traditional model of public administration in similar ways.

The break with traditional models of public administration led to a set of trade-offs that affected the pace and substance of privatization as well as oversight and accountability. Tapping into the private sector for agency employees and using private contractors to fill the remaining personnel deficit allowed the RTC and the THA to construct their organizations quickly and staff them with trained individuals who were often well connected to the very markets the agencies were engaging. Neither agency, however, was well equipped to assess adequately the skill levels of employees and contractors or the conflict-of-interest problems that might be associated with their employment. Such systems of accountability would have taken time to develop and thus would have slowed the process of privatization.

The differential wage systems and pay-for-performance structures reduced recruitment obstacles. Compensation practices bought the agencies flexibility, a capacity to respond to changing environments, and, most important, the ability to learn from experience and incorporate new knowledge quickly into practice. The front-loading of benefits and high salaries, however, reduced the incentive to take a long-term approach and increased the attractiveness of pursuing policies that provided short-term results. Meeting sales goals either individually or as part of a team offered the most immediate recognition of effort and consequently the strongest evidence that money paid up front was well spent. Goals that took longer to develop, such as successful restructuring in Germany or the implementation of a successful affordable housing program and minority- and women-owned contracting system in the United States, did not offer nearly the attractive recognition or rewards. Working to ensure that oversight and accountability measures were effectively and correctly implemented also lacked the appeal of rapid sales. From the perspective of employees, these other goals and oversight measures were performance liabilities to the extent that they detracted from the ability to garner recognition for sales work.

Differing wages reduced the organizational capacity to pursue policies that required high levels of coordination and favored those policies such as rapid privatization that typically required very little coordination between parts of the agency. Merit pay and wage differentials also undermined the individual's attachment to the organization and created conflicts or inequities within the organization. This made it difficult to pursue policies that required more complex patterns of interdependence. RTC and THA employees had little attachment to their organizations and conflict within the agencies was high.

Organizational structures also led to trade-offs on how privatization was implemented. Eschewing steep hierarchies in favor of ceding discretionary authority to regional and local hubs afforded employees in both agencies the freedom to make decisions quickly. This was particularly true of managing agents in the RTC and firm managers hired by the THA. These managers in both agencies were given significant responsibility and authority to restructure institutions and sell assets.[5] A highly decentralized structure also meant that those closest to the assets and institutions were given the most authority. Public managers who understood the assets best were in a position to make managerial and sales decisions, further enhancing the ease with which divestment could occur. Blurring of the lines of authority enhanced the independence that bureaucrats experienced by weakening the spans of control within both organizations. With only weak or dotted lines of authority employees felt that they had greater freedom to operate.

Organizational structures also weakened oversight and accountability. Under more normal circumstances privatization agents and managers would warrant special precautionary measures, given the short-term nature of their contracts, their private sector background, and particularly, their connections to the industries. Yet the decentralized structures of the organizations, coupled with the absence of clear hierarchies, made it difficult to monitor and oversee their actions. Steps taken to increase accountability were fiercely resisted and often ignored by agents in the field.

The structure adopted by the RTC and THA also made it difficult to pursue or implement policies that required greater levels of horizontal coordination between institutions or firms and vertical coordination within the agency. Efforts by the THA to take a more regional approach to the restructuring of industries in eastern Germany were severely weakened by the THA's decentralized structure that focused on single firms as the unit of analysis rather than industries or geographic areas.

Placing time and budgetary restraints on the various hubs, while at the same time ceding agents significant discretionary authority, also reinforced the position of prospective buyers and investors as the premier customers or clients of both agencies. Buyers, investors, and private sector contractors were the customers with the highest priority because they contributed the most to each hub's speed in divesting itself of its holdings, providing liquidity to the agency and showing results.

Structured Choices

Political principals also designed structures that contributed to the behavior of the two agencies. The structures were formal mechanisms that political principals adopted to constrain the activities of the RTC and THA. They were a means to strike a balance between advocating for the interests of their constituencies and maintaining a cautious distance from any crisis that posed a potential loss of political capital. The structures were important because they established the framework within which operators and managers implemented their mandates.

Executives in both countries succeeded in establishing an elaborate and complex network of controls at the national level that gave executives control over the organizations' central management. At the same time it institutionalized enough distance to give the administration in both countries the opportunity to use the agencies as scapegoats in deflecting public anger over the process. This is what I term "scapegoat governance," and it consisted of internal and external elements.

Inside both organizations, oversight and control were diffuse, complicated, and often informal. Different groups and individuals were ceded control. Jurisdictions were blurred and changed over time, leaving the impression that many managers were in charge. The result was that no single individual or group was truly accountable. Externally both agencies were overseen by a single executive agency closely allied with the administration. In the THA's case it was the Finance Ministry. In the RTC's case it was the Treasury Department. Neither of these institutional placements was natural or predetermined. The governing structures of the RTC and THA ensured legitimacy by spreading oversight responsibilities among several different institutional actors. Germany's Ministry of Finance and the U.S. Treasury Department, however, were "first among equals" in overseeing their respective agencies. The structures developed in both instances served the administrations' goal of ensuring control over the process without being fully associated with the agencies' actions. They served the political purpose of institutionalizing important levers of control that the Bush and Kohl administrations could use to influence the agencies' actions.

Political principals adopted complicated structures for the RTC and the THA that circumvented standard budgetary procedures, which ceded greater authority to the agencies and made it more difficult for opponents of the administration to intervene in the agencies' activities through the funding process. The legislative mandates adopted by the political principals lacked specificity, clarity, and priority which freed the managers of the RTC and THA to define the content of privatization. Finally, their hybrid legal identities—as a mixed-ownership government corporation in the RTC's case and as a public trustee agency (*Anstalt*) in the case of the THA—insulated the agencies, gave them limited oversight and greater flexibility to privatize. As neither public nor fully private organizations, the RTC and THA experienced the best of both worlds in terms of the inability of outside actors to control them.

All of these structures were "political" choices that were the result of enormous conflict among parties with different stakes. The structured choices gave both agencies greater freedom to operate, increasing the importance of administrative characteristics. At the same time, the structures allowed the administrations of Helmut Kohl and George Bush to retain important levers of control.

Task Environments

Although political principals seek to structure the actions of executive agencies, agencies are rarely on automatic pilot. Unplanned or unexpected events occur after structures are in place that can affect the behavior and performance of an organization.

German policymakers significantly overvalued East Germany's industrial assets. They envisioned the THA as primarily engaged in the sale of assets and the equitable dissemination of the receipts to East Germans. American policymakers hoped to avoid the problems of the Federal Asset Disposition Agency (FADA) by making the Federal Deposit Insurance Corporation (FDIC) the foster parent of the RTC. The FDIC's standard practices and procedures for resolving whole institutions proved unsuccessful, however, and forced the RTC to scramble for ways to manage and sell institutions and assets. In both cases, their task environments transformed the agencies and affected their performance and behavior.

Managers of coping organizations confront a unique set of incentives that managers of craft or procedural agencies do not face. In the American case the incentives made it far more likely that managers in the agency would favor easy-to-measure outcomes such as the number of resolutions or asset sales rather than oversight or increased opportunities for minority- and women-owned contracting. The THA focused on what it could easily measure: the numbers of firms and assets sold; the number of jobs guaranteed by buyers; and the amount of investment commitments by buyers. Controls and restructuring received little attention.

Further, the RTC and THA were predisposed to face internal conflict because operators are driven by the situational imperatives they face while managers are driven by the constraints they face, particularly from politically influential constituencies.

Finally, as they managed the unanticipated challenges caused by their task environments, the THA and RTC's demand for external support grew dramatically. The RTC and THA became enormous consumers of contractual services. The heavy reliance on third parties impacted the two organizations in several ways. It increased their capacities but also constrained them because of the limited availability of quality contractors willing to work for the agencies. And the more the agencies became dependent on third parties for substantive assistance, the more influence third parties had in shaping the perceived purpose of the organizations.

National Institutional Context

The RTC and the THA were state organizations engaged in the regulation and creation of property rights. The process involved more than agencies, a set of political principals, or their respective task environments. It also involved what Kenneth Dyson (1992) describes as "institutionalized governance arrangements," macro-level structures that determine how societies are governed.

A country's policymaking environment affects the tradeoffs associated with different administrative structures and organizational forms. Although both were strategic bureaucracies with similar managerial structures and organizational forms, the actions of the THA and RTC varied in important ways. These differences are explained partly by the variation in the way Germany and the United States govern their societies and partly by the fact that while the RTC was created and then managed within an American policy environment, the THA was the rare case of a bureaucracy created under a very different system of governance than the one which operated and oversaw it.

The meaning and structure of the state, markets, and society differ dramatically under the two types of governing systems. Under corporatism in Germany, public agencies play a much smaller role in directly intervening in the affairs of societal groups. The state incorporates groups into the decision making and often cedes regulatory responsibility to competing interests such as labor unions and business peak associations. While bureaucratic discretion is much greater today in Germany than in the United States, oversight resides to a large extent in the relationships between affected organized actors rather than in detailed legal statutes. In the United States, by contrast, the federal government plays a significant direct role in regulating and shaping the activities of societal groups. While interest group pluralism creates such policies, the groups themselves are not held directly responsible for policy implementation. Therefore, such groups have a strong incentive to opt for policies that serve their interests regardless of their impact on society as a whole. Trust and cooperation under such a system are extremely low, and distrust of the state agency is high in all areas except as far as one's own interests are concerned.[6] As a result, oversight is a constant battle, achieved through detailed rules that attempt to cover all contingencies, constant vigilance, and of course, extensive use of lawyers and the court system.

The RTC was created and implemented by an adversarial policy system characterized by a high level of skepticism toward state action, where bureaucrats were held in check by detailed rules. The trappings of the U.S. policy system were clearly evident in the RTC. The pace of privatization, for example, was slowed by rules governing the use of contractors, the structure of sales, and the requirements for appraisals. While such constraints slowed the process of privatization, the rules and reporting requirements reduced the potential for insider abuses and fraud. The policymaking environment mediated many of the outcome biases caused by the internal structures.

In contrast, Germany's unique combination of cooperative federalism and corporatism was largely circumvented by the agency. By German standards the THA was a very large federal bureaucracy that took direct actions that shaped local economies and industries. The THA did (albeit reluctantly) incorporate the presidents of each of the newly created eastern states into its supervisory board following unification. Over time and in response to protests from states, the THA also ceded more of a role in the policymaking process to state governments. But the role of state governments in shaping privatization was minimal. The jurisdiction of the agency's regional offices overlapped with the former East Germany's districts rather than the newly created eastern states. The states' role was primarily to deal with struggling firms and industries that had already been privatized. The five state presidents were greatly outnumbered by corporate executives on the THA Supervisory Board. And as Wolfgang Seibel notes, eastern state governments after the fall of the Berlin Wall lacked the institutional infrastructure, expertise, and history to take on the responsibility of privatization.

Unions were also included on the Supervisory Board of the agency, but they were largely excluded where it counted most—at the firm and regional level of the agency. As with state governments, unions were simply not in a position as institutions following the fall of the Berlin Wall to take on many of the responsibilities of privatization. They lacked organization, infrastructure, and expertise. Executives hired by the THA to manage firms and agents responsible for selling and liquidating firms stated that unions played a negligible role in shaping privatization policies. Some of these THA managers and agents boasted about the absence of union participation that would not have been possible in the West. Unions sought to exert influence in negotiating the severance packages and social plans for workers who were laid off as a result of downsizing, privatization, or closure. But the overall role of unions in shaping privatization was nominal. In short, the THA largely circumvented the German model of strong union participation in decision making. Traditional patterns of intergovernmental relations were also circumvented by making state governments subordinate to the federal government over questions of firm restructuring and privatization. At the same time, the German agency made little effort to adopt American types of checks and constraints on bureaucrats. As a result, the speed and pace of privatization of the THA was much greater than that of the RTC, but insider abuses and oversight problems were much more profound. The THA shared many of the internal features of the RTC, yet the German agency existed in a policy environment that presumed the presence of very different structures. The result was that the U.S. policymaking environment mediated some of the effects that the RTC's internal practices had on the agency's output, but the Federal Republic of Germany's policy system exacerbated biases.

THEORETICAL IMPLICATIONS

The RTC and THA's experiences provide an opportunity to consider the connections between various causal factors analyzed in this study to predict impacts on bureaucratic performance more generally. The following discussion takes an initial step using two typologies, based on the empirical findings of this study, and then suggests a number of hypotheses.

Internal and External Environments

The performances of the RTC and THA illustrate that bureaucratic outcomes are a function of internal and external environments. "Internal environment" refers to the way an organization is managed or governed internally. This includes personnel policies, organizational structures, and the organizational culture of the agency. These factors directly affect the agency's behavior and performance by shaping what Cohen, March, and Olsen call "the collection of choices looking for problems, issues and feelings looking for decisions and decision makers looking for work" (1972; see also Kingdon 1984).

Yet as the RTC and THA's experiences make clear, the impact that the internal environment has on an agency's performance depends upon external factors outside of the control of the agency. These outer layers include first, the structured choices made by legislators that set the institutional framework within which agencies must operate. These structured choices include (1) the financing or budgetary structure of the agency; (2) how specific and consistent legislative mandates are; and (3) the legal identity of the organization.

These factors institutionalized the control that external actors could exercise over the RTC and THA. The complicated financing structures, the imprecise and conflicting mandates, and the public/private hybrid legal identities insulated both agencies.

An additional outer layer that affects the ease with which external actors can control an agency is its task environment. The more observable and measurable outputs and outcomes are the easier it is for external actors to control an organization. Such measures are crucial to monitoring an agency because they not only let external actors know when there is a problem but where in the agency the problem exists. Production organizations are thus the easiest to control. And as the RTC and THA illustrate, coping organizations are the most difficult to oversee and control since the quality of information concerning outputs and outcomes is poor.

The RTC and THA's status as coping organizations coupled with the structures passed by legislators provided the agencies with a great deal of freedom. That freedom, in turn, increased the impact that internal structures had on the behavior and performance of the two agencies. In other words, had external actors been able to exert greater control over the two agencies, the impact of the administrative features would have been lessened.

To simplify and extrapolate from the RTC and THA's experience, consider first two types internal environments: (1) a traditional model of bureaucratic governance and (2) a more market-oriented form of governance.[7] As noted in chapter 1, the traditional model includes steep hierarchies, clear lines of authority, limits on an employee's span of control, centralization beneath a single executive, a merit system based on examinations and acquisition of skills, standardized procedures and hiring practices, long probationary periods, and training programs. By contrast, although a market model has no single definition, Guy Peters notes that there is a basic belief in the virtue of competition as an idealized pattern of exchange and incentives of governance organized around competitive structures (Peters 1996). Many of the RTC and THA's administrative characteristics fall within the market model such as decentralization of authority, private-sector management systems, merit- or performance-based pay systems, reliance on external labor markets for services through contracting, and accountability through contracts and measurable results.

The internal environment's impact on bureaucratic performance, however, is affected by the external environment within which the agency operates. Again, one can simplify the world into two alternatives. One alternative is an external environment within which agencies are highly insulated from external actors. A second alternative is one in which the agency is easily controlled by external actors. The degree of agency autonomy is a function of structured choices and tasks—whether political principals possess both the necessary knowledge and authoritative levers to control the actions of the agency.

Building upon these two sets of simplified assumptions offers a way to begin to consider systematically how four combinations of external and internal environments might influence a public agency's behavior.

Strategic bureaucracies. Like the THA and RTC, strategic bureaucracies are characterized by market-based internal environments coupled with weak external controls. The combination of environments is likely to influence the performance of the agency in several ways. First, the agency is more likely to adopt a very short time horizon, emphasizing immediate outcomes over those that take longer to develop. A competitive internal culture that favors individualized compensation based upon merit will make it difficult to postpone actions that benefit employees today. A decentralized delegation of work makes the administration of a longer-term strategy difficult.

Strategic organizations will also emphasize innovation and entrepreneurship over strict adherence to rules and regulations. The organization is likely to be extremely flexible, with a high capacity for learning, and an ability to respond rapidly to changing environments. These organizational features are the result of private sector backgrounds of employees and their compensation structure that rewards entrepreneurial drive and measurable results rather than commitment to the organization or increased skills.

Coordination is likely to be weakened by the internal competitiveness built into the structure, the high turnover of employees, the acceptance of better-paid contractors directly into the organization's ranks, and the lack of esprit de corps or identification with the values of a public agency.

Finally, weak external controls make it difficult for political principals, such as legislators, to change or "reel in" the agency's behavior. At the same time, the agency is likely to be more prone to "capture" or influence from below by third parties that hired into the organization or contractors upon which the strategic agency relies to carry out its task. Since there is very little socialization and often a high turnover, the historic mission or the legislative understandings of the agency's purpose are likely to be secondary to the employees' immediate and short-term understandings. Employees, and certainly contractors, also intend to work for other private principals in the future. They know that they will be evaluated on the basis of the current values of the private principals, not on the basis of their achievement of the historic or legislative goals of the agency.

Independent bureaucracies. Like the Federal Deposit Insurance Corporation (FDIC), independent bureaucracies are characterized by bureaucratic internal environments coupled with relatively weak external controls. The combination of internal and external environments is likely to affect the performance of the agency in the following ways: First, in contrast to the strategic agency, the independent bureaucracy is likely to take a long-term time horizon since the organizational culture, promotion practices, and compensation provide strong incentives that favor a more long-term view. New recruits enter at the lowest levels, and, following a lengthy probationary period, they see their compensation increase rapidly with seniority and training. Moreover, centralization along with a hierarchical structure means that administering tasks is likely to take longer.

The agency's competitive advantage lies in its thoroughness and professionalism. The independent bureaucracy shares similar features with James Q. Wilson's "craft-based" organization, such as strong reliance on standard operating procedures, lack of flexibility, and commitment to fairness. A modification of Wilson's characterization is that independent bureaucracy enjoys a great deal more insulation from political streams. Therefore, the independent bureaucracy is more likely to stay rooted in its historic mission, even during changing political environments. At the same time, the bureaucratic internal environment reduces the vulnerability to capture by third parties from below.

Controlled bureaucracies. The Social Security Administration or the Internal Revenue Service are examples of controlled bureaucracies and are characterized by bureaucratic internal environments coupled with strong external controls. Once again, these internal and external environmental factors are likely to bias the public organization in certain directions behaviorally. Similar to the independent bureaucracy, the controlled bureaucracy is likely to view its purpose with a much longer time horizon since the culture, hiring, and promotion practices and the compensation policies provide strong incentives that favor a more long-term view. The controlled bureaucracy is also likely to favor alternatives in which the state (as opposed to private actors) plays a significant role in the provision of the public good since the culture views the public organization as central to solving the particular problem or fulfilling the particular need. This biased behavior corresponds to a strong need to establish and maintain a high level of internal coordination that is centralized beneath a single executive. The structure makes the organization less responsive or adaptable than strategic agencies. Controlled bureaucracies, however, enjoy a high capacity to carry out complicated tasks that require significant levels of coordination, thoroughness, continuity, and institutional stability.

Finally, in contrast to the independent bureaucracy, controlled bureaucracies are far more vulnerable to the exigencies of the immediate political environment given the ease with which political principals can control the organization. Its bureaucratic internal environment, however, reduces the opportunities for capture from below by third parties.

Competitive controlled bureaucracies. Characterized by strong external controls coupled with market-based internal environment, competitive controlled bureaucracies occur less frequently in the public sector, largely because the controlled competitive bureaucracy shares the strengths but also the weaknesses of both the strategic agency and the controlled bureaucracy.

The organization is highly innovative and flexible, capable of adapting to changing environment pressures since the culture, promotion, and compensation systems and the delegation of work make the organization particularly receptive to external changes and trends. Performance is biased toward short-term observable goals since benefits are front-loaded and agents have few incentives to consider the long term and strong incentives to favor the short term. Oversight is also likely to be strained by the weakened formal rules of oversight, decentralization of work, and incentives that reward individual accomplishment.

In short, what sets these organizations apart is that internal and external environments appear to influence the organization's behavior in conflicting directions. Political principals possess the authoritative mechanisms to control the agency. However, the market-based internal structures make it difficult for external principals to determine precisely what agents in the organization are doing. Information asymmetries between principals and agents are exacerbated and make the informal means of accountability and control more difficult. Rather than focus on agent outputs, the organization is thus likely to pay particular attention to quantifiable outcomes of the agency since political principals enjoy a much greater level of control over the organization than do strategic agencies.

Finally, because of its vulnerability to the control of political principals as well as third parties, the controlled-competitive agency suffers from the greatest degree of instability. In other words, the agency is poorly insulated from the pressures of the political environment as well as societal environment within which it is engaged.

In sum, the preceding extrapolates from the RTC and THA a set of hypotheses that seek to explain how internal administration and external environments matter in shaping the behavior of public organizations. Missing from this account is the role of the national policy environment. Although the hypotheses can be applied generally across advanced industrial countries, the experience of the RTC and THA suggest that there should be variation across national institutional settings. The final section considers, in a very limited way, how national variation can matter in the case of a small subset of public organizations, namely strategic bureaucracies.

National Settings Matter

Each combination of external and internal environments contributes to a set of trade-offs in how the organization is likely to behave. As noted above, there is no suggestion that trade-offs are predetermined. However, a country's national policymaking environment plays an important role in further mediating the impact of those trade-offs. Although both were strategic bureaucracies with similar managerial structures and organizational forms, the THA and RTC outcomes varied in important ways. These differences are explained partly by the variation in the way Germany and the United States govern their societies and partly by the fact that while the RTC was created and then managed within an American policy environment, the THA is the rare case of a bureaucracy created under a very different system of governance than the one which operated and oversaw it.

Steven Kelman (1992) notes that the U.S. policymaking environment is highly adversarial and short-term oriented. By contrast, Germany's system is more cooperative and capable of taking a longer-term view and adopting more rational-comprehensive policies. Building on the work of Kelman and scholars who have specifically compared German and American policymaking environments, we can ask two questions about the RTC and THA: (1) What happens when a short-term oriented public agency exists within a long-term oriented policy environment?; and (2) What happens with a short-term agency in a short-term policy environments such as the United States?

A matrix presented in Figure 7.1 offers a step toward answering the question by making two sets of simplified assumptions that allow one to generate some hypotheses about how national environments can affect behavior and outcomes of strategic agencies. On one axis is the temporal orientation of the agency. As noted above, whether or not an agency has a short- or long-term time horizon is partly a function of internal and external environments. Here, the focus is primarily on the strategic agency which by design has a short-term time horizon.

The second axis describes the temporal orientation of the national policymaking environment or what Dyson (1992) describes

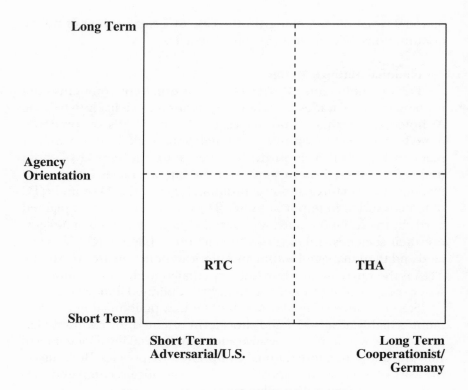

Figure 7.1 Agency and the Policymaking Environment

as macro-governing environment. Chapter 6 described in detail several of the important features that affect a nation's policymaking environment. These include the structure and culture of the state, markets, and bureaucracies. Chapter 6 further pointed out that it is these combinations of cultural and structural factors that create a German national policy environment that fosters the long-term policies. In contrast, those factors create a bias toward a very short term in the American policymaking environment (see Figure 7.1).

One can then consider how the temporal orientation of a public agency mixes with the temporal orientation of the policymaking to produce certain types of behaviors and outcomes.

As a strategic bureaucracy, the RTC had a very short-term time horizon. Its hiring and recruitment practices, organizational culture, and structures reduced the capacity and the possibility that the organization would embrace policies that would have extended the government's role. The public agency is embedded in a policymaking environment characterized by high levels of distrust among societal actors and particularly toward government and the state as an actor. The policy environment itself favors short-term or incremental policies that eschew any type of long-term or rational comprehensive approach. The combination of short-term agency with short-term policymaking environment is likely to contribute to outcomes that include the following and are summarized in Table 7.1.

First, there is likely to be little tolerance for error in auditing and evaluation practices (regardless of cost) because of the strong concerns within an adversarial system for state accountability, fear of scandal, and high levels of overall distrust. Similarly, there are likely to be highly formalized procedures aimed at reducing agent/operator discretion. This formality is partly a function of overall distrust, but particularly a function of interest groups' ability to press for procedural "fairness." Fairness in practice means formalized procedures for using third parties, significant disclosure requirements, and the removal of recruitment decisions away from agency operators.

A further outcome that can also be expected is that courts are likely to play an extensive role in overseeing the agency. Since the 1960s U.S. courts have played an active role in enforcing public policies. Changes in standing requirements and judicial discretion increased the opportunity and likelihood that interested groups will use the courts to hold an agency accountable.

In sum, the combination of a strategic agency embedded within a short-term-oriented policy environment is likely to temper some of the trade-offs indicative of a strategic agency described earlier. Low levels of discretion and high levels of distrust are likely to lessen the potential for scandal and corruption while at the same time making the agency more deliberate.

The THA, as a strategic bureaucracy, shares many of the same features with the RTC except that the German agency existed within a long-term policymaking environment. In addition, it is an

251

Table 7.1

Variation in the Implementation of Reforms

Policies	Germany	United States
Agent Discretion: How much freedom does an agent have to make decisions?	A high level of discretion with minimal reporting requirements.	Low level of discretion with extensive reporting requirements.
	Reason: Public agents traditionally enjoy a great deal of autonomy and the policymaking environment presumes a level of trust among interested actors.	Reason: Public agents must be constantly monitored, they are inefficient, and Congress is in a position to impose strict rules.
Error tolerance: How much tolerance is there for error in auditing and evaluation practices?	High tolerance for error.	Low tolerance for error in auditing and evaluation practices.
	Reason: Public sector actors are treated as experts. In addition, the oversight mechanisms allow for less rigid procedures in auditing and evaluations.	Reasons: Accountability, fear of scandal, and high levels of distrust dictate that audits account for all receipts no matter what the cost.
Contractor recruitment: Is the recruitment of contractors conducted formally or informally?	Very informal occurring through personal connections and employment companies.	Highly formalized procedures to reduce agent discretion.
	Reason: Public sector actors traditionally have a great deal of discretion.	Reason: Contractors, as an interest group, are able to pressure representatives to ensure "fairness." The process is therefore likely to be formal and require a great deal of disclosure. Recruitment decisions are procedurally taken away from the agent.
Contractor discretion: How much freedom is the contractor given?	High level of discretion and low degree of disclosure requirements.	Low level of discretion coupled with extensive reporting requirements.
	Reason: Because they are hired by public sector actors, the contractors are imbued with a similar degree of discretion as the bureaucrats.	Reason: High level of distrust in the system.

252

Table 7.1 (*continued*)

Variation in the Implementation of Reforms

Policies	Germany	United States
Judicial Accountability: What role are the courts likely to play in overseeing the agency	A relatively minimal role in overseeing the agency. Reason: The system of common law and the administrative court's flexibility make it unlikely that the courts will challenge administrative discretion.	Likely an extensive role in overseeing the agency. Reason: Since the 1960s the courts have played an active role in enforcing public policies. Changes in standing requirements and judicial discretion increased the opportunity and likelihood that interested groups will use the courts to hold an agency accountable.
Governance: What type of representation is likely to exist?	Although much less than is typical, probably some form of shared governance of the agency. Reasons: Corporatist system of government.	Representation dominated by business and the financial sector. Reason: Political markets favor concentrated wealthy interests.
Scandal and conflicts of interest: How much scandal and corruption can one expect?	High levels of scandal and corruption. Reason: The mismatch between the orientation of the agency and the policymaking environment. The larger policymaking environment presumes a set of administrative and oversight tools that are absent among strategic bureaucracies.	Low levels of scandal and corruption. Reason: The policymaking environment assumes agencies require close monitoring. Numerous checks are in place to ensure that corruption is minimized and oversight is maintained.

environment in which the central state confers enormous power and responsibility on relevant social groups and state governments while at the same time ensuring that market excesses do not erode levels of social guarantees. The combination of a short-term agency embedded within a long-term policy environment creates a situation in which a number of outcomes are likely.

First, there is likely to be a high level of discretion with minimal reporting requirements largely because public agents traditionally enjoy a great deal of autonomy and the policymaking environment presumes a level of trust among interested actors. Second, there is likely to be a high tolerance for error with deference to the professionalism and expertise of public sector employees. Oversight mechanisms thus allow for less rigid procedures in auditing and evaluations.

Second, the hiring of contractors is likely to occur informally, through personal connections with agency personnel or through employment companies. Again the flexibility and latitude in hiring third parties is largely a function of the high levels of bureaucratic discretion and low degree of disclosure requirements (relative to the adversarial policy environment).

In contrast to the adversarial policymaking environment, the courts are likely to play a relatively minimal role in overseeing the agency. This is because the system of common law and the administrative court's flexibility make it unlikely that the courts will challenge administrative discretion.

Finally, there is a mismatch between the orientation of the agency and the policymaking environment. The larger policymaking environment presumes a set of administrative and oversight tools that are absent among strategic bureaucracies. The result is that the behavioral trade-offs associated with a strategic bureaucracy are likely to be exacerbated. The agency is likely to be less deliberate than the same agency in an adversarial environment. And, more important, the mismatch is likely to make the agency far more vulnerable to scandal and oversight problems.

The implication that flows from this simple typology is that to take a "one-size-fits-all" approach to developing strategic bureaucracies would be a mistake, regardless of how attractive the potential outcomes of strategic bureaucracies might seem. Consider an example.

A June 27, 1998, *New York Times* article titled "Crisis In Banking is Japanese, But Implications Are Global" suggested that in the wake of the Asian economic crisis, countries like South Korea and Indonesia should consider the RTC as a model for resolving the billions in assets resulting from the widespread financial bankruptcies. Although policymakers concerned about Asia's economic problems may view the RTC and THA's rapid privatization as a success story to emulate, rapid privatization is only a part of the story.

Asian countries seemed to be likely candidates for an RTC-style bureaucracy.[8] The financial crisis that erupted in Asia in mid-1997 was caused by many of the features that brought down American financial institutions a decade earlier: inadequate financial supervision, poor assessment and management of financial risk, and financial institutions borrowing large amounts of costly short-term capital to finance poor-quality investments. As a result, the major economies in the region suffered from a significant inventory of poor- and non-performing loans.[9] The inventory of bad loans and failing financial institutions contributed to constraints on credit in the region which further exacerbated the difficulties for economic recovery. In response to the financial crises, a number of countries created agencies akin to the RTC to sell off bad loans and close bankrupt financial institutions. In contrast to the RTC's experience, however, progress has been extremely slow.

The reasons become clear if one looks, in particular, at Japan. First, the size of the loan problem in Asian countries is more severe than the savings and loan crisis was in the United States. Japanese bad loans are estimated at between $550 and $600 billion, which is slightly larger than the $465 billion in assets sold by the RTC. Japan's economy, however, is about half that of the United States. By implication, Japan's bad-loan problem, relative to the size of its economy, is about four or five times as large. This, in turn, has a significant impact on the relative cost of resolution. The RTC and THA experiences were both extremely expensive, despite the expectations by lawmakers that the processes would actually raise revenue for the government. In addition to their administrative and personnel costs, the actions of both agencies required enormous and continual infusions of capital. Given the size of the loan problem relative to the size of their economies, the resolution cost in Asian countries is significantly higher than in the United States.

Second, bad loans are part of the balance sheets of most of Japan's banks. The result is that there are far fewer buyers willing to or capable of purchasing questionable assets or struggling banks. In the United States, bad loans afflicted a relatively small portion of lenders concentrated in a handful of states. Healthy institutions could and did participate in the RTC-held auctions. Finally, and perhaps most important, sick banks matter much more in Japan and other Asian countries than in the United States because Japan's equity markets are less developed, and so are far smaller sources of capital for the private sector. Thus, when the banking system falters or is "cleansed" in some dramatic way, Japanese companies have few alternative sources of money.[10] As a result of these factors, any type of RTC-style action is likely to be far more difficult and face far greater opposition than in the United States.[11] In short, while policymakers concerned about Asia's economic crisis may view the RTC and THA's rapid privatization as a success story to emulate, rapid privatization is only part of the story. As countries around the world confront the difficult challenges associated with transfer of public assets to the private sector, one must be cautious about the lessons drawn from the RTC and THA's experiences.

CONCLUSION

The crises that triggered the creation of the RTC and THA have received a great deal of publicity. We know quite a bit about the savings and loan crisis as well as the events leading up to the collapse of the Berlin Wall. These were clearly historic events. However, as countries around the world confront the difficult challenges associated with transfer of public assets to the private sector, it is the agencies that resolved the crises that offer some of the most important insights and lessons. The crises that gave birth to both organizations provided a unique opportunity to observe and study for the first time such sweeping breaks with the traditional model of public administration. The fact that the experiences occurred at nearly the same point in history in two countries presented an even greater opportunity to compare the experiences in two different national settings. The pay-off is a richer understanding of how market-oriented reforms shape the public goods, the role national policymaking institutions play, and the politics that drive the process.

NOTES

1. Deborah Stone's book *The Policy Paradox* (Stone 1996) includes an excellent chapter on efficiency as a political concept.

2. The THA's management committee ranked each firm's chances. By the end of 1992 only 14.2 percent of firms fell into the two worst categories, five and six, indicating little hope for survivability (Schwalbach and Gless 1996, 188).

3. See Phyllis Dininio's (1999) account of the THA's bias toward restructuring some of the largest firms.

4. In 1991 unemployment in the eastern German states was 10.3 percent. In 1996 the figure stood at 16.7 percent (Schaefers 1997). An articled published in *Neues Deutschland* (23 June 1995), East Germany's former-communist paper, captured the frustration surrounding the THA. The article's headline "Ost Ökonomie ist zum Kümmerling gemacht worden" translates to "The East's Economy Made into Weakling." The article noted: "The policies of the Treuhand, directed by Bonn, contributed to the grandiose destruction of East Germany's industrial capital."

5. Although German managers could also sell assets of the firm, this authority was later limited. In the United States, case managing agents were extremely active selling assets throughout the life of the conservatorship.

6. Thus, for example, opinion polls consistently find that Americans hold Congress in low esteem, yet the rate of reelection is over 90 percent, and citizens typically feel quite good about their own member of Congress.

7. For a good comparison of the traditional model with other administrative models, including the market model, see Peters (1996).

8. For a comparison of the Japanese and American financial crises and resolutions, see Kawahito and Timmons (1999).

9. *Business Week*, in an article titled "The Big Clean Up Begins" (20 July 1998, 46), reported that Japan's banks held $550 billion in bad loans, Thailand's held $36 billion in bad loans, Korean banks owned $90 billion in bad loans, and Malaysia's banks carried an inventory of $25 billion in bad loans.

10. At the end of 1995 total bank credit as a proportion of nominal GNP in Japan was 105 percent compared with 37 percent in the United States (*Economist* Staff 1996).

11. An additional potential difficulty faced by Japan is the close relationship between financial executives and regulators. The common practice known as *ama-ku-da-ri,* or "descent from heaven," moves top ranking bureaucrats and regulators into posts at banks they used to supervise.

Appendix

Interviews

In addition to the print sources cited in this book, a significant number of interviews informed my research, primarily interviews I conducted with elites in the United States and Germany. Two additional sets of interviews were conducted by two separate German academic research teams led by Wolfram Fischer and Nils Diederich, respectively. These supplemental interviews were particularly useful in verifying my own work, developing an understanding of the THA's early period, and determining the factors that led to its enabling legislation.

My comparative project had a very different focus from the earlier THA projects, however, and required a different set of questions and respondents. The interviews I conducted in the United States and Germany fell loosely into two groups: (1) hands-on participants in the RTC and THA, including THA privatization agents and RTC employees charged with selling institutions and assets, managers at THA-owned firms and managing agents of RTC-owned thrifts, managers at the central offices in Berlin and Washington and in the regional offices; and (2) German parliamentarians who served on committees in the lower house (*Bundestag*), which oversaw the THA, and U.S. congressional staff members who served on congressional committees charged with crafting FIRREA and overseeing the activities of the RTC. I used a structured questionnaire with two different forms, one for hands-on participants and another for legislative overseers.

I used several criteria as guides in identifying respondents. First, given the decentralized nature of both agencies, I made sure to speak with a mix of individuals who had experience in the field offices as well as the central office. Second, I made sure I spoke to individuals who were directly involved in the sale or managing of assets. And third, it was important that respondents had been connected to the agencies (as employees, contractors, managers, or overseer) for at least two years. This final criterion was important because both agencies changed so dramatically. I felt that a sense of history, albeit a brief one, was critical for understanding the factors that went into these agencies' outputs.

In both cases, initial interviews were set up through communications officers. These initial interviews led to the identification of a potential set of respondents who worked in the agencies. My initial contacts facilitated further connections within the agencies. Parliamentarians and legislative staff members and U.S. and German auditors were contacted directly for interviews; several journalists, and academics who had written about both agencies were all contacted directly.

Each respondent received an introductory letter with a brief description of the project and a promise of anonymity. I used a structured questionnaire with two different forms, one for legislators and another for hands-on participants. These interviews were with elites, so I used the questionnaire flexibly, dwelling on different aspects with different people and asking a variety of follow-up questions. Most interviews were conducted in person; German interviews were conducted mostly in German, transcribed, and then translated.

THA-RELATED INTERVIEWS

Two members of the Christian Democratic Union in the German Bundestag and former members of the Treuhand Committee. Interviews conducted March 1, 1996, in Bonn.

Four members of the Social Democratic Party in the German Bundestag and former members of the Treuhand Committee. Interviews conducted March 1–3, 1996, in Bonn.

Two members of the Free Democratic Party in the German Bundestag and former members of the Treuhand Committee. Interviews conducted March 1–3, 1996, in Bonn.

Treasurer of the Party of the Democratic Socialist (PDS). Interview conducted December 1, 1995, in Berlin.

Former manager of a large electrical appliance firm hired by the THA. Served on the supervisory board of several other THA-owned firms. Interview conducted May 30, 1995, in Oldenburg.

THA privatization agent who worked in the Dresden regional office. Later worked for the internal auditor of the THA. Interview conducted June 15, 1996, in Berlin.

THA privatization agent who worked in the central office. Interview conducted April 30, 1996, in Berlin.

Contractor and privatization agent for the THA. Initially worked in Leipzig and later Berlin. Interview conducted July 15, 1996, in Berlin.

Privatization specialist in the central office Berlin. Interview conducted May 14, 1996, in Berlin.

THA director in charge of contractors. Interview conducted July 5, 1996, in Berlin. Personnel specialist. Interview conducted July, May 1996, Berlin.

Two auditors at the THA and BvS. Interviews conducted July 2, 1996, in Berlin, Germany.

Several professors of political science who had studied the THA extensively.

Former contractor who worked on large THA privatizations. Interview conducted November 28, 1995, in Berlin.

Executive committee member at IG Metall. Interview conducted June 12, 1996.

THA director of firm development. Interview conducted in June 1996 in Berlin.

Former THA Management Committee contractor. Also worked in the management of the Revision, the THA's internal auditing department. Multiple interviews conducted between March and June 1996 in Berlin.

Business director in the controlling department (C1). Interview conducted December 6, 1995.

THA manager charged with setting up management systems and staffing for 300 large firms in heavy machinery, textiles, and electrical. Worked in the regional and central offices. Interview conducted February 22, 1996, in Berlin.

Manager of THA-owned electrical firm. Interview conducted February 15, 1996.

Privatization agent who worked for a THA-sister agency charged with real estate disposition. Interview conducted November 4, 1995.

Union steward at a large manufacturing company that was privatized. He later worked as a staff member for an SPD parliamentarian. Multiple interviews conducted in February and March 1996 in Schwedt.

THA contractor who worked full time with the Management Committee. Interview conducted July 1996 in Berlin.

THA personnel manager and developer. Interview conducted June 19, 1996, in Berlin.

Der Spiegel reporter who had written extensively on the THA. June 1996 by phone in Berlin.

Privatization contractor and manager within the THA's liquidation division. Interview conducted May 17, 1996, in Berlin.

Special assistant to THA President Birgit Breuel. Multiple interviews conducted May 6–8, 1996.

Privatization agent and contractor who worked in the regional offices. Interview conducted May 14, 1996, in Berlin.

RTC-RELATED INTERVIEWS

Securitization specialist who had worked in California and in Washington. Interview conducted March 11, 1994, in Washington, D.C.

Professor of Real Estate at Southern Methodist University. Interview conducted June 6, 1995, in Dallas, Texas.

Executive Assistant to Bill Rolle. Multiple interviews conducted in March and August 1995, in Washington, D.C.

Owner of a large real estate firm that had contracted with the RTC. Interview conducted June 6, 1995, in Dallas, Texas.

Real estate editor for the *Dallas Morning News* who covered the RTC's activities extensively through the 1990s. Interview conducted June 5, 1995, in Dallas, Texas.

Former president of a large savings and loan. Interview conducted June 3, 1995, in Dallas, Texas.

Sales director for the RTC in Dallas. Interview conducted June 1, 1995, in Dallas, Texas.

Real sales director in Dallas. Interview conducted June 1, 1995, in Dallas, Texas.

RTC public affairs director. Interview conducted June 1, 1995, in Dallas, Texas.

RTC real estate appraiser. Interview conducted June 7, 1995, in Dallas, Texas.

RTC director of loan sales. Interview conducted June 6, 1995, in Dallas, Texas.

RTC manager. Interview conducted June 1997, in Newport Beach, California.

RTC contractor and chairman of real estate research firm. Interview conducted June 7, 1995, in Dallas, Texas.

Senior GAO evaluator who worked extensively on the RTC. Interview conducted June 1, 1995, in Dallas, Texas.

Contracting manager. Interview conducted in Washington, D.C. March 20, 1997.

Senior GAO auditor. Interview conducted March 14, 1995, in Washington, D.C.

RTC contractor (appraiser). Interview conducted June 1997, in Phoenix, Arizona.

GAO auditor. Interview conducted March 21, 1995, in Washington, D.C.

Director of RTC Southwest consolidated office and former managing agent. Interview conducted in Phoenix, Arizona June 17, 1997.

National sales center director. Interview conducted March 1995 in Washington, D.C.

Former Housing Banking Committee staff person and assistant to Henry Gonzales (D-TX). March 20, 1995, in Washington, D.C.

Former RTC managing agent. Interview conducted in Phoenix, Arizona June 25, 1997.

GAO examiner. Had previously worked for the Federal Home Loan Bank Board and the Federal Savings and Loan Insurance Corporation. Interview conduct March 3, 1995, in Washington, D.C.

Resolutions manager. Interview conducted in Washington, D.C., on March 23, 1995.

Resolutions manager. Interview conducted in Washington, D.C., on March 24, 1995.

Executive secretary of the RTC Oversight Board. Interview conducted in March 1995 in Washington, D.C.

Staff of House Banking Committee member involved in the oversight of RTC and the creation of FIRREA. Interview conducted March 17, 1995.

Legislative staff director for the majority on the House Banking Committee during the passage of FIRREA. Interview conducted March 15, 1995.

RTC manager and lawyer. Interview conducted March 1994 in Washington, D.C.

Staff lawyer on the Housing Banking Committee. Helped to draft FIRREA. Interview conducted in March 1994 in Washington, D.C.

RTC oversight board member. Interview conducted March 14, 1994, in Washington, D.C.

Director of national auctions program. Interview conducted March 20, 1995, in Washington, D.C.

Affordable housing specialist. Interview conducted June 1995 in Dallas, Texas.

Securitizations specialist. Interview conducted August 5, 1997, in Washington, D.C.

Managing agent. Interview conducted June 1997 in Newport Beach, California.

RTC director of representations and warranties. Interview conducted in August 1997 in Washington, D.C.

RTC manager. Interview conducted June 1997 in Newport Beach, California.

Managing agent. Interview conducted June 25, 1997, in Phoenix, Arizona.

Managing agent. Interview conducted June 1997 in Milwaukee, Wisconsin.

Managing agent. Interview conducted June 1997 in Phoenix, Arizona.

RTC lawyer and former conservatorship contractor. Interview conducted in June 1997 in Newport Beach, California.

GAO examiner. Interview conducted March 16, 1995, in Washington, D.C.

Former counsel to the Senate Banking Committee. Previously worked for the Federal Savings and Loan Insurance Corporation. Interview conducted March 17, 1994.

Managing agent. Interview conducted June 1997 in Newport Beach, California.

References

Akerlof, G. A., A. K. Rose, J. Yellen, and H. Hessenius. 1991. East Germany in from the Cold: The Economic Aftermath of Currency Union. *Brookings Papers on Economic Activity* 1: 1–115.

Albert, Michel. 1993. *Capitalism vs. Capitalism.* London: Whurr.

American Banker. 1996. Top 100 U.S. Bank Holding Companies. 28 March, 6.

Badaracco, Joseph. 1985. *Loading the Dice: A Five-Country Study of Vinyl Chloride Regulation.* Cambridge: Harvard Business School.

Baumann, Michael. 1994. Die Treuhand und das kleine Einmaleins der Privatisierung. *Frankfurter Rundschau,* 23 June, 20.

Benz, Arthur. 1989. Intergovernmental Relations in the 1980s: Recent Trends and Developments. *Publius: Journal of Federalism* 19: 203–20.

Benz, Arthur, and Klaus Goetz, eds. 1996. *A New German Public Sector.* Hampshire, England: Dartmouth.

Blau, Peter. 1955. *The Dynamics of Bureaucracy.* Chicago: University of Chicago Press.

BMF. 1991. *Die Einkommensstrukturen der Vorstände größerer Treuhand Unternehmen und der Vorstandsmitglieder der Treuhandanstalt.* Bonn: Bundesministerium für Finanzen.

———. 1993. Konzept der Bundesregierung zur Sicherung und Erneuerung industrieller Kerne durch die Treuhandanstalt in den neuen Bundesländern. In *Dokumentation 11*, edited by Treuhandanstalt. Berlin: Treuhandanstalt, 722–23.

————. 1994. *Bericht zur Personal- und Vergütungsstruktur der Treuhandanstalt und der funktionalen Beteiligungsgesellschaften der Treuhandanstalt.* Bonn: Bundesministerium der Finanzen. Nr. 10/94.

Borcherding, Thomas. 1977. *Budgets and Bureaucrats: The Source of Government Growth.* Durham, N.C.: Duke University Press.

Bowers, Jeryl. 1992. The Resolution Trust Corporation's Override Regulation: Freedom for Intrastate Branch Banking. *University of Chicago Law Review* 59: 691–717.

Boyes, Roger, and Charles Bremner. 2000. Tycoon Holds Key to Kohl Bribes Claim. *The [London] Times*, 11 January, 1.

Braun, Dietmar. 1993. Who Governs Intermediary Agencies? Principal-Agent Relations in Research Policy-Making. *Journal of Public Policy* 13 (2): 135–62.

Breuel, Birgit. 1993a. Erhaltung industrieller Kerne in Ostdeutschland? *Wirtschaftsdienst*, February, 60.

————. 1993b. *Treuhand Intern Tagebuch.* Frankfurt, Germany: Ullstein.

Brickman, Ronald, Sheila Jasanoff, and Thomas Ilgen. 1985. *Controlling Chemicals: The Politics of Regulation in Europe and the United States.* Edited by S. Jasanoff and T. Ilgen. Ithaca, N.Y.: Cornell University Press.

Buchanan, James. 1977. Why Does Government Grow? In *Budgets and Bureaucrats: The Sources of Government Growth*, edited by T. E. Borcherding. Durham, N.C.: Duke University Press.

Bundesrechnungshof. 1992. *Mitteilung über die Prüfung der Verfahrensweise der Treuhandanstalt bei der Privatisierung von Unternehmen.* Berlin.

————. 1993. *Prüfung von Ausgaben der THA für den Einsatz externer Sachverständiger bei der Privatisierung von Unternehmen der THA.* Berlin.

BvS. 1995. *Final Report of the THA.* Berlin: Bundesanstalt für vereinigungsbedingte Sonderaufgaben.

REFERENCES

Cadel, Georg. 1994. *Die Kontrolle der Treuhand-Anstalt and ihrer Unternehmen durch das Finanzministerium, den Rechnungshof und das Parlament.* Berlin: Freie Universität Berlin.

Campbell, Jon, and Leon Lindberg. 1991. The State and the Organization of Economic Activity. In *Governance of the American Economy,* edited by J. Rogers Hollingsworth, Jon Campbell, and Leon Lindberg. Cambridge: Cambridge University Press.

Carlin, Wendy. 1994. Privatization and Deindustrialization in East Germany. In *Privatization in Central and Eastern Europe,* edited by S. Estrin. Harlow, Essex, England: Longman Group Publishers, 127–75.

Carlin, Wendy, and Colin Mayer. 1994. The Treuhandanstalt: Privatization by State and Market. In *The Transition in Eastern Europe,* edited by O. Blanchard, K. Froot, and J. Sachs. Chicago: University of Chicago Press, 189–207.

———. 1995. *Structure and Ownership of East German Enterprises.* Berlin: Wissenschaftszentrum Berlin fuer Sozialforschung. FS I 95-305.

Carlin, Wendy, and Peter Richthofen. 1995. *Finance, Economic Development and the Transition: The East German Case.* Vol. FS I 95–301, *WZB Discussion Paper.* Berlin: Wissenschaftszentrum Berlin für Sozialforschung.

Cassell, Mark. 2001. Privatization and the Courts: How Judicial Structures Shaped German Privatization. *Governance* 14 (4): 429–55.

CBO. 1991. *The Cost of Forbearance during the Thrift Crisis.* Washington, D.C., Congressional Budget Office.

———. 1993. *Resolving the Thrift Crisis.* Washington, D.C., Congressional Budget Office.

Christ, Peter, and Ralf Neubauer. 1991. *Kolonie im eigenen Land. Die Treuhand, Bonn und die Wirtschaftskatastrophe der fünf neuen Länder.* Berlin: Rowohlt.

Cloes, Roger. 1991. Die parlamentarische Kontrolle der THA. *DtZ* 8: 291–92.

―――. 1992. Die Treuhandanstalt und ihre Kontrolle. *Die Bank* 7: 377–82.

Cohen, Michael, James March, and Johan Olsen. 1972. A Garbage Can Model of Organizational Choice. *Administrative Science Quarterly,* March, 1–25.

Cohen, Roger, and John Tagliabue. 2000. Big Kickbacks Under Kohl Reported. *New York Times,* February 7, Section A, Page 11.

Congressional Record. 1989. 101st Cong., 1st sess. Vol. 135, pt. 10, S104030.

Cooper, Wendy. 1993. The Treuhand's Troubled Legacy. *International Investor* May: 48–55.

Crawford, John. 1991. $30 Billion RTC Salvage Bill Awaits President's OK. *Congressional Quarterly,* 23 March, 734.

Crouch, Colin, and Wolfgang Streeck, eds. 1997. *Political Economy of Modern Capitalism.* New York: Sage Publications.

Czada, Roland. 1996a. The THA and Its Environment of Politics and Interest Groups. In *Treuhandanstalt: The Impossible Challenge,* edited by W. Fischer, H. Hax and H. K. Schneider. Berlin: Akademie Verlag, 148–73.

―――. 1996b. The Treuhandanstalt and the Transition from Socialism to Capitalism. In *A New German Public Sector,* edited by A. Benz and K. Goetz. Brookfield, Vt.: Dartmouth Publishing Co., 93–118.

Dahl, Robert. 1947. The Science of Public Administration: Three Problems. *Public Administration Review* 7: 1–11.

Deeg, Richard. 1999. *Finance Capitalism Unveiled: Banks and the German Political Economy.* Ann Arbor: University of Michigan Press.

Demaree, Allan. 1990. The New Germany's Glowing Future. *Fortune Magazine,* 3 December, 147.

Dempsey, Judy. 1993. Treuhand Head Administers a Painful Cure. *Financial Times,* 4 October, 3.

―――. 1994. Treuhand's Final Debt to Total DM270 bn. *Financial Times,* 26 July, 2.

REFERENCES

Der Spiegel. 1991. Wer kennt einen, der passt? *Der Spiegel,* 14 January, 90–93.

———. 1994. Bedienen sie sich nur. *Der Spiegel,* 26 September, 40–41.

———. 1996. Rote Lampen. *Der Spiegel,* October, 104–6.

Der Spiegel Staff. 2000. Zwei Drittel der Kanzleramtsdaten gelöscht. *Der Spiegel,* 28 June.

Derlien, Hans-Ulrich. 1990. Historical Legacy and Recent Developments in the German Higher Civil Service. *European Journal of Political Research* 18: 349–72.

———. 1992. Professionalisierung und Säuberung. In *Verwaltungsreform und Verwaltungspolitik im Prozeß der deutschen Einigung,* edited by W. Seibel, A. Benz, and H. Maeding. Baden-Baden: Nomos.

———. 1996. Patterns of Postwar Administrative Development in Germany. In *A New German Public Sector?* edited by A. Benz and K. Goetz. Brookfield, Vt.: Dartmouth Publishing Co., 27–44.

DGB. 1993. *Informationsdienst,* Bundespressestelle des Deutschen Gewerkschaftsbundes.

Die Presse. 1991. Karriere in Deutschland: Auch Österreicher sind gefordert und gesucht. *Die Presse,* 15 March.

Dill, William. 1958. Environment as an Influence on Managerial Autonomy. *Administrative Science Quarterly* 2 (March): 409–43.

Dininio, Phyllis. 1999. *The Political Economy of East German Privatization.* Westport, Conn.: Praeger.

Dobek, Mariusz. 1993. *The Political Logic of Privatization: Lessons from Great Britain and Poland.* Westport, Conn.: Praeger.

Dodds, Paul, and Gerd Wächter. 1993. Privatization Contracts with the German Treuhandanstalt: An Insider's Guide. *The International Lawyer* 27 (1): 65–90.

Donahue, John. 1989. *The Privatization Decision.* New York: Basic Books.

Drost, Helmar. 1993. The Great Depression in East Germany: The Effects of Unification on East Germany's Economy. *East European Politics and Societies* Fall: 458.

Durr, Karoline. 1993. Treuhandanstalt Gives Young Staff Passport to the Business Fast Track. *The Wall Street Journal*, 25 August, 1, 5.

Dyson, Kenneth. 1986. The State, Banks and Industry. In *State, Finance and Industry*, edited by A. Cox. Brighton: Wheatsheaf.

———. 1992. Theories of Regulation and the Case of Germany: A Model of Regulatory Change. In *The Politics of German Regulation*, edited by K. Dyson. England: Dartmouth.

Economist Staff, The. 1990. Who'll Bid for Dallas? *The Economist*, 2 June, 24.

———. 1992. Hand of Kindness. *The Economist*, 21 March, 71.

———. 1996. Moral Hazard Has Played a Part in Japan's Banking Disaster, Too. *The Economist*, 27 April, S24.

Emerson, Richard. 1962. Power-Dependence Relations. *American Sociological Review* 27 (February): 31–40.

Esser, Josef. 1989. Symbolic Privatisation: The Politics of Privatisation in West Germany. In *The Politics of Privatisation in Western Europe*, edited by J. Vickers and V. Wright. London: Frank Cass and Co. Ltd., 105–21.

Estrin, Saul, ed. 1994. *Privatization in Central and Eastern Europe*. England: Longman Group Publishers.

Feddersen, Dieter. 1991. GDR Émigrés and Property Rights. *Politics and Society* 23: 41–61.

Fesler, James, and Donald Kettl. 1996. *The Politics of the Administrative Process*. Second edition. Chatham, N.J.: Chatham House Publishers.

Fichter, Michael. 1993. A House Divided: A View of German Unification as It Has Affected Organized Labor. *German Politics* 2 (1): 21–39.

Fieberg, Gerhard, and Harald Reichenbach. 1992. *Vermögensgesetz*. Munich: Deutscher Taschenbuch Verlag C. H. Beck.

Finn, Peter. 2001. Settlement Reported in Kohl Scandal. *Washington Post*, February 9, A22.

Fischer, Wolfram, Herbert Hax, and Hans-Karl Schneider, eds. 1996. *Treuhandanstalt: The Impossible Challenge.* Berlin: Akademie Verlag.

Fischer, Wolfram, and Harm Schröter. 1996. The Development of the Treuhandanstalt. In *Treuhandanstalt: The Impossible Challenge,* edited by W. Fischer, H. Hax and H. K. Schneider. Berlin: Akademie Verlag, 17–40.

Fisher, Marc. 1991. The Grinding Gears of Reunification. *Washington Post,* 10 March, H1.

Flassbeck, Heiner, and Wolfgang Scheremet. 1992. Wirtschaftliche Aspekte der deutschen Vereinigung. In *Die Gestaltung der deutschen Einheit. Geschichte—Politik—Gesellschaft,* edited by E. Jesse and A. Mitter. Bonn and Berlin: Bouvier Verlag, 279–311.

Fligstein, Neil. 1990. *The Transformation of Corporate Control.* Cambridge: Harvard University Press.

Freese, Christoph. 1995. *Die Privatisierungstätigkeit der Treuhandanstalt.* Frankfurt: Campus.

Friedrich, Carl. 1978. The Struggle for Organizational Survival. In *Bureaucratic Power in National Politics,* edited by F. Rourke. Boston: Little, Brown.

Froomkin, A. Michael. 1995. Reinventing the Government Corporation. *The University of Illinois Law Review,* 543–634.

Ganske, Joachim. 1991. Spaltung der Treuhandunternehmen. *Der Betrieb* 15: 791–97.

GAO. 1983. *Congress Should Consider Revising Basic Corporate Control Laws.* Washington, D.C., General Accounting Office.

———. 1990. *RTC Asset Management: Contracting Conrol Need to Be Strengthened.* Washington, D.C. General Accounting Office. GAP/T–GGD–89–11.

———. 1991a. *Government Contractors: Are Service Contractors Performing Inherently Governmental Functions.* Washington, D.C., General Accounting Office. GGD–92–11.

———. 1991b. *A More Flexible Contracting-Out Policy is Needed.* Washington, D.C., General Accounting Office. GAO/GGD–91–136.

———. 1991c. *Resolution Trust Corporation: Policies, Procedures, Practices and Results.* Washington, D.C., General Accounting Office.

———. 1991d. *RTC: Evolving Oversight on Interim Servicing Arrangements.* Washington, D.C., General Accounting Office. GAO/GGD–91–120.

———. 1991e. *RTC: Progress Under Way in Minority- and Women-Owned Business Outreach Program.* Washington, D.C., General Accounting Office. GAO/GGD–91–138.

———. 1992a. *Affordable Multifamily Housing Program Has Improved but More Can Be Done.* Washington, D.C., General Accounting Office. GAO/GGD–92–137.

———. 1992b. *Asset Valuation Reviews and Cost Tests.* Washington, D.C., General Accounting Office. GAO/GGD–92–17R.

———. 1992c. *High-Risk Series: Resolution Trust Corporation.* Washington, D.C., General Accounting Office. GAO/HR–93–4.

———. 1992d. *Review of RTC Fitness and Integrity Certifications for Western Storm.* Washington, D.C., General Accounting Office. GAO/GGD–93–31R.

———. 1992e. *RTC: Asset Pooling and Market Practices Add Millions to Contract Costs.* Washington, D.C., General Accounting Office. GAO/GGD–93–2.

———. 1992f. *RTC: More Actions Needed to Improve Single-Family Affordable Housing Program.* Washington, D.C., General Accounting Office. GAO/GGD-92-136.

———. 1992g. *RTC: Preliminary Results of Western Story Investigation and Related Contracting Deficiencies.* Washington, D.C., General Accounting Office. GAO/T–GGD–92–16.

———. 1992h. *RTC: Review of Information Reporting Requirements for Asset Management Contractors.* Washington, D.C., General Accounting Office.

———. 1992i. *RTC: Status of Loans and Other Assets Inventory System.* Washington, D.C., General Accounting Office. GAO/IMTEC–92–35BR.

REFERENCES

———. 1992j. *RTC: Survey Results on RTC's Communication and Real Estate Marketing.* Washington, D.C., General Accounting Office. GAO/GGD–92–134BR.

———. 1992k. *RTC Western Storm Follow-up.* Washington, D.C., General Accounting Office. GAO/GGD–93–8R.

———. 1993a. *Controls Over Asset Valuations Do Not Ensure Reasonable Estimates.* Washington, D.C., General Accounting Office. GAO/GGD–93–80.

———. 1993b. *Executive Bonuses: Information on FDIC's and RTC's Executive Bonus Program.* Washington, D.C., General Accounting Office. GAO/GGD–94–15.

———. 1993c. *Government Management: Status of Progress in Correcting Selected High-Risk Areas.* Washington, D.C., General Accounting Office. GAO/T–AFMD–93–1.

———. 1993d. *Resolution Trust Corporation: Funding, Organization, and Performance.* Washington, D.C., General Accounting Office. GAO/T–GGD–93–13.

———. 1993e. *Resolution Trust Corporation: Oversight of SAMDA Property Management Contractors Needs Improvement.* Washington, D.C., General Accounting Office. GAO/GGD–94–62.

———. 1993f. *Resolution Trust Corporation: Status of Management Efforts to Control Costs.* Washington, D.C., General Accounting Office. GAO/GGD–94–19.

———. 1993g. *RTC: Number and Types of Legal Matters.* Washington, D.C., General Accounting Office. GAO/GGD–93–50FS.

———. 1993h. *RTC: Data Limitations Impaired Analysis of Sales Method.* Washington, D.C., General Accounting Office. GAO/GGD–93–139.

———. 1994a. *Failed Financial Institutions: RTC/FDIC Risk Fraud and Mismanagement by Employing Those Deemed Culpable.* Washington, D.C., General Accounting Office. GAO/OSI–95–1.

———. 1994b. *Resolution Trust Corporation: Better Analyses Needed Before Terminating Asset Management Contracts.* Washington, D.C., General Accounting Office. GAO/GGD–94–181ML.

————. 1995. *High-Risk Series: Quick Reference Guide.* Washington, D.C., General Accounting Office. GAO/HR–95–2.

Gaus, John. 1950. Trends in the Theory of Public Administration. *Public Administration Review* 10: 160–72.

Geppert, Mike, and Stefan Schmidt. 1993. *Von der 'DDR AG' zur Treuhandanstalt in Liquidation?* Wissenschaftszentrum Berlin für Sozialforschung. FS II 93–202.

Gerschenkron, Alexander. 1976. *Economic Backwardness in Historical Perspective.* Cambridge: Harvard University Press.

Gerth, H. H., and C. Wright Mills, eds. 1958. *From Max Weber: Essays in Sociology.* New York: Oxford University Press.

Giamo, Susan. 1994. Health Care Reform in Britain and Germany: Recasting the Political Bargain between the State and the Medical Profession. Ph.D. dissertation, Department of Political Science, University of Wisconsin–Madison.

Goodnow, Frank. 1900. *Politics and Administration: A Study in Government.* New York, N.Y.: Russell & Russell.

Gormley, William Jr., ed. 1991. *Privatization and Its Alternatives.* Madison: University of Wisconsin Press.

Griffin, John. 1992. Privatization and Financial Capitalism. Unpublished manuscript.

————. 1994. Investment and Ownership in a Volatile Economy: Big Banks and the Case of East German Economic Transition. *Politics and Society* 22 (3): 389–420.

Gulick, Luther. 1937. Notes on the Theory of Organization. In *Papers on the Science of Administration,* edited by L. Gulick and L. Urwick. New York: Institute of Public Administration, 1–45.

Hall, John, and Udo Ludwig. 1993. Creating Germany's Mezzogiorno? *Challenge* (July/August): 38–44.

Hall, Peter. 1986. *Governing the Economy: The Politics of State Intervention in Britain and France.* New York: Oxford University Press.

Hart, Jeffrey. 1992. *Rival Capitalists.* Ithaca, N.Y.: Cornell University Press.

Hassard, John, and Denis Pym, eds. 1995. *The Theory and Philosophy of Organizations.* London: Routledge.

Helm, Toby. 2001. Kohl Escapes Prosecution. *The Daily Telegraph,* 19 February, 19.

Henkel, Regina. 1991. Zwistigkeit und Frust und Fremdheit. *Manager Magazin,* 162–70.

Hickel, Rudopf, and Jan Priewe. 1994. *Nach dem Fehlstart.* Frankfurt am Main, Germany: S. Fischer.

Hilferding, Rudolf. 1910. *Das Finanzkapital.* Vienna.

Hill, Edward. 1990. The S&L Bailout: Some States Gain, Many More Lose. *Challenge,* May–June: 37–45.

Hirsch, Paul, Stuart Michaels, and Ray Friedman. 1987. "Dirty Hands" Versus "Clean Models." *Theory and Society* 16: 317–36.

Hoffmann, Lutz. 1993. *Warten auf den Aufschwung. Eine ostdeutsche Bilanz.* Regensburg: Transfer Verlag.

Hollingsworth, J. Rogers, Robert Boyer, and Wolfgang Streeck, eds. 1997. *Contemporary Capitalism: The Embeddedness of Institutions.* New York: Cambridge University Press.

Hollingsworth, Rogers, Wolfgang Streeck, and Philippe Schmitter, eds. 1994. *Governing Capitalist Economies.* New York: Oxford University Press.

Homann, Fritz. 1991. Treuhandanstalt: Zwischenbilanz, Perspektiven. *Deutschland-Archiv,* December.

IG Metall. 1991. *Zur solidarischen Finanzierung der sozialen Einigung.* Frankfurt am Main, Industriegewerkschaft Metall.

Ikenberry, John. 1988. Conclusion: An Institutional Approach to American Foreign Policy. *International Organization* 42 (1): 219–43.

Iversen, Torben. 1999. *Contested Economic Institutions.* Cambridge: Cambridge University Press.

Iversen, Torben, Jonas Pontusson, and David Soskice, eds. 2000. *Unions, Employers, and Central Banks.* Cambridge: Cambridge University Press.

Kampe, Dieter. 1994. *Wer uns kennenlernt, gewinnt uns lieb*. Berlin: Rotbuch Verlag.

Kampe, Dieter, and Rudolf Wallraf. 1991. Alles muß hoppla-hopp gehen: Interview mit Detlev Rohwedder. *Der Spiegel*, 28 January, 55–61.

Katzenstein, Peter. 1982. West Germany as Number Two: Reflections on the German Model. In *The Political Economy of West Germany*, edited by A. Markovits. New York: Praeger.

Katzmann, Robert. 1980. *Regulatory Bureaucracy: The Federal Trade Commission and Antitrust Policy*. Cambridge, Mass.: MIT Press.

Kaufman, Herbert. 1960. *The Forest Ranger: A Study in Administrative Behavior*. Washington, D.C.: Resources for the Future.

———. 1965. The Growth in the Federal Personnel System. In *The Federal Government Service*, edited by W. Sayre. Englewood Cliffs, N.J.: Prentice-Hall, 1–30.

Kawahito, Kiyoshi, and Douglas Timmons. 1999. American and Japanese Experiences of the Financial Industry Crisis in the 1980s and 1990s. *Japan Studies Review* 3: 61–86.

Kelman, Steven. 1981. *Regulating America, Regulating Sweden: A Comparative Study of Occupational Safety and Health*. Cambridge, Mass.: MIT Press.

———. 1992. Adversary and Cooperationist Institutions for Conflict Resolution in Public Policymaking. *Policy Analysis and Management* 11 (2): 178–206.

Kemmler, Marc. 1994. *Die Entstehung der Treuhandanstalt: Von der Wahrung zur Privatisierung des DDR-Volkseigentums*. New York: Campus Verlag.

Kerber, Markus, and Wilfried Stechow. 1991. Das Treuhandaußenrecht. *Deutsche Zeitschrift für Wirtschaftsrecht* 3: 105–15.

Kern, Horst, and Charles Sabel. 1996. The THA: A Trial Ground for Developing New Company Forms. In *The Impossible Challenge*, edited by W. Fischer, H. Hax, and H. K. Schneider. Berlin: Akademie Verlag, 478–500.

Kettl, Donald. 1991a. Accountability Issues of the Resolution Trust Corporation. *Housing Policy Debate* 2 (1): 93–114.

———. 1991b. The Savings and Loan Bailout: The Mismatch between the Headlines and the Issues. *PS: Political Science* September: 441–47.

———. 1993. *Sharing Power: Public Governance and Private Markets.* Washington, D.C.: Brookings Institution Press.

———. 1997. The Global Revolution in Public Management: Driving Themes, Missing Links. *Journal of Policy Analysis and Management* 16 (3): 446–62.

Khademian, Anne. 1996. *Checking on Banks: Autonomy and Accountability in the Three Federal Agencies.* Washington, D.C.: Brookings Institution Press.

Kingdon, John. 1984. *Agendas, Alternatives and Public Policies.* Boston: Little, Brown.

Klemmer, Paul. 1990. Modernisierung der ostdeutschen Wirtschaft als regionalpolitisches Problem. *Wirtschaftsdienst* 11: 557–75.

Kloepfer, Michael. 1996. The Treuhandanstalt under Public Law. In *Treuhandanstalt: The Impossible Challenge,* edited by W. Fischer, H. Hax, and H. Schneider. Berlin: Akademie Verlag, 40–85.

Kocka, Jürgen. 1970. Vorindustrielle Faktoren in der deutschen Industrialisierung. In *Das kaiserliche Deutschland: Politik und Gesellschaft 1870–1918,* edited by M. Stuermer. Düsseldorf: Droste Verlag.

———. 1980. The Rise of Modern Industrial Enterprise in Germany. In *Managerial Hierarchies,* edited by A. Chandler and H. Daems. Cambridge: Harvard University Press.

Kooiman, Jan, ed. 1993. *Modern Governance.* London: Sage Publications.

Kristensen, Peer Hull. 1997. National Systems of Governance and Managerial Prerogatives in the Evolution of Work Systems: England, Germany, and Denmark Compared. In *Governance at Work,* edited by R. Whitley and Peer Hull Kristensen. Oxford: Oxford University Press, 3–48.

Kriz, Margaret. 1989. Hurry-up Auctioneers. *National Journal* 21 (40): 2457–61.

Kühl, Jürgen. 1993. Unternehmensentwicklung von Treuhandunternehmen und privatisierten ehemaligen Treuhandfirmen vom Ende der DDR bis Ende 1992. Paper read at Erfahrung und Perspektiven des Transformationsprozesses, April, at Mannheim.

———. 1997. Privatization and Its Labour Market Effects in Eastern Germany. In *Lessons from Privatization*, edited by R. V. d. Hoeven and G. Sziraczki. Geneva: International Labour Office, 119–42.

Küpper, Hans-Ulrich, and Robert Mayr. 1996. Contract Drafting and Contract Management by the Treuhandanstalt. In *Treuhandanstalt: The Impossible Challenge*, edited by W. Fischer, H. Hax, and H. K. Schneider. Berlin: Akademie Verlag, 317–49.

Lasswell, Harold. 1950. *Politics: Who Gets What, When and How.* New York: P. Smith.

Lee, Peter. 1992. Common Goals, Divided Loyalties. *Euromoney,* February, 40–44.

Lehmbruch, Gerhard. 1990. The Organization of Society, Administrative Strategies and Policy Networks. In *Political Choice, Institutions, Rules and the Limits of Rationality*, edited by R. Czada and A. Windhoff-Heritier. Frankfurt: Campus Verlag.

———. 1991. Die deutsche Vereinigung. Strukturen und Strategien. *Politische Vierteljahresschrift* 32: 585–604.

———. 1992. The Institutional Framework of German Regulation. In *The Politics of German Regulation*, edited by K. Dyson. Brookfield, Vt.: Dartmouth.

Lichtblau, Karl. 1993. Privatisierungs- und Sanierungsarbeit der Treuhandanstalt. *Beiträge zur Wirtschafts- und Sozialpolitik.* 209 (4). Köln: Institut der Deutschen Wirtschaft.

Litan, Robert. 1990. Getting Out of the Thrift Crisis Now. *Brookings Review.* Winter, 241–45.

Long, Norton. 1949. Power and Administration. *Public Administration Review* 9: 257–64.

Luft, Christa. 1992. *Treuhandreport. Werden und Vergehen einer deutschen Behörde*. Berlin: Aufbau Verlag.

REFERENCES

MacDonald, Heather. 1995. The Resolution Trust Corporation's Affordable Housing Mandate: Diluting FIRREA's Redistributive Goals. *Urban Affairs Review* 30 (4): 558–79.

Marissal, Matthias. 1993. *Der Politische Handlungsrahmen der Treuhandanstalt.* New York: Peter Lang.

Marshall, Jeffrey. 1993. Learning from the RTC. *United States Banker,* September: 28–37.

Martin, Joanne. 1992. *Cultures in Organizations.* New York: Oxford University Press.

Martin, Todd. 1991. No sale: RTC's Many Miscues In Selling Off Property Rattle Local Markets. *Wall Street Journal,* 28 March, 1.

Marx, Manfred. 1985. *Die Notwendigkeit und Tragweite der Untersuchungsmaxime in den Verwaltungsprozeßgesetzen.* Frankfurt am Main: Peter Lang.

Mayntz, Renate, and Hans-Ulrich Derlien. 1989. Party Patronage and Politicization of the West German Administrative Elite. *Governance* 2: 384–404.

Mayntz, Renate, and Fritz Scharpf. 1975. *Policy-Making in the German Federal Bureaucracy.* Amsterdam: Elsevier.

Mazmanian, Daniel, and Paul Sabatier. 1983. *Implementation and Public Policy.* Glenview, Ill.: Scott, Foresman.

McCubbins, Mathew, and Timothy Schwartz. 1984. Congressional Oversight Overlooked: Police Patrols Versus Fire Alarms. *American Journal of Political Science* 29: 721–48.

Meier, Kenneth. 1980. *Politics and the Bureaucracy: Policymaking in the Fourth Branch of Government.* North Scituate, Mass.: Duxbury Press.

Meriam, Lewis. 1939. *Reorganization of the National Government.* Washington, D.C.: Brookings Institution Press.

Merton, Robert. 1940. Bureaucratic Structure and Personality. *Social Forces* 18: 560–68.

Moe, Ronald. 1983. *Administering Public Functions at the Margin of Government: The Case of Federal Corporations.* Washington, D.C., Congressional Research Service. 83–236.

Moe, Terry. 1989. The Politics of Bureaucratic Structure. In *Can the Government Govern?* edited by J. Chubb and P. Peterson. Washington, D.C.: Brookings Institution Press, 267–329.

———. 1990. The Politics of Structural Choice: Toward a Theory of Public Bureucracy. In *Organization Theory from Barnard to the Present and Beyond*, edited by O. Williamson. New York: Oxford University Press.

Moe, Terry, and Michael Caldwell. 1994. Institutional Foundations of Democratic Government. *Journal of Institutional and Theoretical Economics (JITE)* 150 (1): 171–95.

Myritz, Reinhard. 1992. Elite ohne Alternative: Zur Situation der Führungskräfte in ostdeutschen Unternehmen. *Deutschland Archiv* 5: 475–83.

Nägele, Frank. 1994. Strukturpolitik wider Willen? *Aus Politik und Zeitgeschichte* B43–44: 43–52.

Nick, Harry. 1995. Die Schuldenlegende. In *Vereinigungsbilanz: Fünf Jahre deutsche Einheit*, edited by K. Steinitz. Hamburg: VSA Verlag.

Niskanen, William. 1971. *Bureaucracy and Representative Government.* Chicago: Aldine, Atherton.

Nolte, Dirk. 1994. Industriepolitik in Ostdeutschland am Beispiel des Bundeslandes Sachsen. *Aus Politik und Zeitgeschichte* 17 (April): 37–45.

North, Douglass. 1991. *Institutions, Institutional Change and Economic Performance.* New York: Cambridge University Press.

Osborne, David, and Ted Gaebler. 1992. *Reinventing Government: How the Entrepreneurial Spirit is Transforming the Public Sector, From Schoolhouse to Statehouse, City Hall to the Pentagon.* Reading, Mass.: Addison-Wesley.

Ouchi, William. 1981. *Theory Z: How American Business Can Meet the Japanese Challenge.* Reading, Mass.: Addison-Wesley.

PDS. 1994. *Blickpunkt Treuhandanstalt.* Berlin: Matthias Kirschner Verlag.

REFERENCES

Perry, James. 1986. Merit Pay in the Public Sector: The Case for a Failure of Theory. *Review of Public Personnel Administration* 7: 57–69.

Peters, Guy. 1996. *Governing: Four Emerging Models.* Lawrence: University Press of Kansas.

Pfeffer, Jeffrey, and Gerald Salancik. 1978. *The External Control of Organizations: A Resource Dependence Perspective.* New York: Harper and Row.

Pierre, Jon, ed. 1995. *Bureaucracy in the Modern State.* England: Elgar Publishing.

Pizzo, Stephen, Mary Fricker, and Paul Muolo. 1989. *Inside Job: The Looting of America's Savings and Loans.* New York: Random House.

Pressman, Jeffrey, and Aaron Wildavsky. 1973. *Implementation.* Berkeley: University of California Press.

Priewe, Jan. 1991. Logik des Kahlschlags. *Blätter für deutsche und internationale Politik* 2: 208–15.

———. 1993. Privatisation of the Industrial Sector: The Function and Activities of the Treuhandanstalt. *Cambridge Journal of Economics* 17: 333–48.

Rainey, Hal. 1992. On the Uniqueness of Public Bureaucracies. In *The State of Public Bureaucracy,* edited by L. Hill. Armond, N.Y.: M. E. Sharpe.

Revision. 1993. *Revisionsbericht: Vereinbarung anläßlich des Ausscheidens von THA-Mitarbeitern.*

Ripley, Randall, and Grace Franklin. 1986. *Policy Implementation.* Chicago: Dorsey Press.

Rom, Mark. 1996. *Public Spirit in the Thrift Tragedy.* Pittsburgh: University of Pittsburgh Press.

Rosenblatt, Robert. 1989. Authors of S&L Bailout Irked at Soaring Costs. *Los Angeles Times,* November 2, D1.

———. 1990. Banking Panel Angry Over 'Timid' Pace of S&L Cleanup. *Los Angeles Times,* February 1, D2.

Rosenblatt, Robert, and James Bates. 1989. S&L Mop-Up Agency; History's Biggest Fire Sale. *Los Angeles Times*, August 11, A1.

RTC. 1991. *Annual Report.* Washington, D.C.: Government Printing Office.

————. 1996. *Statistical abstract : August 1989/September 1995.* Washington, D.C.: Resolution Trust Corporation's Office of Planning, Research, and Statistics. 1061–K–01.

RTC Office of the Inspector General. 1992. *Asset Valuation Methods and the Appraisal Review Process.* Washington, D.C. Audit Report A92–016.

Rüsken, Walter. 1995. Beweis durch beigezogene Akten. *Betriebsberater,* 761.

Sako, Mari. 1994. Neither Markets nor Hierarchies: A Comparative Study of the Printed Circuit Board Industry in Britain and Japan. In *Governing Capitalist Economies,* edited by R. Hollingsworth, W. Streeck and P. Schmitter. Oxford: Oxford University Press, 17–42.

Schäfers, Bernhard. 1997. *Politischer Atlas Deutschland.* Bonn: J. H. W. Dietz.

Schatz, Klaus-Werner. 1996. Comment on Herbert Hax, "Privatization Agencies: The Treuhand Approach." In *Economic Aspects of German Unification: Expectations, Transition Dynamics, and International Perspectives,* edited by P. Welfens. Berlin: Sprenger.

Schaub, Günter. 1993. Die Rahmenvereinbarung der Treuhandanstalt mit Gewerkschaften und ihre Richtlinien. *Neue Zeitschrift für Arbeitsrecht,* 673–79.

Schein, Edgar. 1985. *Organizational Culture and Leadership.* San Francisco: Jossey-Bass.

Schmeckebier, Lewis Meriam and Lawrence. 1939. *Reorganization of the National Government.* Washington, D.C.: Brookings Insitution.

Schmidt, Helmut. 1993. *Handeln für Deutschland.* Berlin: Rowohlt.

Schmidt, Klaus-Dieter, and Uwe Siegmund. 1996. Privatisation Strategies. In *The Treuhandanstalt: The Impossible Challenge,* edited by W. Fischer, H. Hax, and H. K. Schneider. Berlin: Akademie Verlag, 211–40.

Schneider, Anne. 1995. *Policy Design for Democracy.* Lawrence: University Press of Kansas.

Schuppert, Gunnar. 1992. Die Treuhandanstalt. Zum Leben einer Organisation im Überschneidungsbereich zweier Rechtskreise. *Staatswissenschaft und Staatspraxis* 2: 186–210.

Schwalbach, Joachim, and Sven Gless. 1996. Supporting Companies Capable of Being Restructured on Their Way to Privatization. In *Treuhandanstalt: The Impossible Challenge,* edited by W. Fischer, H. Hax, and H. K. Schneider. Berlin: Akademie Verlag, 177–210.

Schwenn, Kerstin. 1995. Über Erfolg oder Misserfolg der THA ist noch nicht entschieden. *Frankfurter Allgemeine Zeitung.*

Seibel, Wolfgang. 1992. Necessary Illusions: The Transformation of Governance Structure in the New Germany. *Toqueville Review* 13: 178–97.

———. 1994. Strategische Fehler oder erfolgreiches Scheitern? Zur Entwicklung der Treuhand 1990–1993. *Politische Vierteljahresschrift* 35: 3–39.

———. 1997. Privatization by Means of State Bureaucracy? The Treuhand Phenomenon in Eastern Germany. In *Restructuring Networks in Post-socialism: Legacies, Linkages, and Localities,* edited by G. Grabher and D. Stark. New York: Oxford University Press, 284–304.

Seibel, Wolfgang, and Stefan Kapferer. 1996. The Organizational Development of the Treuhandanstalt. In *The Treuhandanstalt: The Impossible Challenge,* edited by W. Fischer, H. Hax and H. K. Schneider. Berlin: Akademie Verlag, 111–47.

Seibel, Wolfgang, and Sandra Lavenex. 1997. Ethical Challenges in a Time of Change-Germany. Paper read at Ethics in the Public Sector meeting, November 2–3, Paris.

Seidman, William. 1993. *Full Faith and Credit.* New York: Times Books.

Selznick, Philip. 1949. *TVA and the Grass Roots.* Berkeley: University of California Press.

Shonfield, Andrew. 1969. *Modern Capitalism.* London: Oxford University Press.

Sinn, Gerlinde, and Hans-Werner Sinn. 1992. *Jumpstart: The Economic Unification of Germany.* Cambridge, Mass.: MIT Press.

Sirleschtov, Antje. 1991. 12000 Manager werden die Chefetagen räumen müssen. *Neue Zeit,* August 18.

Sitte, Ralf, and Hartmut Tofaute. 1996. *Beschäftigungsbilanz der Treuhandanstalt.* Düsseldorf: Wirtschafts und Sozialwissenschaftliches Institut in der HBS, 27.

Skowronek, Stephen. 1982. *Building a New American State: The Expansion of National Administrative Capabilities, 1877–1920.* Cambridge: Cambridge University Press.

Smid, Stefan. 1990. *Rechtssprechung: zu Rechtsfürsorge und Prozess.* Berlin: Heymann.

Smyser, W. R. 1993. *The German Economy.* New York: St. Martin's Press.

Southern, David. 1993. Restitution or Compensation. *German Politics* 2 (3): 436–49.

Southern Finance Project. 1992a. *Fortunate Sons: Three Years of Dealmaking at the Resolution Trust Corporation.* Charlotte, N.C.: Southern Finance Project.

———. 1992b. *Under New Management: The S&L Crisis and the Rural South.* Charlotte, N.C.: Southern Finance Project.

Spoerr, Wolfgang. 1993. *Treuhandanstalt und Treuhandunternehmen zwischen Verfassungs-, Verwaltungs- und Gesellschaftsrecht.* Köln.

Stechow, Wilfried, and Markus Kerber. 1991. Die Treuhandanstalt im Spannungsverhältnis zwischen öffentlichem und privatem Recht. *Deutsche Zeitschrift für Wirtschaftsrecht* 2: 49–52.

Stone, Deborah. 1996. *The Policy Paradox.* New York: Norton.

Streeck, Wolfgang, and Philippe Schmitter. 1985. *Private Interest Government: Beyond Market and State Financial Reform.* Beverly Hills, Calif.: Sage Publications.

Suhr, Heinz. 1991. *Der Treuhandskandal: Wie Ostdeutschland geschlachtet wurde.* Frankfurt am Main: Eichborn Verlag.

Süss, Walter. 1992. Eine Behörde verkauft die ostdeutsche Volkswirtschaft. *Das Parlament,* 3 March, 3.

THA, DGB, DAG. 1991. Gemeinsame Erklärung von Deutschem Gewerkschaftsbund, Deutscher Angestelltengewerkschaft,

Treuhandanstalt zum Interessenausgleich und Sozialplan. *Zeitschrift für Wirtschaft* 10: 690–92.

Thelen, Kathleen, Sven Steimo, and Frank Longstreth. 1993. *Historical Institutionalism in Comparative Analysis.* New York: Cambridge University Press.

Thompson, James. 1967. *Organizations in Action.* New York: McGraw-Hill.

Thrift Depositor Protection Oversight Board. 1995. *The Role of Citizen Advisory Boards in the Federal Government's Resolution of the S&L Crisis.* Washington, D.C.

Thurow, Lester. 1992. *Head to Head: The Coming Economic Battle among Japan, Europe, and America.* New York: William Morrow and Co.

Tolliday, S., and Jonathen Zeitlin, eds. 1986. *The Automobile Industry and Its Workers.* Cambridge: Cambridge University Press.

Treuhandanstalt. 1990. *Leitlinien der Geschäftspolitik der Treuhandanstalt.* Berlin.

———. 1994a. *Dokumentation 11.* Edited by R. Drewnicki, C. Freese, C. Hossbach, H. Schmidt, W. Schoeder, A. Wandersleben, and I. Wienen. Berlin: Jovis Verlagsbüro.

———. 1994b. *Dokumentation 14.* Edited by R. Drewnicki, C. Freese, C. Hossbach, H. Schmidt, W. Schoeder, A. Wandersleben, and I. Wienen. Berlin: Jovis Verlagsbüro.

———, ed. 1994c. *Dokumentation 13.* Edited by R. Drewnicki, C. Freese, C. Hossbach, H. Schmidt, W. Schoeder, A. Wandersleben, and I. Wienen. Berlin: Jovis Verlagsbüro.

Tucker, Vicki, Patti Meire, and Phyllis Rubinstein. 1990. The RTC: A Practical Guide to the Receivership/Conservatorship Process and the Resolution of Failed Thrifts. *University of Richmond Law Review* 25 (1): 1–52.

Tulluck, Gordon. 1965. *The Politics of Bureaucracy.* Washington, D.C.: Public Affairs Press.

U.S. House. 1989. Financial Institutions Reform, Recovery, and Enforcement Act of 1989 Conference Report to Accompany H.R. 1287. 101st Cong., 1st sess. H. Rept. 101–222.

————. 1990a. *Briefing Paper on the Operation and Performance of the Resolution Trust Corporation.* Banking, Finance and Urban Affairs Committee, 101st Cong., 1st sess. Dec. 5.

————. 1990b. *Hearing on the Supervision, Regulation and Insurance, Regarding RTC's Personnel Management of Institutions in Conservatorship.* RTC Task Force on Banking, Finance and Urban Affairs. 101st Cong. 2nd sess. June 15.

————. 1990c. *Year end Asset Sales, Institutions Resolution, Management, and Strategic Plan.* RTC Task Force of the Committee on Banking, Finance and Urban Affairs. 101st Cong. 2nd sess. December 11.

————. 1991. *Report to the Subcommittee on Financial Institutions Regulations and Insurance.* RTC Task Force of the Committee on Banking, Finance, and Urban Affairs. 102nd Cong. 1st sess. March 11.

————. 1993. *Status Report on the Resolution Trust Corporation.* U.S. House Subcommittee on General Oversight, Investigations, and the Resolution of Failed Financial Institutions of the Committee on Banking, Finance and Urban Affairs. 103rd Cong. 1st sess. February 23.

————. 1994. *Resolution Trust Corporation's Minority and Women-owned Business Programs.* Subcommittee on General Oversight, Investigations, and the Resolution of Failed Financial Institutions. 103rd Cong. 2nd sess.

————. 1995. *Oversight of the Resolution Trust Corporation.* Subcommittee on General Oversight and Investigations of the Committee on Banking and Financial Services. 104th Cong. 1st sess. May 16.

U.S. Senate. 1990. *Oversight of Resolution Trust Corporation Contracting.* Subcommittee on Federal Services, Post Office and Civil Service of the Committee of Governmental Affairs. 101st Cong. 2nd sess. September 24.

————. 1991. *Oversight Structure of the RTC.* Subcommittee on Consumer and Regulatory Affairs of the Committee on Banking, Housing, and Urban Affairs. 102nd Cong. 1st sess. Oct. 23.

———. 1992a. *The RTC and the Western Storm Project.* Committee on Banking, Housing and Urban Affairs. 102nd Cong. 2nd sess. March 11.

———. 1992b. *Second Hearing on the Semiannual Report of the Resolution Trust Corporation.* Committee on Banking, Housing and Urban Affairs. August 5.

———. 1993a. *Contracting Problems at the Resolution Trust Corporation: Homefed.* Subcommittee on Regulation and Government Information of the Committee on Governmental Affairs. 103rd Cong. 1st sess. February 19.

———. 1993b. *Resolution Trust Corporation: Whistleblowers.* Committee on Banking, Housing and Urban Affairs. 103rd Cong. 1st sess. September 23.

Vandell, Kerry, and Timothy Riddiough. 1991. The Impact of RTC Dispositions on Local Housing and Real Estate Markets. *Housing Policy Debate* 2 (1): 49–92.

———. 1992. Auctions as a Disposition Strategy for RTC Real Estate Assets: A Policy Perspective. *Housing Policy Debate* 3 (1): 117–41.

Verwaltungsgericht (Administrative Court). 1991. Anteilsveräußerung durch Treuhandanstalt. *Neue Juristische Woche* 6: 377–79.

Vickers, John, and Vincent Wright, eds. 1989. *The Politics of Privatisation in Western Europe.* New York: Frank Cass & Co.

Vogel, David. 1981. The "New" Social Regulation in Historical and Comparative Perspective. In *Regulation in Perspective,* edited by T. McCraw. Cambridge: Harvard University Press, 155–86.

Vonnemann, Wolfgang. 1991. Die Treuhandanstalt und Ihre Töchter stehen zueinander nicht in dem behaupteten konzernrechtlichen Verhältnis. *Handelsblatt,* 28 November, 1.

Wagner, Heinz. 1993. Der Gewerkschaftsaufbau in den Neuen Bundesländern - untersucht am Beispiel von Verwaltungsstellen der IG Metall. Diplomarbeit, Political Science, Free University, Berlin.

Waldman, Michael. 1990a. Testimony on Oversight of the Resolution Trust Corporation. Washington, D.C., House Banking,

Finance, and Urban Affairs Committee. 101st Cong. 2nd sess. 6 December 1990, 495–515.

———. 1990b. *Who Robbed America?* New York: Random House.

Waldo, Dwight. 1948. *The Administrative State: A Study of the Political Theory of American Public Administration.* New York: The Ronald Press.

Weimar, Robert. 1990. Treuhandanstalt und Treuhandgesetz. *Betriebs-Berater* 35/36: 10–15.

———. 1991. Gesellschaftsrechtliche Zweifelsfragen beim Umgang mit Treuhandunternehmen. *Der Betrieb* 46: 2373–78.

———. 1992a. Die Gesamteröffnungsbilanz der Treuhandanstalt. *Zeitschrift für Wirtschaft* 6: 378–86.

———. 1992b. Grundsatzfragen im Recht der UmwVO-Gesellschaften. *Zeitschrift für Wirtschaft* 2: 73–83.

———. 1993a. Die Treuhandanstalt im Verwaltungsprivatrecht. *Zeitschrift für Wirtschaftsrecht* 1: 1–14.

———. 1993b. Haushaltsrechtliche Instrumente der Treuhandanstalt gegenüber ihren Beteiligungsunternehmen. *Die Öffentliche Verwaltung* 1: 2–10.

———. 1993c. Rechte von Treuhandunternehmen. *Der Betrieb* 16: 821–25.

———. 1993d. *Treuhandgesetz: Kommentar.* Stuttgart: Kohlhammer.

Westerman, Harm. 1996. The Legal Framework and Its Changes. In *Treuhandanstalt: The Impossible Challenge,* edited by W. Fischer, H. Hax and H. K. Schneider. Berlin: Akademie Verlag, 86–112.

Whitney, Craig. 1997. Why Blair's Victory May Not Travel Well to Europe. *New York Times,* May 4, 3.

Wiarda, Howard. 1997. *Corporatism and Comparative Politics.* Edited by G. Mahler, *Comparative Politics Series.* New York: M. E. Sharp.

Wild, Klaus-Peter. 1991. Die Treuhandanstalt ein Jahr nach Inkrafttreten des Treuhandgesetzes - eine aktuelle Zwischenbilanz. In *Treuhandunternehmen im Umbruch,* edited by P. Hommelhoff. Cologne: Kommunikationsforum GmbH, 1–15.

REFERENCES

Wilson, James Q. 1989. *Bureaucracy.* New York: Basic Books.

Wilson, Woodrow. 1887. The Study of Administration. *Political Science Quarterly* 2 (June): 197–222.

Witte, John. 1992. Public Subsidies for Private Education. *Educational Policy* 6 (June): 206–27.

Witte, John F., and Chris Thorn. 1994. *Fourth-year Report, Milwaukee Parental Choice Program.* Madison, Wis.: La Follette Institute of Public Affairs.

Wolter, Henner. 1992. *Treuhandanstalt und Treuhandunternehmen als qualifizierter faktischer GmbH - Konzern?, Graue Reihe - Neue Folge 45.* Düsseldorf: Hans Boeckler Stiftung.

Wright, Vincent. 1994. Industrial Privatization in Western Europe: Pressures, Problems and Paradoxes. In *Privatization in Western Europe,* edited by V. Wright. New York: St. Martin's Press, 1–43.

Index

accountability: clear lines of authority, lack of, 103–06 (*see also* scapegoat governance); compliance, voluntary, 54–59; designing a system of (*see* scapegoat governance; structural choice); employment contracts and, 52–53; financial, 132–33, 146–50; legal identity and, 157–62; monitoring systems, 54, 64–68; patterns of, 6–8, 53–55, 69–70, 232; sanctions/penalties, 54; standards, 54, 59–65

Adair, Jack, 59, 73n21

administration: institutional environment (*see* governance); organizational culture (*see* organizational culture); organizational structure (*see* organizational structure); personnel (*see* personnel management); supervisory governance, 132; variables and implications of, 11–12, 75–78, 118–23, 234–38, 243–44. *See also* public bureaucracy; structural choice

Administrative Court of Berlin, 159–60

Administrative State, The (Waldo), 18

Affordable Housing Advisory Board (AHAB), 140, 152

Affordable Housing Disposition Plan (AHDP), 39–40

Affordable Housing program, 6, 58, 63, 121

agency, governmental. *See* public bureaucracy

AHAB. *See* Affordable Housing Advisory Board

AHDP. *See* Affordable Housing Disposition Plan

Akerlof, George, 187

Allocation Act (1991), 96

analytical approach: case selection, 19–20; interviews, 259–60; methodology and data, 20–21; organization-centered, 16–19

arena setting, defined, 225n5

ATLAS. *See* Ausgewählte Treuhandunternehmen vom Land Sachsen angemeldet zur Sanierung

Ausgewählte Treuhandunternehmen vom Land Sachsen angemeldet zur Sanierung (ATLAS), 45, 122, 224

Bagger-, Bugsier- und Bergungsreederei GmbH, 72n16
Balz, Manfred, 163
BankAmerica, 28
banks, German, 181–85, 191n6
Bellino GmbH & Co., 72n16
Benz, Arthur, 201
Birkhold, Sylvia, 116
Bowsher, Charles, 84
Braun, Dietmar, 15, 173–74
Bremer Vulkan, 7
Breuel, Birgit: decentralized structure, 97–98; firms, restructuring of, 44; fundraising activities, 147; the "Industrial Core," 71n10; and the Kohl administration, 142; leadership of, 169n28; legal identity, 158–59; legislative mandate, 155; organizational leadership of, 117; personnel management, 103, 128n35; scapegoat, the Treuhandtalt as, 166n2
Bundesrechnungshof (Federal Audit Office), 7, 65, 121
bureaucracy. See public bureaucracy
Bureaucracy (Wilson), 171
Bush, George, 132, 148, 175

Cadel, Georg, 103–04
Caldwell, Michael, 132
Carlin, Wendy, 5
Casey, Albert, 82, 84, 89, 92–93, 126n21
CDU. See Christian Democratic Union party
Chamber Court of Berlin, 159

Christian Democratic Union (CDU) party, scandal surrounding, 22n5, 54
Citibank, 28
City Savings, 105–06
civil service, German and American compared, 202–06
Clarke, Robert, 167n7
Cohen, Michael, 243
COMECON. See Council for Mutual Economic Assistance
competitive controlled bureaucracy, 247–48
compliance. See accountability
contractors: authority, lack of clear and, 104; dependence on, 15; hiring of, 60–62, 63–64, 87–89; implications of using, 15, 173, 190, 235–36; minority and women (see Minority and Women-Owned Business program); reports required from, 221; short-term, implications of, 121–22
controlled bureaucracy, 247
Cooke, David, 94–95, 140–41
corporatism, 200–201
Council for Mutual Economic Assistance (COMECON), 185–86
courts: American, 251; German, 161, 170n34–35
Creative Privatization Program, 44–45
Czada, Roland, 46, 208, 212, 226n16

Dean, Allan, 138
Derlien, Hans-Ulrich, 206
Deutsche Angstellten-Gewerkschaft (German Union for Employees), 209
Deutscher Gewerkschaftbund (Federation of German Trade Unions), 156, 209

Dill, William, 172

Dininio, Phyllis, 43, 45, 86, 147

divestment: challenges of, xiv–xv. *See also* privatization

domain consensus, defined, 173

Donahue, John, 18

Downs, Anthony, 57

dumping, protection of local markets from, 6, 41–42

Dyson, Kenneth, 182, 195–96, 225n4, 240, 249

economy and society, German and American compared, 200–202

EKO Stahl GmbH, 72n15

Elf-Aquitane, 22n5

employment and investment guarantees, the Treuhandstalt and, 25, 35, 46–53, 167n11

environment: institutional (*see* governance); internal and external of bureaucratic agencies, 243–45; policymaking, 249–56; pollution of, 188; task (*see* task environment)

Environmental Framework Law (*Umweltrahmengesetz*), 188

FADA. *See* Federal Asset Disposition Agency

Faser AG, 52

FDIC. *See* Federal Deposit Insurance Corporation

Federal Asset Disposition Agency (FADA), 140, 174–75

Federal Audit Office (Bundesrechnungshof), 7, 65, 121

Federal Deposit Insurance Corporation (FDIC): compensation, 92; governance and oversight, 140; impact of, 15; as independent bureaucracy,
246; location of, 1; organizational culture, 107; as organizational model, 175–79, 222, 239; personnel challenges and, 80, 84–86

Federal Savings and Loan Insurance Corporation (FSLIC), 108, 140, 174–75, 190–91n1

Federation of German Trade Unions, (*Deutscher Gewerkschaftbund*), 156, 209

Fesler, James, 54

Final Report of the Treuhandanstalt, 51

Financial Institutions Recovery Reform and Enforcement Act (FIRREA): conservator or receiver, powers of, 127–28n34; creation of the Resolution Trust Corporation, xiv; funding structure, 148–50; governing structure, 138–39, 141; legislative mandate, 5–6, 25, 151–53; repudiation of leases and contracts, power to, 102; secondary goals, 35, 40–41, 231; standards for sale of assets, 63

firms: East German, valuation of, 180–81; growth of American, 225n7; restructuring of, 6, 13, 35, 42–46, 69–70, 154–56, 162–66, 231–32

FIRREA. *See* Financial Institutions Recovery Reform and Enforcement Act

Fisher, Marc, 183

Fogel, Richard, 80

Forest Service, U.S., 107

Freyend, John von, 71n12

Friedrich, Carl, 11

Froomkin, Michael, 149, 157, 168n14

FSLIC. *See* Federal Savings and Loan Insurance Corporation

Gaebler, Ted, 173
Gellert, Otto, 167n4
GEMSU. *See* German Economic,
    Monetary, and Social Union
General Accounting Office, U.S.:
    accountability and lack of
    controls, 7–8, 58–59, 63–64, 68,
    73n26, 121, 232; affordable
    housing program, 39–41;
    contractors, reports required
    from, 221; downsizing, 102;
    field offices, function of, 101;
    legal actions, number and
    type, 219; organizational
    structure, 105
German Economic, Monetary, and
    Social Union (GEMSU),
    182, 184
German Institute for Economic
    Research, 45–46
German Union for Employees
    (*Deutsche Angstellten-
    Gewerkschaft*), 209
Gerschenkron, Alexander, 191n6
Goetz, Klaus, 201
Gohlke, Rainer, 135
Goldman Sachs, 105–06
governance, 195–96, 240–43; civil
    service, German and U.S.
    compared, 202–06; economy
    and society, German and U.S.
    compared, 200–202; impact of,
    15–16; and performance,
    German and U.S. compared,
    222–24; the Resolution Trust
    Corporation and, 216–22;
    scapegoat (*see* scapegoat
    governance); the state, German
    and U.S. compared, 198–200;
    structures, German and U.S.
    compared, 196–98; supervisory,
    132; the Treuhandstalt and,
    206–16. *See also* structural
    choice

Gramm, Phil, 179
Gulick, Luther, 22n6

Hall, Peter, 23n12
Halm, Gunter, 135
Hamilton, Alexander, 199
Hart, Jeffrey, 202
Hemmnisbeseitigungsgesetz (Obstacles
    Removal Law), 187
Henkel, Hans-Olaf, 167n4
Herzog, Roman, 22n8
Hickel, Rudopf, 66
High Administrative Court of
    Berlin, 160
Hilferding, Rudolf, 191n6
Hitler, Adolf, 2
Hobbes, Thomas, 199
Hoffmann, Lutz, 184
Homefed Federal Savings Bank, 59
Honecker, Erich, 83
Hope, C. C., Jr., 167n7
housing, and the Resolution Trust
    Corporation, 5–6, 13, 39–41,
    151, 231
Hove, Andrew, Jr., 167n7

IG Metall, 156
Ikenberry, John, 23n12
independent bureaucracy, 246–47
Innerrevision, 65–66
institution, defined, 224–25n1
institutional environment. *See*
    governance

Jackson, Andrew, 204
Japan, 255–56

Kampe, Dieter, 65–66, 70, 116
Kapferer, Stefan, 61, 97, 103,
    128n35
Katzenstein, Peter, 225n6
Kaufman, Herbert, 107
Kearny, Daniel, 145–46
Keating, Charles, 190–91n1

Kelly, Lamar, 92
Kelman, Steven, 249
Kemmler, Marc, 43
Kennedy, Joseph, 148
Kerber, Markus, 159
Kettl, Donald, 54, 63, 138, 141, 201–02
Kingdon, John, 107
Kloepfer, Michael, 155
Koch, Alexander, 117, 123n6
Koehler, Claus, 167n4
Kohl, Helmut: bribery scandal and, 7, 22n5, 54; legislative mandate, 155; politics and structural choice, 132, 138; predictions by, 180, 183; private sector recruitment, 83
Krause, Wolfram, 135
Kreditanstalt für Wiederaufbau, 6
Küpper, Hans-Ulrich, 155
Kühl, Jürgen, 46, 53

Lasswell, Harold, 19
Lavenex, Sandra, 203
Lee, Peter, 184–85
Lehmbruch, Gerhard, 23n12, 198, 225n1
Leibinger, Bethold, 167n4
Lennings, Manfred, 167n4
Leyson, André, 167n4
Ludewig Group, 138

MacDonald, Heather, 39–41
Madison, James, 199
de Maizière, Lothar, 154, 181
Management KGs. See Management Kommanditgesellschaften
Management Kommanditgesellschaften (Management KGs), 44, 119, 122
March, James, 243
markets, German and American conceptions of compared, 200–202

Martinelli, Michael, 93–94
Marx, Manfred, 161
Mayr, Robert, 155
McKenna, W. F., 175
Meier, Kenneth, 172
Merton, Robert, 205
methodology: case selection, 19–20, 259–60; organization-centered approach, 16–19; qualitative case study, 20–21
Milken, Michael, 191n1
minorities, and the Resolution Trust Corporation, 5–6, 13, 35–38, 152, 221, 231
Minority and Women-Owned Business (MWOB) program, 6, 35–38, 58, 63, 116, 121, 231
Minority- and Women-Owned Legal Firm (MWOLF), 38, 221
mission, of an organization, 12
Modrow, Hans, 153, 180
Moe, Terry, 14, 69, 131–32, 146
Müller-Armack, Alfred, 201
MWOB. See Minority and Women-Owned Business program
MWOLF. See Minority- and Women-Owned Legal Firm

Nägele, Frank, 143
national settings, organizational behavior and, 249–56
Niethammer, Frank, 167n4
nomenclatura, 81
North, Douglass, 23n12

Obstacles Removal Law (Hemmnisbeseitigungsgesetz), 187
Odewald, Jens, 124n10, 134, 167n4
Olsen, Johan, 243
Ordnungspolitik, 198
Ordo-liberals, 198, 200
organizational culture, 11, 75–77, 106–07, 120–21; integration of cultures, 114–18;

organizational culture (*continued*)
    multiple cultures, presence of,
    107–14
organizational mission, 12
organizational structure, 11–14,
    75–77, 96, 119, 236–38; clear
    lines of authority, lack of,
    103–06, 237; decentralized
    operations, 96–103, 236–37
Osborne, David, 173
oversight. *See* accountability

Pastuzek, Horst, 167n4
Paul, David, 93
personnel management, 11–12,
    75–77, 118–19; challenges of,
    78–81; compensation, 87–94,
    116, 236; hiring and
    recruitment, 82–90, 235–36;
    training, 94–95, 235
Peters, Guy, 244
Piltz, Klaus, 167n4
policymaking environment, 249–56
politics. *See* governance; structural
    choice
Politics of Structural Choice (Moe), 146
Price Waterhouse, 59
Priewe, Jan, 66, 141–42
principal-agent relations, 171–74.
    See also contractors; task
    environment
privatization: assets, types of, 27–28;
    comparison of cases, 23n14;
    forms of, 29–30; legislative
    mandate, 25–26; political
    elements of, 19, 230–34;
    secondary goals and the process
    of, 5–6; speed of, 4–5, 26–27,
    30–34, 223–24. *See also*
    divestment
public bureaucracy: classical models,
    variation from, 75–78;
    competitive controlled, 247–48;
    controlled, 247; control of (*see*

accountability); German and
    American compared, 202–06;
    independent, 246–47;
    institutional environment of
    (*see* governance); internal and
    external environments, 243–45;
    legal identity, 133, 156–62;
    principal-agent relations,
    171–74 (*see also* contractors; task
    environment); strategic (*see*
    strategic bureaucracy);
    structural choices shaping,
    131–33 (*see also* structural
    choice); task environment and
    (*see* task environment); theory
    and puzzling performance,
    9–10, 69; third parties,
    dependence on, 15. *See also*
    administration

real estate and financial markets:
    concerns regarding, 13;
    protection from dumping, 6,
    41–42, 231
Real Estate Owned Inventory System
    (REOIS), 68
Rechsstaat, 202–03, 205
REFCORP. *See* Resolution Funding
    Corporation
regulatory culture, defined, 225n1
Reinventing Government (Osborne
    and Gaebler), 173
REOIS. *See* Real Estate Owned
    Inventory System
Resolution Funding Corporation
    (REFCORP), 149
Resolution Trust Corporation
    (RTC): accountability, 6–8,
    53–55, 57–60, 62–64, 67–68,
    232; assets, types of, 27–28;
    contractors, hiring of, 60,
    63–64, 88–89; creation and
    mission, xiv, 3–4, 12; economic
    and political concerns

regarding, 12–14; funding structure, 147–50; headquarters of, 1–2, 115; institutional environment, 216–22, 240–43 (*see also* governance); legal actions against and by, 218–20; legal identity, 133, 156–58; legislative mandate, 25–26, 133, 150–53; organizational culture (*see* organizational culture); organizational structure, 100–106 (*see also* organizational structure); oversight and scapegoat governance, 133–34, 138–41, 144–46; personnel management (*see* personnel management); privatization, forms of, 29–30; as a public bureaucracy, 9–10, 77–78; scandal and fraud, 8, 54; secondary goals, 5–6, 13, 25, 35–42, 69, 178, 231; speed of privatization, 4–5, 32–34; as a strategic bureaucracy (*see* strategic bureaucracy); structural choices shaping the (*see* structural choice); task environment, 174–79, 189–90, 239–40; third parties, dependence on, 15; winners and losers from the actions of, 232–33

Ressortprinzip, 204

restitution, 186–87

restructuring of firms. *See* firms, restructuring of

Rickert, Dieter, 81, 124n11

Riddiough, Timothy, 34, 41

Robson, John, 145

Rohwedder, Detlev: economic transformation, speed of, 183; governance and, 208; killing of, 169n28; leadership of, 124n10; leadership of East German firms, 123n6; organizational structure, 167n3; recruitment, 81, 124n8; restitution laws, 186; restructuring of firms, 223; valuation of East German firms, 180

Rolle, William, 92, 117–18, 176

Roosevelt, Franklin, 205

RTC. *See* Resolution Trust Corporation

RTC Completion Act of 1993, 140, 150

RTC Funding Act of 1991, 41, 150

RTC Refinancing, Restructuring, and Improvement Act of 1991 (RTCRRIA), 37, 140, 168n15

RTCRRIA. *See* RTC Refinancing, Restructuring, and Improvement Act of 1991

Rubin, Robert, 168n17

Rueter, Martin, 57

Ryan, John, 38, 123n3

Ryan, Timothy, 167n7

SAMDAs. *See* Standard Asset Management Disposition Agreements

scapegoat governance, 133–34, 238; external controls, 141–46; internal controls, 134–41

Schering AG, 66

Schirner, Kurt, 135

Schmidt, Helmut, 2, 13

Schmidt, Klaus-Dieter, 31, 64–65

Schmitter, Philippe, 200

Schroeder, Patricia, 150

securitization, 128–29n42

Seibel, Wolfgang: contractors, use of, 61; early years of the Treuhandstalt, 115; government institutions in eastern Germany, 242; labor unions, 215;

Seibel, Wolfgang (*continued*)
  legal rules, flexibility of, 203;
  organizational structure, 97,
  103, 136; organizational
  structure and personnel,
  128n35; personnel, 109–10,
  125n16; unification and
  governmental institutions, 207
Seidman, Harold, 158
Seidman, L. William: assets, quality
  of, 177; the legislative mandate,
  152; organizational leadership
  of, 117; organizational
  structure of the RTC, 103–04,
  140, 144–45
Shonfield, Andrew, 191n6, 201–02
Siegmund, Uwe, 31
Sinn, Gerlinde, 184
Sinn, Hans-Werner, 184
Skowronek, Stephen, 204
Slattery, Jim, 150
Smyser, W. R., 198
social market economy
  (*sozialmarktwirtschaft*), 200
SOEs. *See* state-owned enterprises
sozialmarktwirtschaft (social market
  economy), 200
Splitting Law (1991), 165–66
Stabsstelle für Besondere
  Aufgaben, 65
Standard Asset Management
  Disposition Agreements
  (SAMDAs), 101
state, the, German and American
  compared, 198–200
state-owned enterprises (SOEs),
  28, 42
Stechow, Wilfried, 159
strategic bureaucracy, 229–30,
  245–46; national setting and,
  249–56; politics of privatization,
  230–34
Streeck, Wolfgang, 200
structural choice, 14, 131–33, 166,
  238–39, 243–44; financial

accountability, 132–33, 146–50;
  legal identity, 133, 156–66;
  legislative mandates, 133,
  150–56; scapegoat governance
  (*see* scapegoat governance)
Sullivan, Carmen, 95, 126n29
Süss, Walter, 209

task environment, 14–15, 171–74,
  239–40, 244; impacts of, 188–90;
  of the Resolution Trust
  Corporation, 174–79; of the
  Treuhandstalt, 179–88
Taylor, William, 126n22, 141
THA. *See* Treuhandstalt
third parties. *See* contractors
Thompson, James, 172–73
Tränker, Ludwig, 55
Treuhand Act, 134, 154–56, 161,
  168–69n26
Treuhand Credit Act of 1992
  (*Treuhand-Kreditaufnahmegesetz*),
  147, 159
Treuhand Investigatory
  Committee, 8
Treuhand-Kreditaufnahmegesetz
  (Treuhand Credit Act, 1992),
  147, 159
Treuhandstalt Law, 6, 25, 42, 231–32.
  See also Unification Treaty
Treuhandstalt (THA):
  accountability, 6–8, 53–57,
  59–62, 64–67, 70, 232; assets,
  types of, 28–29; central offices
  of, 2, 115; contractors, hiring of,
  60–62; creation and mission, xiv,
  3–4, 12, 23n10; economic and
  political concerns regarding,
  12–14; funding structure,
  146–47; institutional
  environment, 206–16, 240–43
  (*see also* governance); labor
  unions and, 209–15; legal
  identity, 133, 156, 158–66;
  legislative mandate, 25–26, 133,

153–56; organizational culture (*see* organizational culture); organizational structure, 96–100, 103, 106 (*see also* organizational structure); oversight and scapegoat governance, 133–38, 141–44; personnel management (*see* personnel management); privatization, forms of, 30; as a public bureaucracy, 9–10, 77–78; public identity, implications of, 162–66; scandal and fraud, 7–8, 54, 232; secondary goals, 5–6, 13, 25, 35–36, 42–53, 69–70, 231–32 (*see also* firms); speed of privatization, 4–5, 30–32; as a strategic bureaucracy (*see* strategic bureaucracy); structural choices shaping the (*see* structural choice); task environment, 174, 179–90, 239–40; third parties, dependence on, 15; winners and losers from the actions of, 233

Umweltrahmengesetz (Environmental Framework Law), 188
Unification Treaty: agency financing, 146–47, 159; legislative mandate, 154; the management committee, 138; positioning within the government, 141–42;

restitution claims, 186; the Treuhandstalt Law, 6, 25
unions, German: in a corporatist system, 200–201; elite bargaining, participation in, 209–15; restructuring over rapid privatization, favoring of, 156; supervisory board, representation on, 134, 242; wage agreements, 187

Vandell, Kerry, 34, 41
van Tilburg, Jahan, 167n4
Vento, Bruce, 37, 179
Vogel, David, 225n7
Vulkan. *See* Bremer Vulkan

Wagner, Herman, 83, 124n8, 125n19
Waigel, Theo, 142
Waldo, Dwight, 18–19
Weber, Max, 77, 90, 203
Western Storm Project, 59
Wiarda, Howard, 225n6
Wild, Klaus-Peter, 135–36
Wild, Peter, 83
Wilson, James Q., 20, 171–72, 179, 190, 246
Wilson, Woodrow, 90, 205
Wirth, Tim, 3
Witte, John, 23n15–16
women, and the Resolution Trust Corporation, 5–6, 35–38, 152, 221, 231. *See also* Minority- and Women-Owned Business (MWOB) program

DATE DUE